A. Artisans' District
B. Elven Quarter
C. Gatehouse and Bridge defences
D. Merchants' District
E. Residential District
F. Shipyards' District
G. The Town Hall Quarter

1. Bowmen's Guild-hall
2. Bridge Street
3. Butchers' Quay
4. Gaol
5. Gatehouse
6. Glittering Gate
7. Granaries and Warehouses
8. Guard barracks
9. Hospital
10. Market-pool
11. Market square
12. Merchants' Guild-hall
13. River trade Tollhouse
14. Street of bowyers and fletchers
15. Tollhouse
16. Town-hall
17. Town watch barracks
18. Water-gate

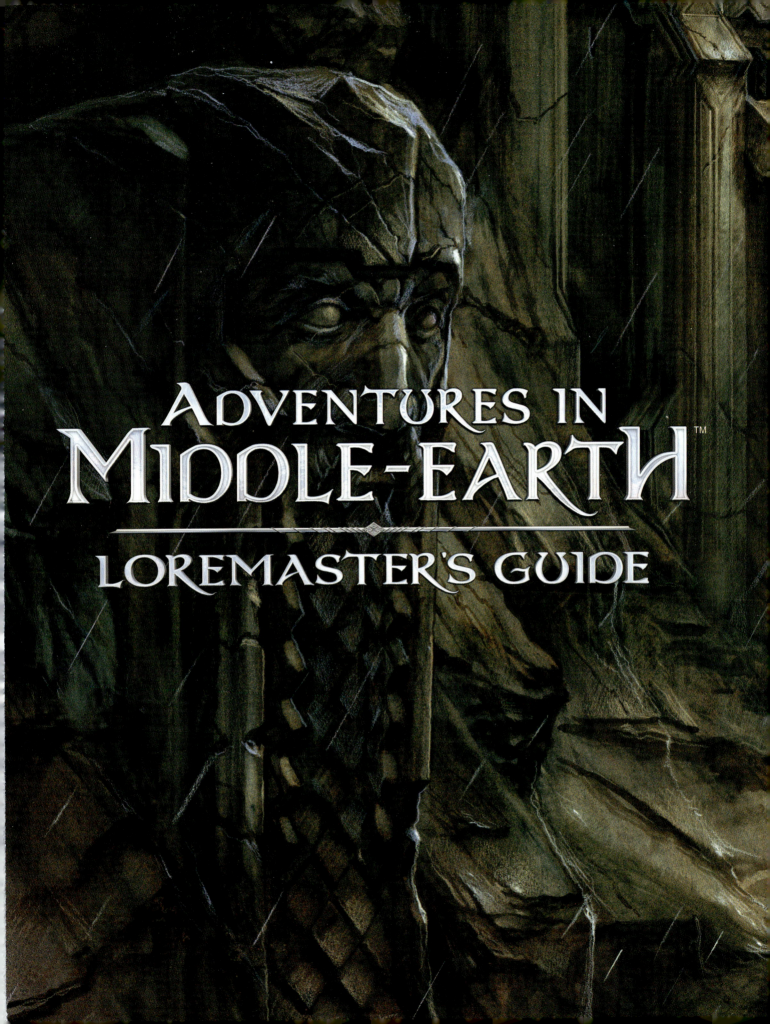

– CREDITS –

Creative Direction by Dominic McDowall and Jon Hodgson

Designed and Written by Walt Ciechanowski, Steve Emmott, Jon Hodgson, TS Luikart, Dominic McDowall, Francesco Nepitello, David Rea, Jacob Rodgers, Gareth Ryder-Hanrahan and Ken Spencer

Cover Art by Ralph Horsley

Illustrated by Andy Hepworth, Jon Hodgson, John Howe, Tomas Jedrusek, Sam Manley, Jan Pospisil, Scott Purdy, Naomi Robinson and Egil Thompson

Maps by Paul Bourne

Edited by Amanda Valentine with Dominic McDowall and Francesco Nepitello

Graphic Design and Layout by Paul Bourne

Proofreaders: Jacob Rodgers, assisted by David Rea

Special thanks to Jacob Rodgers

Based on *The One Ring Roleplaying Game* by Francesco Nepitello and Marco Maggi

© Sophisticated Games Ltd 2017   © Cubicle 7 Entertainment Ltd 2017

www.cubicle7.co.uk

ISBN: 978-0-85744-311-3
SKU: CB72301

Product Identity: The following items are hereby identified as Product Identity, as defined in the Open Game License version 1.0a, Section 1(e), and are not Open Content: All trademarks, registered trade-marks, proper names (characters, place names, etc.), new rules, classes, items, virtues, backgrounds, places, characters, artwork, sidebars, and trade dress. Open Game Content: The Open content in this book includes material taken from the Systems Reference Document. No other portion of this work may be reproduced in any form without permission.

Published by Sophisticated Games Ltd, 3 Andersen Court, Newnham Road, Cambridge CB3 9EZ, UK and Cubicle 7 Entertainment Ltd, Suite D3, Unit 4, Gemini House, Hargreaves Road, Groundwell Industrial Estate, Swindon, SN25 5AZ, UK

The One Ring, Middle-earth, The Hobbit, The Lord of the Rings, and the characters, items, events and places therein are trademarks or registered trademarks of The Saul Zaentz Company d/b/a Middle-earth Enterprises and are used under license by Sophisticated Games Ltd and their respective licensees. All rights reserved. No part of this publication may be reproduced, stored in a retrieval system, or transmitted, in any form or by any means, electronic, mechanical, photocopying, recording or otherwise, without the prior permission of the publishers.

Printed in Lithuania

~ contents ~

Setting and the Tale of Years 8

Chapter One expands the setting information presented in the *Player's Guide*, and is packed with detail and inspiration for the Loremaster. Here you will learn a great deal more about Wilderland, the geographic setting for an *Adventures in Middle-earth* campaign. All the significant regions and locations are discussed, and the Tale of Years presents a timeline of events in the history of the Third Age. Finally a guide to Lake-town brings this bustling settlement to life as the base of your company's initial adventures. And who can say what the future holds?

Welcome to Middle-earth	10
Wilderland	10
The Tale of Years	10
Using the Sources	10
Assembling a Company	11
King Bard's Proclamation	11
Wilderland & Beyond	12
The Lands about the Mountain	12
Lake-town	14
The Land of the Beornings	15
The Land of the Woodmen	16
Mirkwood	18
Other Lands	20
The Tale of Years	21
Old Lore	21
Recent Past	24
Gathering Shadows	25
Wilderland Player's Map	27
A Guide to Lake-town	28
Gatehouse and Bridge Defenses	28
Merchants' District	29
Artisans' District	30
Elven Quarter	32
The Town-Hall Quarter	32
Residential District	34
Shipyards District	34
New Fellowship Phase	35
Undertakings for Lake-town	36

Before the Game 38

Chapter Two provides Loremasters with guidance on planning a game and detailing some of the themes useful for building effective Middle-earth gaming sessions. Some clear beacons to the kind of game you'd like to play are offered as navigational aids to the Loremaster.

Before the Game	40
Precepts of Middle-earth Play	40
Miles Are Miles	40
Years Are Long	41
All Enemies of the One Enemy	42
The Long Defeat in a Fallen World	42
Deliverance Arrives As All Seems Lost	42

The Adventuring Phase 44

Chapter Three covers the primary activity of an *Adventures in Middle-earth* game – the Adventuring phase. The role of the Loremaster is thoroughly examined, with lots of hints on how to perform the task with aplomb. The idea of Tolkien's Canon is also explored, and there's a round up of important rules for the Adventuring Phase. Lastly a handful of optional rules for character virtues are presented..

The Loremaster	46
The Middle-earth Loremaster	47
The Qualities of a Good Loremaster	47
Tolkien's Canon	48
Adventuring Rules	50
Rests	50
Exhaustion	52
Inspiration	52
Multiclassing	53

Journeys Expanded 54

Chapter Four offers guidance for running journeys in your games. This includes suggestions for ways to describe Middle-earth as your Player-heroes travel through it, explores resting on the road, suggestions for how to handle breaking or unexpectedly ending a journey, as well as providing the underlying rules so that you can create your own journey event tables.

Journeys	56
Rests on the Road	57
Describing Middle-earth	58
Interrupting Journeys	59
Experience on the Road	61
Making your own Journey Events Tables	61

Non-Player Characters and Audiences Expanded 64

Chapter Five gives the Loremaster copious inspiration for creating and playing effective non player characters of Middle-earth, from the barkeep at the Green Dragon Inn to Gandalf the Grey. This chapter also provides a gallery of useful NPCs with their stats and expectations.

Folk Along the Way	66
Playing Members of the Free Folk	67
Characters of Middle-earth	68
Audiences	80
Planning Audiences	80
Running Audiences	82

Adversaries and Battle 86

Chapter Six provides inspiration and guidance for using monsters in Middle-earth. New rules for customising your Middle-earth adversaries with a range of abilities and actions are included, along with a set of rules expanding the use of location and scenery in battle. There is also a Wilderland bestiary containing a variety of Orcs, Trolls, Spiders, Wargs and Vampires.

Adversaries	88
Battle in Middle-earth	88
Scenery in Combat	90
The Wild	90
Woodland	91
Mirkwood	93
Ruins	94
Caves	95
Atmosphere	96
Weather	96
A Wilderland Bestiary	97
Orcs	97
Mordor-Orcs	100
Spiders of Mirkwood	105
Trolls	107
Wolves of the Wild	111
Werewolves	113
Vampires	114
Creature Actions and Abilities	116
List of Creature Actions & Abilities	116
Creature Bonus Actions	118
Creature Reactions	118
Troupe Abilities, Actions and Bonus Actions	118
Especially Strong Abilities and Actions	119
Creature Specific Actions and Abilities: Orcs & Goblins	120
Creature Specific Actions and Abilities: Trolls and Ogres	120
Creature Specific Actions and Abilities: Spiders	121
Creature Specific Actions and Abilities: Wargs and Wolves	121

Wondrous, Legendary and Healing Items 122

Chapter Seven explores matters arising from straight-forward material wealth like gold and silver, as well as less commonly found artefacts and legendary weapons. Some additional options for more magical healing are also covered.

Treasure and Rewards	124
Out of Character Treasure Hunters	124
Go to the Source	125
What Is Gold For?	126
Wondrous Artefacts	127
How Wondrous Artefacts Work	127
Discovering the Blessings of an Artefact	127
Artefact Bonus	127
Magical Results	128
Not-so-Subtle Magic	130
Blessings Tables	131
Other Wondrous Artefacts	131
Legendary Weapons and Armour	132
Creating Legendary Weapons and Armour	132
How Legendary Weapons and Armour Work	134
Discovering Qualities	134
Enchanted Qualities	135
Magical Healing	139

Magic in Middle-earth 140

Chapter Eight describes the role of magic in Middle-earth and how you can add more to your game should you so wish. A list of appropriate Open Gaming License spells is also featured.

The Magic of Middle-earth	142
Meddling in the Affairs of Wizards	142
Creating Your Own Magic	143
Options for Adding Magic	144

The Fellowship Phase 146

Chapter Nine details the Fellowship phase from the perspective of the Loremaster, providing detail on the group narrative arising during this player-controlled phase of play. Sanctuaries, Patrons and Undertakings are all examined.

The Fellowship Phase	148
If They Split Up	148
If They Stay Together	149
Ending a Fellowship Phase	149
How Long is a Fellowship Phase?	150
Experience Points	150
Sanctuaries	151
Recovery	151
Removing Conditions	151
Shared Location	151
Undertakings	151
The Open Virtue Undertaking	151
Beginning Point of an Adventuring Phase	152
Focus	152
What Does Opening a Sanctuary Mean?	152
Further Undertakings	153
Gain an Open Virtue	153
Gain a Cultural Virtue	153
Influence Patron	153
Patrons	154
Adventures in Middle-earth Player's Guide Errata and Rules Clarifications	155
Index	156

FOREWORD

Middle-earth is an incredible setting, by turns both epic and personal. Its moments of impossible heroism and sacrifice dwell alongside touching, gentle moments that shine a light on our own natures, and the nature of our world. But you already know that.

When we set out on this publishing journey we knew that it would be long and hard and that there would be dangers along the way. What we could not have predicted was just how well the *Adventures in Middle-earth Player's Guide* would be received.

Building on what had already been laid down in *The One Ring Roleplaying Game*, we were able achieve what we set out to do – to bring our love of Middle-earth gaming, and the answers we'd already found to the many questions such an endeavour raises, to the widest possible audience.

The challenge in achieving this was not a small one. Many had expressed the thought that the 5th Edition rules-set had certain inherent ideas that would be hard to work with and still impart the flavour and feel of Middle-earth.

That never worried us too deeply. We know that players of this game are clever people enjoying complex, nuanced games with deep characters and immersive moments. We've had plenty of those ourselves using these rules across a variety of settings. We also knew that we had great material and ideas that translate into any rules-set, and that the team tasked to do it was a strong one.

Something that I was delighted to discover was just how strong the 5th Edition rules are. While they maintain their traditional clear focus on fairness and balance, there is a lot of room for whomever is running the game to tailor the rules as they see fit. There are wide range of options, and different 'official' ways to play.

This really appeals to all of us working on *Adventures in Middle-earth*. Because first and foremost this is *your* game. *You* are best placed to know your players, *you* can find out what they enjoy and what they're looking for from any given roleplaying game session. We aim to offer a range of additional options and inspiration that empowers *you* to make the Middle-earth roleplaying experience you want to be a part of.

Since it falls to me to write these opening words, I can take this opportunity to sing the praises of the team leader that instilled this player-focused approach across the board — Dom McDowall. Dom rarely gets the credit he deserves for the sheer volume of creative work he brings to our games. If it's here, or in any other Cubicle 7 tome or boxed set, he's had a hand in shaping it. He's also way too modest to ever point this out. *Adventures in Middle-earth* would not be here without Dom's creativity, drive and vision.

"All we have to decide is what to do with the time that is given us"

Jon Hodgson, 2016

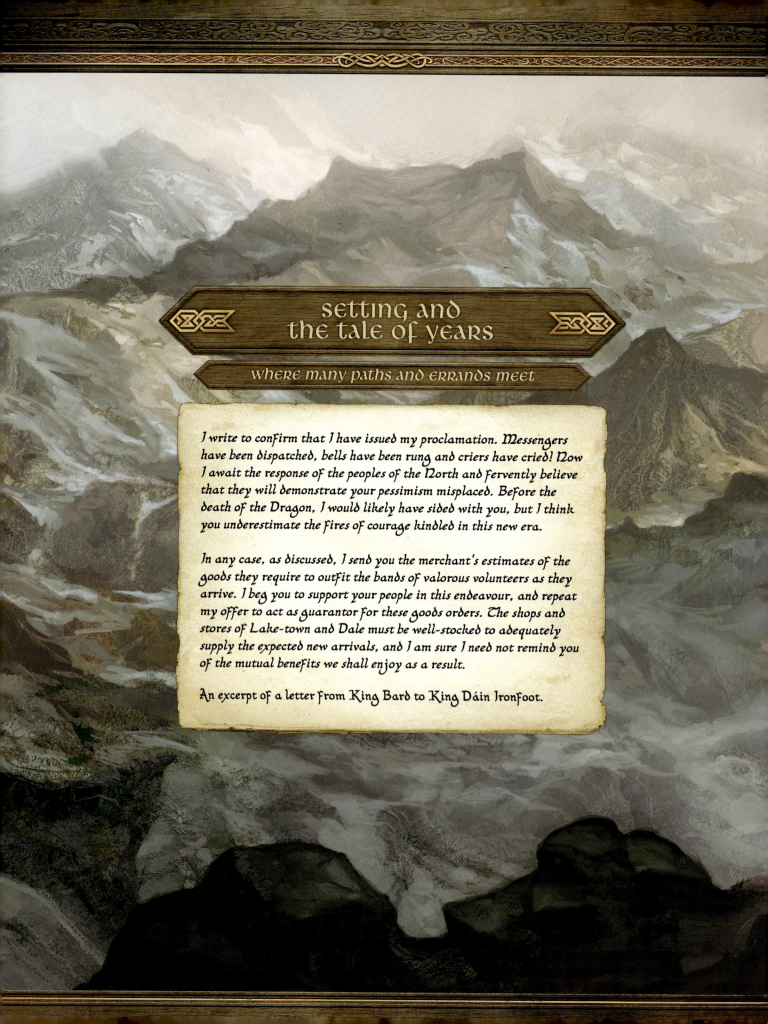

Setting and the Tale of Years

where many paths and errands meet

I write to confirm that I have issued my proclamation. Messengers have been dispatched, bells have been rung and criers have cried! Now I await the response of the peoples of the North and fervently believe that they will demonstrate your pessimism misplaced. Before the death of the Dragon, I would likely have sided with you, but I think you underestimate the fires of courage kindled in this new era.

In any case, as discussed, I send you the merchant's estimates of the goods they require to outfit the bands of valorous volunteers as they arrive. I beg you to support your people in this endeavour, and repeat my offer to act as guarantor for these goods orders. The shops and stores of Lake-town and Dale must be well-stocked to adequately supply the expected new arrivals, and I am sure I need not remind you of the mutual benefits we shall enjoy as a result.

An excerpt of a letter from King Bard to King Dáin Ironfoot.

Welcome to
- Middle-earth -

... suddenly his hand met what felt like a tiny ring of cold metal lying on the floor of the tunnel.

In the year 2941 a number of important events usher Wilderland into a new age: the death of Smaug, the Battle of Five Armies, the restoration of the Kingdom under the Mountain and of Dale, and the discovery of the Ruling Ring by Bilbo Baggins. The decade following these momentous events sees the Free Peoples savour an unexpected respite: men gather under the banners of ambitious kings and chieftains, raising their heads to look beyond their old and restrictive borders for the first time in a long while, and adventurers dare once again to follow forgotten roads in search of renown. From a gaming perspective, this is a very suitable time to set up a new campaign in Wilderland. It is a period that is well known to readers, but its chronology is missing the detail of later times, allowing for all sorts of adventures.

Adventures in Middle-Earth 'officially' starts in the year 2946. By this time, the heroes have adjusted to the new status quo and have five years of active adventuring in front of them before the year 2951 offers the Loremaster the opportunity to close the first part of a campaign with a bang as the Shadow returns. This rude awakening shatters the peaceful optimism of recent years, a dramatic event that proves particularly effective if the early years have been spent playing simpler adventures.

This chapter contains the background material needed to start playing a game set at the end of the Third Age. The information is supposed to be used more as a toolkit rather than as a rigid script – the last thing it should do is limit your creativity as a Loremaster or your players. By introducing the locations, personalities and events presented here, Loremasters and players will be able to set up a great number of Adventuring and Fellowship phases that will be both entertaining and faithful to the source material. The aim of the material found in this chapter is to establish the foundations of an ongoing series of adventures based initially around a focused location (for example, the cities of Esgaroth and Dale) and eventually ranging across Wilderland, an area full of opportunities for exploration and excitement. The period of relative peace offers the Loremaster a chance to present adventures rich with wonder and discovery, set in a simpler narrative style, well-suited to the mood of the tale narrated in *The Hobbit.*

Wilderland

Wilderland is a wide region. Leagues and leagues of unexplored terrain lay in front of heroes in search of adventure, and well-known and beloved locales await players eager to discover them once again from a new personal perspective. Wilderland, of course, is only a portion of Middle-earth – wide lands lay outside its borders, beyond the mountains and south of the forest. *Adventures in Middle-earth* will explore all these lands in more detail in future supplements.

The Tale of Years

The chronologies found in this volume record events from the past and provide an outline of things yet to come. Most entries are drawn directly from the available sources; others have been developed for the game, striving to attain a certain level of internal consistency. The result is a timeline composed of events great and small, giving a historical context to the deeds of the heroes.

Combining the happenings described here with your own adventures will help you achieve a deep level of participation in the setting. Moreover, the presented events serve as plot elements that may be developed into complete adventures.

Using the Sources

The background material found in this chapter has been written to be as complete as possible, but of course the best reference material is Tolkien's books themselves. A Loremaster in need of inspiration or a player looking for the most faithful description of a place can simply crack their books open and look for the relevant chapters; although spirited discussions of the 'correct' interpretation of a particular passage should be kept for after the game!

As you explore Wilderland, *The Hobbit* is the book to keep handy, but several pages in *The Lord of the Rings* concern themselves with what happened before Frodo's time. However, this doesn't mean that every time that a character encounters someone or visits a place the Loremaster should search through hundreds of pages for the tiniest bit of reference material.

Assembling a Company

The composition of the group of characters is very important, as no other gaming element has a comparable influence on the type of campaign that will take shape during play. Assembling the right group of adventurers is therefore a step that should be considered with the greatest care.

To facilitate this decision, this chapter offers a standard solution, one that should easily accommodate the choices made by the players during character creation: The default campaign starts in 2946, on the occasion of the first Gathering of Five Armies, a celebration held in Dale for the first time, five years after the eponymous battle.

Newly created heroes may be adventurers that have been attracted to Lake-town by the clamour surrounding the event, or by King Bard's proclamation. They may have ended up there on their own, or they might have accompanied an official emissary. If the Loremaster wants the campaign to feature characters as personalities of importance, the adventurers might even be those emissaries themselves! Whatever the details, the Gathering of Five Armies provides a quick and easily customisable option.

King Bard's Proclamation

Five years after the fabled Battle, the Free Peoples came once more to Dale, for the first festival called the Gathering of Five Armies, to remember and to celebrate the death of Smaug. The wise among them also speak of the defeat of the mysterious Necromancer, who was driven from Mirkwood around the same time by the White Council.

In the months before the Gathering, King Bard of Dale sends heralds and messengers out across Wilderland, who proclaim the king's words:

And so, Free Peoples of the North, gather up your courage and bring it to me. I have plans for the North such as you will scarce believe, but I need your strength to turn plan to deed. In return for playing your part in our rebirth, I will pay well in gold, land and the satisfaction of knowing you lead your people from the shadows into a brighter future.

This new age of Wilderland is a fragile thing. 2941 was a year of great triumph – the orcs were scattered, the Dragon slain, the Necromancer banished – but the Shadow still lies on Middle-earth. All the good that was done can be undone, all that joy can be turned to sorrow and ash, unless heroes arise to defend the Free Peoples and safeguard this fragile dawn.

Wilderland & Beyond

...what I have heard seems to me for the most part old wives' tales, such as we tell to our children. All that lies north of Rohan is now to us so far away that fancy can wander freely there.

The Adventurer's Map of Wilderland (see page 27) shows the regions found to the east of the Misty Mountains, as far as the river Redwater. It's an area measuring approximately 600 miles across from west to east and 500 miles from north to south. Most of it is occupied by the forest of Mirkwood, and the peoples inhabiting it claim the lands around it or very close to it, if not inside it. This section contains several entries detailing various features shown on the Loremaster's Map (see the end papers at the back of this guide). Lake-town, is described in greater detail as it is uniquely situated between both Forest and Mountain and is likely to chosen as the base of operations for a newly-formed company of adventurers.

The Lands about the Mountain

Some of the most powerful realms of the Northlands can be found in the vicinity of the isolated peak known as the Lonely Mountain.

Dale

Dale is a city of Men built on the western bank of the Running River. It rises in a valley between the southern arms of the Lonely Mountain, where the river turns around the town making a wide loop before resuming its southward course. Its foundations were first laid by Northmen almost four hundred years ago. For two centuries, the city enjoyed a close alliance with the Dwarves of the Kingdom under the Mountain and grew rich and prosperous, extending its power to the east over the lands between the Running River and Redwater. Many kings passed down their crown to their heirs, until the city was destroyed when Smaug descended on the Dwarf kingdom.

Dale remained a deserted ruin for the best part of two centuries, its power a dream remembered only in sad songs sung in Lake-town and in smaller settlements scattered along the Running River.

Dale was reclaimed in the year 2941 by Bard, a descendant of its former lords and slayer of the Dragon, when news of his great deed attracted many Men from the west and south. With the re-founding of the Kingdom under the Mountain the city is returning to its former splendour as the products of skilled Dwarven hands issues again from the Front Gate of Erebor to be sold in the markets of Dale, along with the wares made by local craftsmen and the foreign goods brought upstream by boats coming from Lake-town.

The last four years have seen the completion of most of the restoration works, including crenellated walls and bell towers, but great labours are undertaken every month as trading blooms and wealth increases. Dwarf stonemasons are seen working everywhere, as they supervise the building of new fountains and pools and the raising of new bridges stretching across the waterways. Dwarf craftsmen busy themselves with the paving of the streets using stones of different colours (from which the streets take their names). The countryside to the south and west of the Mountain is once again home to vast farmlands providing food for the city population and, especially, for the Dwarf colony under Erebor. Farmers are enlarging their fields every year, getting nearer and nearer to the great forest of Mirkwood and the northernmost extensions of the Long Marshes.

Erebor

The Lonely Mountain has been known as the lair of Smaug the Dragon for almost two centuries. Today, Erebor is again the seat of the King Under The Mountain and the most prosperous colony of Durin's Folk. It is an isolated peak, rising to the east of Mirkwood and south of its greater neighbours, the Grey Mountains. The Mountain is tall enough to be covered in snow until spring is underway, and extends over a wide area. Its slopes separate in six great spurs, long steep-sided ridges that fall towards the plains to the south and west, and in the direction of the Waste and its tumbled lands to the north and east.

The waters of the River Running spring from the roots of the Mountain, where the two southernmost spurs of the peak meet in a great cliff-wall. Here, the stream flows swiftly out of the Front Gate of the Dwarven stronghold and then winds a wide loop over the valley of Dale, before finally turning away from the Mountain on its way to the Long Lake.

Since the death of the Dragon, the followers of King Dáin have been busy cleansing all the passages of their underground kingdom, to free them from the stench of the worm that permeated every corner. Then, they started delving ever deeper, to carve halls and streets under the earth befitting a rich and powerful kingdom. In just a handful of years they have restored all the upper levels of their stronghold, and reopened many lower passages and tunnels that the Dragon blocked to defend his hoard.

Dale Adventure Seeds

◈ Odvarr of Dale was once a farmer in lands east of the Long Lake. He was wounded in the Battle of Five Armies, but his heroism in the fray won him many gifts from King Bard, and so Odvarr remained in Dale as it was rebuilt. Now, his daughter Kelda has come of age and will soon marry, so Odvarr seeks heroes to reward if they travel to his old farmstead and ensure it is safe and secure so he can gift it to his daughter.

◈ King Bard sees his new kingdom surrounded by good fertile land to be settled, but the Desolation of the Dragon left terrible scars on the world, and all the old maps were burnt. He needs heroes to go out and chart the borders of his new kingdom.

◈ The descendants of folk who fled the old town of Dale when the Dragon came have long memories. They remember that their ancestors were once wealthy lords who dwelt in great stone houses, and tales of buried gold and ancestral heirlooms have been passed down from one generation to the next. Now the Dragon is gone, and those ancestral holds can be reclaimed. The heroes might be employed to find the site of some long-lost mansion or tower, and to drive away any rival thieves and treasure-hunters.

Erebor Adventure Seeds

❖ Someone has been hunting the ravens of the Lonely Mountain. The culprit strikes at night and brings down its victims with a stone, but if it is thrown or flung from a sling, none can say. The Dwarves of Erebor are understandably upset about this and offer a rich reward for whoever can catch the murderer and bring them alive to King Dáin.

❖ Parties of Dwarves are making their way to Erebor from all across Middle-earth. They bring news from all the far flung corners of the world, and the knowledge gathering in Erebor is vast. If an adventurer needed to hear news from far away, Erebor, or the road toward it would be a place to start. Equally this gathering of families and clans can bring about problems of its own. Problems that outsiders might be best suited to solve.

The Iron Hills

The easternmost outpost of the Dwarves is the fortress of the Iron Hills. These hills have little in the way of silver or gold, the toys of the Dwarves, but are obviously rich in their servant iron. The great forges and smithies in the hills turn out weapons and armour in great profusion, and the doughty dwarves of the Iron Hills are the strong right arm of the King Under The Mountain.

Lake-town

Since the great days of old, when a powerful realm of Northmen stretched far from the Lonely Mountain, there has been a city upon the Long Lake. Grown out of a small community born along its western shore, the village of Esgaroth became a trading port when families of merchants decided to move there from Dale. They built warehouses, and great residences to live in and closely follow the coming and going of their goods. For many years thereafter the boats of the Lake-men were seen going up and down the river, their holds filled with gold and their decks crowded with warriors in armour, ready to bring war to distant lands. When Smaug descended on Erebor almost two hundred years ago, the town of Esgaroth was miraculously spared. Dale wasn't so fortunate, and those inhabitants who were able to escape its ruin with their lives were forced to seek asylum among the Lakemen. But in time, even the town along the shore had to be abandoned for fear of the Dragon, and the Lake-men built new dwellings directly on the surface of the Long Lake itself, in the hope that its deep, cold waters might keep them safe from the fire. Lake-town was born, and it endured under the shadow of the Mountain until the night Smaug fell upon it, and it disappeared in a cloud of steam and sparks.

Today, a great wooden bridge runs out from the western shore to reach the city of Esgaroth, built anew a few miles to the north of the spot where the bones of Smaug rest undisturbed. Larger than before, the new home of the Lake-people is also constructed upon stilts made of huge forest trees driven into the bottom of the lake, and its buildings, quays and streets bustle with the activities of a folk enjoying a greater level of prosperity than ever before. Skilful Elves from the kingdom of Thranduil have helped in the reconstruction, and their cunning art is visible in the many arches that bend as gracefully as tree boughs across the wider streets, and in the delicate frets that grace several house facades.

To this day Esgaroth remains a free city, governed by a Master elected from among the old and wise. He conducts the affairs of his office from a Great House in the main Market-place, on behalf of the people of Lake-town and advised by an assembly of councillors. His duty is to safeguard and preserve the peace and riches of the city, administering its trades and policies. In recent years Esgaroth has started to suffer from the proximity of the city of Dale: fearing for the independence of Lake-town, the Master of Esgaroth is tightening his trading and political relations with the Woodland Realm.

The Wood-elves have always been welcome in Lake-town, and they sent much sought-after help when the city was destroyed by Smaug. Elves have never stopped being an everyday sight for the Lake-men, both along the quays and in the houses of the most fashionable and influential merchant families.

Find out about Lake-town in more detail on page 28.

The Long Marshes

The lands opened wide about him, filled with the waters of the river which broke up and wandered in a hundred winding courses, or halted in marshes and pools dotted with isles on every side…

The narrow belt of land flanking both sides of the River Running where it touches the eastern eaves of Mirkwood has been turned into a trackless swampland by the flooding of the river waters over too many years to count. But in more recent times, relentless rains and even a couple of earthquakes have seen the Long Marshes expand their boundaries north, to reach and engulf even the course of the Forest River where it exits Mirkwood to the east. By 2946, the Long Marshes cover an area more than one hundred miles long from north to south, from the eastern borders of the Woodland Realm to the shores of the Long Lake, and south beyond the Mountains of Mirkwood.

To enter the Long Marshes, a traveller needs only follow the River Running as it goes south beyond the Long Lake, or the Forest River to the west. Often, the marshes will offer the same sight, regardless of the chosen direction: a wide, treeless expanse of mires and pools of sullen waters, unmoving but for the river course that stirs them. Here, thick mists rise in the morning, and lift only with the approaching of midday. But the fog never really disappears; rather it changes into a transparent vapour, capable of turning the brightest light of the Sun into the palest radiance. The dreariness of the region is multiplied where the marshes meet Mirkwood. Under the shadows of the forest all sounds of nature are utterly silenced and only chill breezes move the drooping branches of the trees that rise from the waters.

The Land of the Beornings

The borders of the land falling under Beorn's rule are defined by how far his followers are willing to go to pursue their enemies. To this day, this includes territories around both sides of the Great River near the Carrock. Since the day that Beorn decided to become a leader of men, his followers have come to live close to his house, building homesteads and small fortified settlements along the edge of Mirkwood, from the Old Forest Road up to the Forest Gate.

Beorn's House

Beyond a belt of ancient oaks and a very tall thornhedge, the House of Beorn encloses a wide area including gardens, wooden barns, stables and sheds, and a great house not very different from a traditional Northmen hall (see Northmen Great House on page 149 of the *Player's Guide*); rows of bell-shaped bee-hives show that Beorn's eating habits haven't changed since Bilbo's visit (even if it is plain that he doesn't enforce them on his followers, who

live mostly by hunting). It is here that Beorn can be found most of the times (at least during the day), holding council with the older and mightier among his followers, receiving foreigners and guests or baking his famous cakes.

The Land of the Beornings Adventure Seeds

- The Beornings protect the Old Ford from bandits and other dangers, and have made many enemies in doing so. When thieves attack the guards at the ford and murder several of them, can the adventurers track down the killers? And was the attack ordered by merchants embittered by the Beorning's high charges for crossing the River?

- Beorn will not suffer the trapping or hunting of animals on his lands. If he catches a band of wandering misfits tucking into venison, what will be asked in payment? Can the company turn an extremely angry Beorn into a patron?

- A shepherd claims that his young daughter was stolen and eaten by the Eagles of the North. The Eagles have stolen many of his sheep over the years, he says, and he knows the signs of their predations. Now, he demands that the heroes hunt down the King of the Eagles and extract justice for his loss. Can the company find out what really became of the girl? Might the keen-eyed Eagles be witnesses to the misdeed if they are not responsible for it?

The Carrock

The Carrock is a great hill of stone breaking the current of the river in the upper reaches of Anduin, to the north of the Old Ford. An ancient flight of steps starting from a small cave at the foot of the hill leads to a flat space on top. A stony ford joins the Carrock to the eastern shore of the Great River, but not to its western shore.

High Pass

A pass going over the Misty Mountains, connecting Wilderland to the western lands. The High Pass is known to most people as it is often a preferred route to the Redhorn Gate and the pass going over the mountains at the source of the Gladden River. Watching over the pass to free it from the threat of Goblins is one of the duties that Beorn requires from his folk, an obligation that the Beornings are glad to fulfil.

Old Ford

The Old Ford is the point where the Old Forest Road crosses the Great River. Once, a great stone bridge stood here, and the ruins of its foundations can still be seen in the drier season when the river is shallower. The ford is watched constantly by the Beornings, who also meet here to trade with other folks (mainly the Woodmen).

The Land of the Woodmen

The valleys along both sides of the Great River and the western eaves of Mirkwood are the home of the Woodmen. Numerous, brave and well-armed, they populate a land that is constantly imperilled by many threats. The Woodmen of Wilderland are not united under a crown, but are divided into several Houses, as they call a group of clans or families who dwell together in the same great hall under a common token of kinship. Every house is ruled by its council of Elders, a circle of the old and wise. In times of need, the Elders from all houses meet at a folk-moot, a great gathering where the most important decisions concerning the Woodmen at large are taken. There are four main Houses of Woodmen in Wilderland: the House of Mountain Hall, the House of Woodland Hall, the House of Woodmen-town and the House of Rhosgobel.

Mountain Hall

This is the main settlement of the Woodmen on the west side of the Great River. It is hidden in a narrow valley east of the Misty Mountains, where a turbulent stream runs amid steep walls of rock and around grassy knolls and pine-covered hills. The village itself is located where the river loops around an area of grassland set against the stony shoulder of the mountains. It is not protected by a stockade or hedge, as the watercourse has been widened and deepened, making the village accessible only by a dirt road cut along the stream where it passes the nearest to the rock face.

Many villagers work in mines dug into the mountains to the west, searching in the recesses of the earth for metals prized by all inhabitants of the vales of the Great River: copper, tin and iron. It is a dangerous trade, as many creatures lurk in the dark under the mountains, waiting patiently for the unwary.

The Land of the Woodmen Adventure Seeds

- The Woodmen dig mines into the Misty Mountains. The resulting ore is smelted in Mountain Hall and then poured into ingots for transport down the winding path and across the river to the other Woodmen settlements. The Woodmen guard this trade themselves, but with more and more being lost en route, something is amiss. Is it the predications of especially bold bandits, or something more sinister? Or is there some internal strife between the Woodmen families that is at the root of things?

- The Wizard Radagast has urgent business in the south, but fears that evil things in the forest will take advantage of his absence if he leaves Rhosgobel. He asks a Scholar among the heroes to temporarily masquerade as the Wizard, so no-one suspects that Rhosgobel lies undefended. Can the heroes fool the Spiders and their spies by pretending to be Radagast for a season?

- Old tales speak of another people, akin to the Woodwoses of the South, who once dwelt in the deep parts of the forest when Mirkwood was yet Greenwood the Great. The barrows and strangely carved statues of this vanished people can yet be found by those who dig deep enough in the wood. What became of this folk, and what did they leave behind?

Rhosgobel

Rhosgobel is the name of the place where the abode of Radagast is found, on the southwestern edge of Mirkwood just one hundred miles north of the naked hill where Dol Guldur rises. Its name ("Brown hay") comes from the high thorn-hedge that separates the area from the nearby forest. The Brown Wizard has been living here since before the Northmen came to the vales of Anduin. His presence has been greatly beneficial to the Woodmen, and over time a small village has sprung up; here the Woodmen dwell under one roof, the long House of the folk, as is their custom.

The Great Hall of Rhosgobel

This great building has its back to the wood and its face to the Great River, with two doors opening to the north and south. Radagast comes here often, although he usually prefers to reside in his own house some distance to the south of the great hall, a small cottage with a thatched roof inhabited by all sorts of birds.

Woodland Hall

Woodland Hall lies fifty miles to the south of the Old Forest Road, in a wide clearing cut in the forest by generations of axe-wielding Woodmen. It is the largest community of Men to be encountered within the borders of the wild wood, a village protected by a very tall hedge and a stout stockade, raised beside a river flowing south from the Mountains of Mirkwood.

Woodmen of all ages search for fish among the eddies of the Dusky River with bow, spear, net or line, as its waters are considered wholesome this far from the foulest depths of the forest. They also wash the gravel of its shallows looking for gold, brought here by the waters of the river from the roots of the mountains to the north. The great house of Woodland Hall is a very large building, built on a hillock whose sides have laboriously been made sheer on all sides but one, increasing its defensibility.

The Great Hall of Woodland Hall

Among the great houses of the woodland folk this is probably the most magnificent. Generations of carpenters once spent long hours with knife and gouge in hand to carve life-like images of beasts, warriors and women into the tough wood of the trees of Mirkwood. Every door and window-post, every pillar, rafter and beam tells a different tale, sometimes harkening back to times now forgotten, when the Woodmen lived in different lands. Such craft has never been equalled again, leaving the Woodmen of today to wonder at the cunning of their forefathers.

Adventures in Middle-earth

Woodmen-town

Woodmen-town lies forty miles to the south of Woodland Hall. It is a smaller settlement, lying in a clearing among the trees where the forest stream heads west, turning before the wood rises into low hills beyond its eastern shore. Several homesteads cluster around an ancient great house, built by a hero of the Woodmen when the Shadow was first banished from Mirkwood. With a history going back for more than nine hundred years, the House of Woodmen-town is the source of the most prominent families of the Woodmen (even if Woodland Hall is the largest dwelling of their folk). Its council of Elders is given precedence in all folk-moots, and many war-leaders have been chosen among its warriors and chieftains. Woodmen-town suffered greatly from the threat of the Shadow and, when noisome mists and vapours started to issue once again from Dol Guldur four centuries ago, many Woodmen left the village.

It is only thanks to the actions of the Wizard Radagast that Woodmen-town wasn't completely deserted. Today, many Woodmen are returning, as the darkness recedes from the western borders of the forest and birds and animals return to enliven the oak and beech woods with their cries.

The Hall of Balthi

This great house takes his name from a legendary hero of the folk. Under its roof the Woodmen keep their greatest treasure, a wondrous lamp burning with an everlasting blue light, the product of a craft so ancient it comes from a time before the reckoning of Men. It is held aloft by chains fastened to a beam of the roof. The lamp is encased in a fair and clear blue glass like a sapphire, wrought by craftsmen of the folk with figures in gold showing a young warrior, not much more than a boy, leading an elderly figure holding a staff through the woods, and advancing together towards a dark fortress on a hill. The Woodmen attribute the lamp with prodigious healing powers, and the great house is considered a hallowed place by all the Houses of the Woodmen.

Mirkwood

Described by many as "the greatest of the forests of the Northern world", Mirkwood is a sea of woodland measuring more than 400 miles from north to south and 200 miles from east to west, at the point where the Old Forest Road crosses its width. It extends across the very

middle of Wilderland, and its presence has shaped the history of the region for centuries. Nobody knows exactly what lies within its borders, as no one has thoroughly explored it.

The days when the Elvenking enforced his rule over all of Greenwood the Great are long gone, and the wild wood has reclaimed its hundreds of streams and shadowy vales, its clearings, bogs, hills and mountains. The creatures that inhabit it have become "queer and savage", as Beorn once put it, like the ever-present black squirrels, the thousands of black moths that crowd around any traveller carrying a source of light, and the hundreds of black butterflies that fly above the tree-tops. Many darker things have descended from the mountains that rise in the middle of the forest or have issued out of the pits of Dol Guldur, to breed and multiply in the dim shadows. Fortunately for all who live near its edge, the forest has grown less dark since the Necromancer was driven from his stronghold in the south of Mirkwood, and some think that it will soon be possible to open the Old Forest Road to traffic once again.

Mirkwood Adventure Seeds

- You may not step off the path yourself, but what will you do to help another who has done so? Danger can visit the door of even the best equipped adventurers when they agree to help the foolhardy or ill-prepared in Mirkwood. Where have they gone, and what has happened to them after they left the safety of the path? And are you so cold hearted as to leave them to an evil fate?

- There is no wood near the Lonely Mountain – the fires of the dragon burnt the pines that once grew atop the heights. Now, with both Dale and Erebor reclaimed and under reconstruction, there is a powerful hunger in the north for timber. The sounds of saws and axes disturb the peace of eastern Mirkwood as Dalish foresters labour to feed this demand – but it is never wise to cut down trees beloved by Elves, or trees that are deep-rooted in darkness...

Heart of Mirkwood

Trackless and unconquered by the light, the Heart of Mirkwood is the rotten core of the forest. Here the trees have huge, gnarled trunks, their twisted branches are heavy with strands upon strands of ivy and their roots are so tangled that in some places it is impossible to set foot upon the open ground. Many creatures have made their lair in this region, the darkest part of the forest, and most Spiders seem to emerge from its remote corners. Nothing that goes on two legs is welcome here, and not even the boldest of Orcs dares to enter.

Northern Mirkwood

This region borders with the Woodland Realm, where the Forest River cuts the northernmost portion of Mirkwood neatly in half. Despite its proximity to the realm of Thranduil, this area is very dark, and dense cobwebs stretch from tree to tree; the clear sign of the presence of Spiders. For a while now, the only viable way across Mirkwood has been found here, where the Forest Gate admits entrance to the Elf-path. This is a trail made by the Silvan Elves, and it is protected by the Elvenking's magic from being overgrown or blocked by cobwebs. Near its eastern end, a small forest river interrupts the path with dark, swift waters said to carry an enchantment capable of making anyone who drinks from it drowsy and forgetful.

Mountains of Mirkwood

The Mountains of Mirkwood were once known by the Elves as the Dark Mountains because of the colour of their slopes, covered by dense forests of dark fir. With the passing of the centuries the name assumed a different interpretation, as the Dark Lord's most hideous creatures began to haunt the range. It is from cold caves under these mountains that the great bats that participated in the Battle of Five Armies came from, and many returned there to mend their wounds and brood upon their defeat. From a spring among these mountains the Enchanted Stream flows to meet the Forest River to the north, as do several other brooks and creeks that lose themselves in winding courses among the trees of Mirkwood or in the Long Marshes to the east.

Southern Mirkwood

Southern Mirkwood was the land of the Necromancer. His dark tower sits upon a hill surrounded by a forest of dark firs. From its gate issue dozens of paths and trails that spread like a web across the region, the roads once used by his many servants, spies and soldiers. Today, the vast fortress of Dol Guldur is empty and silent, but the presence of its former master echoes still in its many dark halls and chambers. His malevolent will weighs upon the region like a curse, and his influence is felt by anyone who tries to approach it, and by those creatures that still lurk in the area, waiting.

The Narrows of the Forest

Approximately 140 miles south of the Old Forest Road, the width of the forest narrows until it measures less than 100 miles across. This tapering 'waist' was created centuries ago by the work of a powerful folk of Northmen that once lived in the lands to the west of the wild wood. The large indentation along the eastern border of Mirkwood is all that is left of their realm. They cleared it by felling many trees for the building of their homes and to make space for their pastures.

Several paths made by the Silvan Elves used to cross the entire width of the Narrows of the Forest, and other folks made use of them when the Elvenking forsook these lands. Today, many Woodmen know where these tracks start but nobody knows whether they lead anywhere or simply disappear where the forest is darker. Stories tell of how these paths are haunted by Wood-wights, restless ghosts of Northmen who died as slaves when an enemy folk took their land, centuries ago.

Western Mirkwood

The wide portion of the forest that extends to the west of the Mountains of Mirkwood is as dark and dreary as most of the wild wood. Here, the Old Forest Road used to enter Mirkwood, approximately thirty miles east of the Old Ford. Also known as the 'Dwarf-road', the Old Forest Road used to run across the forest for over 200 miles, to emerge where it was interrupted by the Running River. At the time of the journey of Bilbo, the road was said to be used by Goblins and overgrown by vegetation. Five years later, the situation might have improved as the Orcs have been severely diminished at the Battle of Five Armies, and the road might soon be opened again.

Woodland Realm

The area of Mirkwood to the north of the Forest River is claimed by the Elvenking as his own domain. In another age of the world, the Elvenking sat at court on the hill of Amon Lanc, where today stands the dreaded fortress of Dol Guldur. But the day came when the King left his realm to bring war upon the Enemy at the head of a powerful host, and never returned. His mourning son took his place on the throne, and retreated north with his people. When, centuries, later the forest darkened and Orcs and Spiders spread under its shadows, the Elvenking withdrew again, finding sanctuary in a stronghold under the earth, not far from the eastern side of Mirkwood.

Today his subjects dwell in wooded valleys of ancient oaks and beeches, along the river that runs out of the Grey Mountains to the north and flows into the Long Marshes to the east. Here, they live in houses and huts built upon the surface of the forest and high up on the branches of the trees.

The Halls of the Elvenking

Protected by magic and by great doors of stone, the underground fortress of the Wood-elves is a palace and treasury for their King, a refuge for their folk and a prison for their enemies. The Halls are built into a system of caves underneath a great hill, and host many comfortable chambers and passages, including the royal residence of King Thranduil. A subterranean watercourse flows under the hill where the wine cellars of the palace are located, along with the deep dungeons reserved for those who must be kept prisoner at the orders of the King.

Other Lands

To the north stretch the Grey Mountains where the Dwarves long delved, and the Withered Heath, the ancient breeding ground of Dragons. Beyond them lie the frozen wastes, enshrouded in cold mists and dark legends.

To the east lay endless plains where strange tribes dwell and multiply, until the day a new king or chieftain will once again harness their hatred and bring them to war against the west.

The West

To the west extend the Misty Mountains, a range of forbidding peaks riddled by Goblin tunnels and mines, running for almost 800 miles from the far north to the south. Beyond is the haunted land of Eriador, where once great kingdoms reigned, but now the lands are mostly empty. The Elves of Eregion are gone; so too are the men of the North-Kingdom of Arnor. Only scant remnants remain – the hidden valley of Rivendell, the Dúnedain, and the Grey Havens, last outpost of the Elves on the hither shore. The Dúnedain patrol the old East-West road, and guard the Shire of the Hobbits and the human settlement of Bree-land from orcs, trolls and worse things that have crawled out of the shadows of Angmar.

Near the Havens lie the Blue Mountains, another dwarf-hold where Thorin Oakenshield and his companions once dwelt. Now, dwarves hurry east along the road, eager to return to their ancestral halls under the Lonely Mountain. It was in Eriador that Thorin met the wizard Gandalf the Grey, and made the acquaintance of Mr. Bilbo Baggins, esq., treasure-hunter extraordinaire.

It is the Dwarves who bring news west, and so their tales shape the impressions the Hobbits and Bree-folk have of Wilderland. When the Dragon ruled in Erebor, the dwarves described Wilderland as being full of perils and sorrow. Now, they speak of a new King Under The Mountain and new hope in the north. King Bard's call has reached even the taprooms of *The Prancing Pony* and *The Green Dragon*, and some in the west look to Wilderland to seek their fortunes.

The South

The River Anduin flows through Wilderland, and on past the Falls of Rauros to the southlands: the rolling fields of Rohan, and the land of Gondor, the last remnant of vanished Numenor. For all of the Third Age, Gondor has kept watch on the Enemy's realm of Mordor, and battled with the forces of Minas Morgul. Gondor is much diminished from its days of glory: the city of Osgiliath has been abandoned, and there is no king in Minas Tirith any more, only a line of stewards. Still, even the faded glory of Gondor outshines every other free realm in Middle-earth, and the alliance of Gondor and Rohan makes the southlands a formidable force in this age of the world.

Gondor historically paid little heed to Wilderland – the attention of the Tower of Guard has ever looked to the east. Still, the fall of the Dragon and the rise of Dale has brought cheer even to the distant south. With the Necromancer gone and the shadow lifted from Mirkwood (at least for now), there are more traders and adventurers on the roads than ever before. This is, sadly, destined to be only a brief respite, for in a few years' time the Dark Lord will return to Mordor and Gondor will once again be under siege.

And if Gondor falls, the forces of evil will march across all of Wilderland...

The Tale of Years

Three timelines have been included in this section: the first (**Old Lore**) presents facts mainly concerning the ancient history of relevant areas of Middle-earth and the folks inhabiting it; the second (**Recent Past**) offers information that is considered common knowledge to most starting adventurers; the third chronology (**Gathering Shadows**) outlines current and possible future developments that can be witnessed or affected by the heroes themselves.

Old Lore

"Long ago in my grandfather Thrór's time our family was driven out of the far North..."

The information presented in most entries below may be revealed to a character belonging to the folk most concerned with the information and proficient in Lore. Entries in *italics* are reserved for the Loremaster's eyes, as they relate facts known only to a few (if anyone at all).

Year 1050
About this time, a shadow takes shape in Greenwood the Great. The forest is darkened and Orcs and Spiders begin to spread from the Naked Hill in the south. The Silvan Elves confine themselves to the northernmost regions of the forest, and Men begin to call it Mirkwood. *The earliest tales of the Hobbits relating to their Wandering Days seem to indicate that they once came from these areas.*

Year 1980
The Dwarves of the line of Durin delve too deep under the Misty Mountains and awaken an ancient evil. After millennia of prosperity, the vast halls of Khazad-dûm, Wonder of the Northern world, are abandoned the following year, its inhabitants driven out by fear and death.

Adventures in Middle-earth

Year 1999

Thrain I, King of Durin's folk and distant ancestor of Thorin Oakenshield, comes to the Lonely Mountain and founds a dwarf-kingdom. There, the Dwarves discover their most prized treasure, the Arkenstone, known also as the Heart of the Mountain.

Year 2063

In the past centuries, the increase in power of the Necromancer of Dol Guldur has been responsible for the slow but steady diminishing of the inhabitants of the vales of the Great River. In the year 2063, the Wizard Gandalf finally enters the fortress to investigate the matter (songs and legends of the Woodmen have him led through Mirkwood by the young son of a hunter).

The evil power dwelling in Dol Guldur retreats when faced by Gandalf's challenge and flies to the East. The Wizard returns from the pits of the fortress carrying a treasure, and gives it to the Woodmen for safekeeping (see Woodmen-town on page 18). This begins the period known to the Wise as the Watchful Peace, a truce that will last for four hundred years.

The shadow over Mirkwood weakens and many folks that were forced to leave return to their lands: the Woodmen multiply and prosper in the following years, establishing settlements both east and west of the Great River.

Year 2210

Thorin I, son of Thrain, removes the royal house of Durin's folk from Erebor to abide in the Grey Mountains. He carries the Arkenstone with him, as part of the royal treasure.

Year 2460

After four centuries of hiding, the Dark Lord secretly returns to Dol Guldur. His strength is increased, and his dark thoughts are felt by all malevolent creatures. The Ring heeds the call of its maker and stirs from its resting place.

Mirkwood darkens once again as evil things are called back and creep into the forest. In the following decades, many people choose to leave the region and go south.

Year 2463

At the request of the Lady Galadriel, a White Council of the Wise and Powerful is formed to unite the forces of the West against the Shadow. Saruman the White, who has long studied the Enemy and his servants, is chosen to lead it. The Elvenking of Northern Mirkwood is invited to join, but refuses.

It is around this year that Déagol, a Stoor Hobbit, finds the One Ring while swimming in the Gladden River. It does not remain in his possession for long, as his friend Sméagol murders him to get it for himself. In the

following years Sméagol is estranged from his people, and eventually seeks refuge under the Misty Mountains.

Year 2480
Answering commands issued from their master in Dol Guldur, the Orcs begin to spread in the dark places beneath the Misty Mountains. From Mount Gundabad in the north to Moria in the south they secretly strengthen every stronghold, barring all the passes into the lands west of the mountains.

To respond to the increasing threat from the mountains, the Woodmen of the western river vales raise their burg at Mountain Hall, building upon the foundations of an older fortification.

Year 2510
Following a great battle, Eorl the Young, lord of the Horsefolk of the north, leads his people from the upper vales of the river Anduin to live as free Men in the plains of Calenardhon, far in the distant south. He becomes the first King of the Mark of the Riders.

Year 2570
Late in the reign of Náin II, a plague of Dragons begins to afflict the Dwarven mansions in the Grey Mountains. The Dwarves face a long and terrible war.

Year 2589
The Dragons of the northern waste spread south to prey on the Dwarves. King Dáin I and his second son Frór are slain by a Cold-drake while barring the gates to their halls.

Year 2590
Thrór, the eldest son of Dáin I and heir to the kingship, restores the royal house to its ancient seat in Erebor. The Arkenstone is brought back to its place in the Great Hall of Thrain, and with it returns a great part of Durin's folk. They mine and tunnel the roots of the Mountain, enlarging the subterranean kingdom building huge halls and greater workshops. Another group of Dwarves is led eastward by his brother Grór, the third son of Dáin: under his rule they eventually settle in the Iron Hills. About this time, several clans of Northmen living along the River Running move north to be closer to the Lonely Mountain. They befriend the Dwarven colony of Erebor, attracted by the opportunities offered by the brisk trade with the Iron Hills.

The city of Dale prospers, and the following hundred years see it become the capital of a strong kingdom extending far and wide to the East and South.

Year 2740
Dismayed by the increasing forces of both Dwarves and Men of the North, many Orcs resort to raiding the regions west of the Misty Mountains. This threat comes mainly from their stronghold of Mount Gram.

Year 2747
At the Battle of Greenfields, Hobbits of the Shire face and defeat an Orc-band from Mount Gram. Their king, the Orc Golfimbul, is killed by Bandobras Took, better known as the "Bullroarer".

Year 2758
About this time, the wild folks of the East move against their enemies. In the North, the armies of Dale muster under the banner of King Bladorthin, but between the end of 2758 and the first months of 2759, stiff, relentless winds hit the North, covering the lands with snow and ice. The Long Winter has come, and King Bladorthin dies before he sees the end of it. He is succeeded by his young son Girion, who drives his enemies back to the eastern frontiers of the realm.

For five months, the Long Winter causes great suffering and inflicts grievous losses on many peoples. Gandalf the Grey himself intervenes, coming to the aid of the Shire-folk.

Year 2770
One night, Smaug the Dragon descends on the Lonely Mountain spouting flames. The Dwarves are caught by surprise and Erebor is sacked, its inhabitants slain. Warriors from Dale are destroyed too, and Girion their lord is killed. Thrór, the King Under The Mountain, escapes the slaughter by secret means with his son Thráin. They are joined in exile by Thorin, the young son of Thráin.

The Dragon claims the underground halls of Erebor as his lair, and its treasure becomes his hoard. From the Mountain, Smaug starts preying upon the neighbouring lands, killing people and livestock and reducing the surrounding area to a wasteland. Some time later, Dale is deserted and slowly crumbles to ruins.

Year 2790
Thrór, Dwarven King in exile, is captured and slain in Moria by the Great Orc Azog. Preparing a war of vengeance, his son Thráin calls for a great muster of Dwarves.

Year 2793
The Dwarves of Durin's Folk, strengthened by great forces sent from the Houses of the other Fathers of the Dwarves, begin a long and cruel war against the Orcs of the Misty Mountains.

Year 2799
The final battle of the War of the Dwarves and Orcs is fought before the East-gate of Moria. The Dwarves are victorious, and a very young Dáin Ironfoot distinguishes himself by killing Azog singlehandedly. But victory has a bitter taste: the war has greatly reduced the number of Orcs still dwelling in the mountains, but at the cost of a frightful number of lives.

After the battle, the various Houses part ways without attempting to reclaim Moria, and the Dwarves are dispersed again to the four winds: Dáin Ironfoot returns to the Iron Hills. Thráin and his son Thorin wander westwards, to eventually settle in the Blue Mountains to the northwest.

Year 2841
A lust for gold slowly takes possession of Thráin. He resolves to return to Erebor and convinces Balin and Dwalin and a few others to leave the Blue Mountains with him. Their wanderings bring them again beyond the Misty Mountains, until on a dark night Thráin disappears in Mirkwood.

Year 2850
After almost eight hundred years, Gandalf the Grey once again enters Dol Guldur in secrecy. Inside the evil fortress, he finds his darkest fears to be true: the dreaded Necromancer is indeed the dark lord Sauron. Before fleeing the black stronghold, the Wizard encounters the missing Heir of Durin: a stricken Thráin entrusts him with a map and a key and then dies.

Year 2851
The White Council meets in Rivendell to confer about Gandalf the Grey's discoveries in Dol Guldur. He urges a move against the Dark Lord, proposing an attack on his fortress. Saruman opposes Gandalf's advice, asserting that the Council is not yet ready and that for the moment Dol Guldur should not be molested for fear of worse repercussions (at this time, Saruman has already discovered that the One Ring was lost in the Gladden Fields, and does not want any interference in his attempts to find it).

Year 2890
Bilbo Baggins of Bag End is born in the Shire, son of Bungo Baggins and Belladonna Took.

Year 2900
Despite the dangers of Wilderland, many bold men and women make their way back into the vales of the Great River from the South. They are welcomed by Radagast the Brown to 'live in amongst the more pleasant woods in the valleys and along the river-shores'.

Year 2911
An extremely fierce and long cold season begins in November. Remembered as the Fell Winter, its frozen grip doesn't release the regions of the North from snow and ice for five months. Rivers and lakes are frozen over, and white wolves descend from the frozen wastes of the far North. When the frigid winds finally relent in March of the following year, rivers overflow with the melting of the snow and many lands are flooded as a result. It is about this time that the Long Marshes spread extensively, extending from the Old Forest Road to the Forest River.

Year 2931
Aragorn, son of Arathorn, is born on March 1st. He is the direct descendant of Isildur, the last High King of the Men of the West. Two years later, his father is killed while riding against the Orcs of Mount Gram with the sons of Elrond Halfelven. His mother Gilraen takes Aragorn to Rivendell, where he is received by Elrond as foster-son. He is given the name Estel (Hope) and his lineage concealed.

RECENT PAST
... there came one day to Bilbo's door the great Wizard, Gandalf the Grey, and thirteen Dwarves with him...

The following entries report the relevant events that have occurred in the past five years. Entries not in *italics* are to be considered common knowledge for any character coming from the North, as this great news has spread far and wide in Wilderland. Even for characters coming from the South, they have likely heard distorted rumours of what has transpired.

Year 2941

The Wizard Gandalf, Thorin Oakenshield and thirteen Dwarven companions visit Bilbo the Hobbit in the Shire: they set upon a quest to recover the treasure of Durin's Folk and free the North from the threat of the Dragon of Erebor.

Gandalf temporarily abandons the expedition to persuade the White Council to strike decisively against Dol Guldur: this time, Saruman approves and the council sets upon the difficult task. But Sauron yet again anticipates the moves of his enemies and retreats from his fastness: the Dark Power leaves Mirkwood.

A series of unlikely events lead to the death of Smaug and to the destruction of Lake-town. Dáin of the Iron Hills becomes King of the restored Kingdom under the Mountain, while Dwarves, Men and Elves collaborate in rebuilding new cities in Dale and upon the Long Lake.

Year 2942

Bilbo returns to his peaceful life in the Shire. He carries the One Ring with him, not suspecting its true nature. News of the great events that have come to pass spread across the land as he travels home.

The Dark Lord returns to Mordor. He is received by his most powerful servants, the nine Ringwraiths, who prepared for his return in their stronghold of Minas Morgul.

Year 2943

The Master of Lake-town falls victim of the Dragon-sickness and leaves, carrying with him most of the gold given to him by Bard for the help of the Lake-people. Initially helped by some companions, he is then abandoned and dies of starvation in the Waste.

Year 2944

The creature Gollum leaves his lair under the Mountains and begins his search for the thief of the Ring. Some time later, he enters Mirkwood, to eventually reach Esgaroth and even the streets of Dale. For a while he is watched closely by the Wood-elves.

Years 2944-2945

Bard completes the reconstruction of Dale and is crowned King. A new Lake-town is completed on the Long Lake and trade resumes up and down the Running River. Beorn establishes his rule as a great chief at the head of his new followers, soon to be known as the Beornings.

Gathering Shadows

One autumn evening some years afterwards, Bilbo was sitting in his study writing his memoirs...

The following entries describe events concerning Wilderland from year 2946 to 2951. Here no entries are given in *italics*, as all featured events are available for the Loremaster to use in any ways desired. For example, each entry could be expanded to constitute the main plot of an Adventuring phase, or narrated to players as part of the Year's End segment of a Fellowship phase, or simply employed as a descriptive background element.

Some information won't be revealed to players at all, but kept secret until the day it will become known (if it will be discovered at all).

There are no major events recorded in the sources for the first four years, and so a handful of simple ones have been devised for the game (mainly to facilitate the introduction of a new group of heroes). Without earth-shattering occurrences, new characters have plenty of room to develop their adventuring careers before more important occurrences start affecting their lives: in year 2951, the first seeds of the War of the Ring are planted, and a new era for Middle-earth begins.

Year 2946

The Gathering of Five Armies

In the last days of November, on the fifth anniversary of the eponymous battle, a great feast celebrating the victory at the Battle of Five Armies is held in Dale for the first time. People from all neighbouring lands are expected to participate in the revels, as the feast has been arranged to coincide with local celebrations held for the end of the harvest season and the beginning of the colder months of the year.

These celebrations are a great occasion to put together a group of new heroes, so the default assumption of *Adventures in Middle-earth* is that the game starts here and now.

The Council of the North
During the first Gathering, envoys from Lake-town, the Woodland Realm and the Kingdom under the Mountain meet in the presence of King Bard to debate matters concerning Wilderland. The player-heroes may be present as representatives of their own folk, and might even meet each other at the Gathering.

Year 2947
Gollum seeks the One Ring
About this time, Gollum abandons the trail of Bilbo over the Misty Mountains and turns back. He hides in Mirkwood, slowly making his way to the South. His presence fills the forest with dreadful rumours, and among the Woodmen a tale starts to spread, telling of a blood-drinking ghost preying upon the unwary.

Heroes journeying through Mirkwood or spending a Fellowship phase in proximity to the forest might see a glimpse of Gollum.

Year 2948
The Grey Pilgrim
Fearing a possible estrangement between the Folks of the North, Gandalf the Grey visits the courts of Elves, Men and Dwarves. He is considering the possibility of inviting one of their rulers to become a member of the White Council. The choice will be offered either to King Dáin, the Elvenking, King Bard or Beorn. Gandalf will consider his choices, and then present his candidate to the head of the council, the Wizard Saruman.

If the heroes are in a position to be considered as counsellors, Gandalf listens to their advice.

Year 2949
Gandalf and Balin visit Bilbo
Gandalf and Balin journey to the Shire to visit Bilbo Baggins. They arrive at Bag End on one autumn evening. They spend some time together, talking of their adventuring times and about how things are going in Wilderland. Balin doesn't hide his disquiet from his good friend, and tries to convince Bilbo to join him in a new adventure. Bilbo is reluctant, and in the end declines the invitation.

If a hero hails from the Shire, he might actually witness the episode.

Year 2951
Sauron Declares in Mordor
After nine years of preparations, Sauron unveils his presence in the black land of Mordor. He is ready to spread his power far and wide, and begins to rebuild his Dark Tower. His will is bent on gathering a vast army in the black land, and his summons are answered by all sorts of wicked creatures. Gollum is among them, and his path slowly turns in the direction of Mordor.

At this time, characters with at least a permanent Shadow point or a Shadow rating of 3 or more may experience nightmares, mostly visions of the black land, the raising of the Dark Tower, or the Flaming Eye.

The Nazgûl enter Dol Guldur
As his first act of war, Sauron sends the Nazgûl to reclaim his stronghold in southern Mirkwood. Their arrival triggers once again the Darkening of Mirkwood. Rumours of a new Shadow in the South start to be whispered by many folks in the North. Orcs and Goblins are found bearing the symbol of a lidless Eye.

The Return of Arwen
Arwen, daughter of Elrond, returns to Rivendell to visit her father after a long stay in Lórien.

The Departure of Aragorn
On the day of his coming of age (March 1st) Aragorn learns about his true name and heritage from Elrond, his foster-father. From his hands he receives two heirlooms of his House: the shards of the sword Narsil and the ring of Barahir. The next day, Aragorn encounters Arwen for the first time and falls in love with her. Upon learning of her true nature and heritage, Aragorn leaves Rivendell to go into the wild. Many Rangers set out around the same time, spreading out east of the mountains.

Adventures in Middle-earth

a guide to
- lake-town -

Your first *Adventures in Middle-earth* campaign is likely to begin in Lake-town. With Bard's proclamation circulating Wilderland and beyond, adventurers of all kinds are drawn here to help King Bard in his work of establishing his new kingdom of free peoples.

Lake-town is the perfect place for your company to meet and to find work as adventurers. In the default setting of *Adventures in Middle-earth* it is considered the first sanctuary available to a new company. Your company of Player-heroes can quickly build some shared history and expand beyond this starting point if they desire, but it's a truly useful and inspiring place to begin. This section details Lake-town, also known as Esgaroth, five years after the death of Smaug.

Rivalled in the North only by the city of Dale, Esgaroth is a unique sight. In a region where most populated settlements are no larger than a group of farmsteads surrounded by hedges, Lake-town is an island made of timber rising from the waters of the Long Lake, and crowded with roofs, streets and towers.

Esgaroth was originally settled as a trading port when the North was rich and prosperous. It achieved its independence when the Lord of Dale allowed its citizens to appoint a Master, chosen from the old and wise. For centuries, Lake-town has endured thanks to its position, set strategically between the Woodland Realm, the Kingdom under the Mountain, and the city of Dale.

Today Esgaroth is a thriving port, measuring almost thrice the size of the town that Smaug destroyed. Beyond the falls to the south of the Long Lake, the Celduin River runs for many leagues, until it reaches the great inland Sea of Rhûn, past the land of Dorwinion. From there and beyond, travellers arrive in Lake-town aboard trading ships and rafts, bringing wares and goods for sale at the markets of the city. The map of Esgaroth at the front of this guide shows the home of the river-faring Men of the Lake as it appears in the year 2949, when its population has grown to over one thousand people. The following sections give information about the town's different districts, and the buildings contained in them.

GATEHOUSE AND BRIDGE DEFENSES

The great bridge that connects Esgaroth to the shores of the Long Lake ends in a tall **Gatehouse** (5 on the map). It serves the purpose of guarding access to the city, should enemies succeed in taking the defenders unawares so that they are unable to throw down and destroy the bridge. The

gatehouse lets archers attack assailants from a protected vantage point, and murder-holes allow other defenders to rain down rocks on attackers trying to smash the gates. The palisade to the left and right of the Gatehouse allows more archers to target foes on the bridge, catching them in a deadly crossfire. Should the enemy penetrate the Gatehouse, they would find themselves in a killing zone, bordered by the **Tollhouse** (15) and an encircling palisade. From the top of the palisade, rows of archers would rain arrows down on the attackers.

The large **Tollhouse** (15) is defended by stout wooden gates. Here, those who enter the city are inspected and merchants must pay a tax to town officials for the right to enter and sell their wares in the town markets. The **Guard barracks** (8) and the **Bowmen's Guild-hall** (1) stand conveniently close to the palisade defending the Gatehouse, to the left and right of the bridge defences, respectively. A suspended bridge connects the courtyard behind the Guard barracks to a detached building that serves as the town gaol. Here are led those who break the laws upheld by the town council.

Gatehouse and Bridge Defences Adventure Seeds

- With so much trade coming through Lake-town in recent months, the importance – and workload – of the tax collectors and customs inspectors has increased greatly. Bribery is always rife here, and trustworthy heroes may be called upon to investigate particularly egregious cases – or to hunt down a treacherous rogue who's stolen from the tollhouse coffers.

- The opening-up of the north brings strangers who have never visited these lands before. Travellers come up the River Running and the roads from Dorwinion. Some come fleeing the wars of the South; others look for new opportunities, or are simply curious. Still others are spies of the Enemy. When a stranger asks the adventurers about Lake-town, what do they tell her? What purpose lies behind her questions?

Town Guards

A number of armed guards are assigned every day and night to guard the great bridge, to man the various city gates, and to protect the Town-hall and its main occupants - the Master of Esgaroth and his councillors. The Town guard is an armed force under the direct command of the council of Esgaroth, and its main duty is to keep custody of specific assigned places, leaving the job of dealing with any other types of trouble to the Town watchmen.

Guards are trained and equipped at the **Guard barracks** (8). In the case of an armed threat or other serious disturbance, the Town guard is joined by the archers of the Bowman's Guild. The Town guard is ocassionally known to call on hired hands should they need eyes and ears, or perhaps a sword arm, beyond the Town itself.

Merchants' District

The widest gap opening in the middle of Lake-town is the **Market-pool** (10), and the nearby open area is the city's main **Market square** (11). This is certainly the largest and busiest district of the town, where a large share of the town population lives and merchants from distant lands come to meet those of Esgaroth, Dale, Erebor and the Woodland Realm, and where farmers from the nearby lands come to sell their goods.

Boats and barges from the south unload here their cargoes of wine, olive oil, spices and salt, pottery, dyes and other more exotic goods, and fill the town warehouses. Then, they are loaded once again with grain and wool, the handiwork of Dwarven smiths, and with the wares sold by the vendors who manage the stalls of drapers, leather dressers and skinners, shoemakers, saddlers, and other craftsmen.

The trading of livestock is dealt with inside the fenced off area close to the Market-pool; here, farmers sell their cattle, sheep and poultry to the butchers of Esgaroth, who will prepare the meat for sale along Butchers' Quay, together with fish and wild fowl. Farmers who don't have animals to trade are allowed to sell cheese, eggs, roots and herbs along Bridge Street as pedlars.

Everything that can be sold or bought in Lake-town is on offer in this district, with the exception of timber, gold and precious stones - these materials are sold and bought exclusively within the so-called 'Elven quarter'. The finest

alehouses and inns are to be found along Bridge Street, the street that connects the city gates to the Market square. Here, wandering musicians find shelter under its overhanging gables to entertain the passers-by.

The **Merchants' Guild-hall** (12) is one of the largest buildings in Lake-town, and functions as the communal meeting hall and hospital for all the members of the guild of Merchants. An association created for the mutual aid of its members, the guild holds considerable power, as the Master of the city is often chosen from its affiliates. The hall is used by the merchants of the guild to conduct their affairs, as a meeting place for private businesses, and to give assistance to those members that cannot exercise their trade due to old age or sickness. In agreement with the city council, the night-watch starts its progress through the city streets from the Merchants' Guild-hall, as most of the town granaries and warehouses are located in the vicinity. Warning trumpets are always ready to sound from the top of its tower in the case of fire or other impending danger.

> ### Merchants' District Adventure Seed
>
> ◆ Lodin the Half-Blind is a down on his luck musician that can barely keep himself fed and sheltered. He spends most of his days wandering along the quays of the Merchants' District or playing outside the inns of Bridge Street. He knows tales of ancient heroes and lost treasures, and readily uses them to try and earn his keep. One of his tales speaks of a Dwarven expedition to clear the Old Forest Road that failed to return from Mirkwood. It is said that ancient arms and armour, exemplars of the Dwarven craft from before the coming of Smaug, were lost with them.

Merchants

A merchant is a member of a family who prospers by dealing in the buying and selling of wares. Normally, merchants from Lake-town sell local products (like wool, iron tools, painted glass) and buy foreign goods (like wine, spices and salt, dyes for the colouring of textiles) to sell them in the markets of Esgaroth and Dale. Merchants visit both cities regularly and own small fleets of boats to carry their wares up and down the river. Many a firstborn in a merchant family spends a good part of the year abroad, as they are sent to distant markets aboard a merchant vessel to supervise the family business.

Merchants are busy folk, always distrustful of strangers but possibly interested in the services of adventurers who proved trustworthy in the past. Aging merchants and trading matrons are often accompanied by their older children, brash youths with expensive clothes and quick tongues.

Dwarf Smiths

Many tireless smiths work their forges under the Mountain to make weapons, armour and tools that will eventually make their way to the hands of warriors, farmers and craftsmen all over Wilderland. Often, apprentices are sent to the market square of Esgaroth to sell their handiwork to local ironmongers, or to merchants headed to distant lands.

It is said that their work cannot match that of the Dwarven smiths of old, but they still make stout coats of mail and sharp blades and their workshops are always crowded with the young sons of Barding nobles and craftsmen, sent there as apprentices in the hope that one day they will learn the secrets of Dwarven craftsmanship.

Artisans' District

North of the Market-pool, the streets of Lake-town become narrow and twisted. Here, small, two-storied houses lean one against the other, creating a maze of darkened alleys. These are the workshops and living quarters of the many artisans and craftspeople in Esgaroth, a thousand-faceted expression of the burgeoning prosperity of the town.

Many-coloured and fanciful signs hang from the workshop fronts, in the attempt to give some order to the general chaos and identify precisely the trade of each craftsman. But the confusion is only an initial distraction, as the local artisans have divided the quarter neatly, dedicating even the smallest alley to a different trade.

Drapers, leather dressers and skinners, tailors, saddlers and shoemakers give their names to the narrow lanes in the interior of the district. Closer to the Market square is

Millers' Row, where most of the bread bakers have their shops, but the Street of Bowyers and Fletchers is probably the most prominent, with its window shutters painted in black and white checkers.

On the Day of the Black Arrow (1st of November), a procession of artisans carrying aloft the symbols of their trade and led by the Master of the town starts here and opens the festivities known as Dragontide.

With so many of the workshops in the Artisans' District requiring the use of furnaces, ovens or kilns, it should come as no surprise to find here the main barracks of the **Town Watch** (17). Its tall tower lets the watchmen enjoy a good view of the town, and also guards over the nearby merchant warehouses.

Artisans' District Adventure Seed

◈ A jeweller made seven necklaces studded with gemstones that he found in the lake – stones that were once part of Smaug's fabled diamond waistcoat. The dragon-sickness still lies heavily on these stones, and those who wear the necklaces are doomed to go mad. To make matters worse, the dwarves still have claim on those gemstones as part of the hoard of the King Under The Mountain, and the jeweller fled into Mirkwood when dwarves came to his workshop asking questions about the stones. Can the adventurers find the seven necklaces before tragedy strikes?

Craftspeople

Many of the people who come to live in Esgaroth every year are artisans, or become apprentices to some craftspeople, as the city offers many opportunities for those who are willing to exercise or learn a trade. Every year, the Kingdom under the Mountain, the city of Dale and the new Lake-town need more people who can bake bread, sew clothes, make shoes, dye fabrics, weave tapestries, build houses, carts, boats, pottery and so on. Craftspeople are usually peaceful individuals, dedicated to their chosen crafts. Most of the craftspeople of Lake-town operate in small workshops built on the ground floor of a building in the Artisans' district, and live upstairs on the first floor with their families (tanners are the exception, as they are forbidden by decree to exercise their trade within the city, for reasons of the foul smell produced by their work). Artisans and craftspeople often have need of materials that can be hard for normal folk to come by.

Town Watch

When the very foundations of a town are built from wood, its safety relies on ever-watchful eyes, ready to notice the tiniest flicker of an unguarded flame and raise the alarm. The watchmen of Esgaroth are a group of one hundred volunteers who patrol the town at night, ready to quench any unattended fire. For this purpose, every watchman carries a small bucket made with rope sealed with pitch, a small axe, and a small brass trumpet to send a warning blast if help is required. In the case of a larger fire, the watchmen can rapidly retrieve ladders, hooks and other useful equipment from their barracks.

In addition to their duty as firefighters, the watchmen of Lake-town serve as the city's night watch to guard the streets and buildings from burglars, thieves, or other kind of troublemakers. One in every three watchmen (called a 'captain') carries a buckler and a sword. But if any serious threat arises, the watchmen are instructed to sound their warning trumpets and wait for the town guard and the archers of the Bowmen's Guild to show up.

Elven Quarter

The corner to the southwest is entirely occupied by the district known today as the 'Elven quarter', as since the refounding of the town it has been traditionally inhabited by diplomats, emissaries, merchants and traders coming from the Woodland Realm. All timber coming from Mirkwood is bought and sold here, as is most of the production of the Elven woodwrights from Thranduil's kingdom. A canal separates the area from the nearby Merchants' District, and access to the quarter can be gained only by crossing one of its three bridges (or by boat). While nominally everyone is allowed to enter the district freely, anyone who attempts to cross or disembark into the Elven quarter is likely to be approached by two or more armed Wood-elves and questioned about the reasons for their visit. In particular, anyone openly carrying weapons will be stopped and asked to leave their weapons in custody, or turn back. This is probably the most noticeable proof of the power that the Elvenking has over the government of Lake-town.

> ### Elven Quarter Adventure Seed
> ◆ A sure way to gain the respect of the Raft-elves is to take part in one of their many contests, such as running the gunwales of their slim boats, walking ropes strung across the fast-flowing waters, or leaping from one swift moving boat to another. Recently, barrel-riding has become a popular challenge, inspired by the deeds of Thorin's company.

The Dwarves of the **Glittering Gate** (6) are the main exception to the all-Elf population of the district. These goldsmiths and gemcutters and their young Barding apprentices are the only individuals in Lake-town allowed by the Master of Esgaroth to deal in the buying and selling of gems and gold, either wrought or unwrought. Their best customers are mostly Elves, generally on behalf of their king, who is notably fond of jewels, but any adventurer looking for the appraisal of a newly-discovered treasure should come here, as should anyone wanting to have a gem cunningly set upon a necklace, or a ring cast out of gold and engraved.

Raft-elves

Wood-elves from the villages that rise along the shores of the Forest River serve as boatmen for the Elvenking. They man the rafts that are sent up to Lake-town to retrieve the goods needed in the Woodland Realm and can often be seen on its quays, or sitting inside its Town-Hall, drinking and chatting with local dignitaries. They also lead the small and slim boats used by Elves to move about the city. Raft-elves are often more forthcoming with foreigners than the average Elf from Mirkwood, and get along well with the Men of the Lake, unless their allegiance is brought into question.

Silvan Elf Emissaries

A Silvan Elf emissary is a trustworthy follower of the Elvenking, sent to conduct all negotiations as a delegate in a foreign land. As a custom, King Thranduil picks his representatives among the Raft-elves, to profit from their familiarity with the world outside the forest of Mirkwood. Emissaries are usually tactful and subtle diplomats, and attentive observers ready to pick up details that might prove useful in their dealings. They are also ideally placed should the King of the Woodland Realm require the services of a band of adventurers...

The Town-hall Quarter

The area surrounding the **Town-hall** (16) is considered the best quarter of the city. It is accessible only through a gate manned by guards at all times, and it contains the greater houses and the most comfortable lodgings.

When the arrival of many folks from the surrounding areas made it apparent that the new Lake-town was bound to become much bigger than the one destroyed by the fall of Smaug, the older and wealthier merchant families of Esgaroth chose the best spot to build their own residences, and used the tallest and most robust stilts to have the area stand high above the surface of the lake.

As a consequence, the houses here are warmer and drier, and considered generally more wholesome by their affluent denizens. Today, the majority of the town councillors and other officials live in this area, as do the many ambassadors and emissaries who come to Laketown on errands from their rulers (the Elves of Mirkwood being the notable exception).

> ### Town-Hall Quarter Adventure Seed
>
> ◊ Magni Twice-Sunk is a retired merchant of Lake-town who has gained a seat on the town council. As his sobriquet implies, twice he has lost a boat and all its goods to misfortune. While he has been able to more than recover from both incidents, he has never truly forgotten. Each lost boat contained some precious goods that should have survived the ravages of time. Brave men and women are wanted to retrieve these items.

The **Town-hall** (16) dominates the landscape and is the most impressive building of the entire city. Its great hall is the venue for the election of a new Master and where all business discussions which require the presence of community representatives are held. A chamber at the west end is used for the council to meet in private, and is known as the Justice Room, as the councillors gather here especially for court trials. The chamber at the east end is where the town records are kept.

One of the halls that surround the courtyard before the Town-hall has, by agreement with the Master, been given over to the recruitment of adventurers. Here representatives of King Bard post their notices of commission for companies of brave and willing adventurers. In recent times the Adventurer's Hall has become something of a centre of adventuring activity: others in need of assistance know that there are companies for hire to be commissioned, should they have business for such a group.

On a busy day the hall throngs with representatives of merchant families, emissaries from Erebor, messengers, outfitters' agents, Bard's men, recruiters for the Guild of Bowmen, armourers, map makers and sword smiths, and many others come to both serve and hire adventurers.

Barding Nobles

Several eager young men paid homage to Bard when he first announced he was about to reclaim Dale. Today they attend the king in his palace, serving as counsellors, officers and right-hand men, or are sent abroad as his emissaries and diplomats. The wealthiest are keen to aid their King in the hiring of adventurers to expand the kingdom and solve its problems. A Barding noble is a warrior first and foremost, not yet used to the subtlety of politics, something that often put them at odds with the consummate manoeuvrings of their direct counterparts and neighbours, the town councillors of Lake-town.

Dwarf Notables

Since the re-founding of the Kingdom under the Mountain, most able-bodied veterans of the Battle of Five Armies have been charged with some office on behalf of King Dáin. Chief among them are the ten companions who survived the Quest of Erebor: all of them now serve as the King's advisors, stewards, treasurers, chancellors, and envoys. A Dwarf notable belongs to the ruling class of the realm of Erebor; most of them are rich beyond measure, or soon will be as the prosperity of the kingdom increases. Most preserve an adventurous edge, a restless side that might eventually lead them to leave their newfound home. They keep a keen interest in adventuring and adventurers, and are known to hire the occasional band of roving heroes to send out into the wider world on who knows what mysterious business...

Town Councillors

When a successful merchant from Esgaroth retires from their trading activity they might be invited by the Master of the town to join the town council. This invitation cannot be refused, and the new councillor will join their peers at the Town-hall every time that an office requires their presence, for as long as their health will permit. Councillors put their extensive trading experience at the service of the population of Esgaroth, for example discussing river-tolls with delegates from the Woodland Realm or the rent of warehouses with the emissary of King Bard.

A town councillor is often an aging but still energetic individual who is turning his ability in making a profit into something that should benefit his community. If he makes a good career his name might one day be added to the roll of the benefactors of the town, a parchment kept in the town-hall, or even considered for the title of Master of Esgaroth - if he is deemed to be worthy of the honour when the time comes to elect a new Master. The Town Councillors are happy to work with King Bard and his plans, for what is good for Dale is good for Lake-town. But Esgaroth does have its own problems that sometimes need the hand of a band of outsiders prepared to travel the wild.

Residential District

This is the part of the town that has seen the fastest growth since its construction. More stilts are placed every year, and more houses are raised to accommodate the increasing number of farmers, herdsmen, woodsmen and hunters who abandon their former occupations to settle in Lake-town and profit from its prosperity. Originally, only the families of the boatmen, shipbuilders and workers employed in the nearby shipyards district lived here. Their houses were built by decree of the old Master of Esgaroth, and it has been their custom to raise them using materials available to carpenters and shipwrights. This tradition has given the quarter its most peculiar look, with its brightly-painted houses and fronts fitted with ropes and canvas. Today, some of these houses are given to adventurers who have earned the honorific title of *Burgess* (see the *Player's Guide,* pg 201) and can thus live in them as tenants.

The largest great house of the district is the **Hospital** (9), a building erected for the care of the sick, the poor, the old and the infirm of Esgaroth. Several wives serve in this house voluntarily, cleaning, feeding, clothing and housing the sick. The house is high-ceilinged, with tall windows, to let the air circulate freely and dispel any 'bad air' that might linger where the sick are resting.

> ### Residential District Adventure Seed
>
> ◈ Diplomats and ambassadors from the halls of the various Free Folk gather in Dale for the Council of the North. Their journeys home will be perilous, so they may need the protection of doughty adventurers on the return journey. There are worse things on the road than bandits, too – politics and intrigue in Dale may lead to assassins and murder in the wild...

Hospital Healers

Those assisting the sick at the Hospital are wise-folk skilled in the arts of healing illness, wound and hurt. Some of them are learned in herb-lore, and can identify which plants have curative properties and administer cures based on their use. Others are midwives, experienced in caring for women during childbirth, but also capable of setting a broken bone or closing an open wound.

Shipyards District

The shipyard district is entirely given over to the building of rafts, boats and everything else that is needed for the main pursuit of Lake-town: commerce. Every day a small forest of ancient oak-trees is split by an army of carpenters to create the long planks needed to shape the hulls of boats. Smiths hammer on the anvil at any hour of the day to produce the thousands of wrought-iron rivets and roves needed to fix those planks to keels. Hundred of oars are carved out of tall spruce trees. Lengths of rope are stretched taut between the buildings to dry under the sun. Sailcloths are cut and sewn artfully by experienced craftsmen and then painted with the colours of the city. Barrel builders work incessantly to provide the countless containers needed every year to ship out local products or bring in fine wines and other exotic commodities.

> ### Shipyards District Adventure Seeds
> ◆ Lake-town sits upon thousands of timber pilings, packed close together, but still navigable by a small boat. It has been some years since the water beneath the town saw the sun. And floating debris builds up quicker than a shoreman might realise. It also provides ingress to many places within the town above which are otherwise inaccessible, albeit a risky one. The space under Lake-town could be a location for all manner of adventures.

The majority of the boats built here are skiffs and longships commissioned by private merchants, but a number of larger longships have lately been ordered by the town council. The smallest boats are the ones employed in Laketown for everyday use, round-bottomed skiffs allowing for two, four or eight rear-facing oarsmen. Longships used for the transportation of goods or armed men can be between 50 to 80 feet long. They are fitted with oars along almost the entire length of the boat itself, and can have from ten to twenty rowing benches (the Master of town's great gilded boat sports 30 rowing benches). Despite their length, even the largest longships built in Lake-town are designed to be relatively light, as they need to be lifted out of the water and loaded on the wheeled carts used along the Stair of Girion.

Boatmen of Esgaroth

There are many boatmen in Lake-town, from those who man the small boats sent to tow the rafts of barrels coming down from the Forest River, to the more adventurous ones who leave their families for months to lead their ships to lands as distant as Dorwinion and the Sea of Rhûn. They are all very experienced and, especially in the case of the smaller craft, they often own the boat they employ in their activities (the larger longships are often owned by wealthy merchant families instead).

Bowmen of the Guild

A law passed by the new Master and his councillors requires that all inhabitants of Lake-town between the ages of 16 and 35 must train in the use of the short bow

or great bow. While every true Man of the Lake is at least a passable archer, only the best among them are admitted to the Bowmen's Guild. Its members are not men-at-arms, but free men who in times of danger are required to leave their homes to muster at the city gates, as soon as they are summoned by the sound of warning trumpets. The guildsmen do not wear a livery, but they all use dark coloured arrows in their archery (as the Lakemen always did). To this day, all members of the guild keep Bard the Bowman (as they call him) in the greatest esteem, as he was from Esgaroth and a member of the guild, but they despise the Royal Archers of Dale with a passion. Many archers from the guild are exceptional marksmen who were with Bard when he killed the Dragon and fought valiantly in the Battle of Five Armies.

Royal Archers of Dale

The Royal Company of Archers counts fifty members, hand-picked among the best warriors and hunters of Dale to serve as the bodyguard of the king. They are easily recognisable, as they customarily wear black from head to toe. No distinctions of rank or lineage are made in their selection, and every young man in the city dreams of joining the Black Company, as it is often called. Royal archers are supposed to hone their skill at any occasion, and are thus given license to access any place suited for the shooting of arrows (like any open field). At least a dozen archers are found at any time at the Royal Barracks in Dale, either practising by shooting at targets or personally crafting their arrows.

New Fellowship Phase Undertakings for Lake-town

These additional undertakings can be chosen by companions spending a Fellowship phase in Lake-town.

Go to the Market-pool

Men spoke of the (...) wealth over and to spare with which to buy rich things from the South...

Player-heroes spending time in Lake-town can take advantage of the largest market to be found in the North, and spend some of their accumulated wealth to gain some useful items. When heroes choose this undertaking, they can spend 4 Gold Pieces and select one of the options shown below to acquire an item that gives them a bonus of +1 to all rolls made using the corresponding skill. Each option can be taken up to two times, for a total bonus of +2 (representing an upgrade of the original item, or a new, additional item of the same type).

For example, Lifstan visits the market to buy himself a lyre. He spends 4 Gold Pieces, and gains a bonus to checks when he used the lyre equal to +1. In a later Fellowship phase, he returns to the same luthier to have his lyre newly strung with silver cords for another 4 Gold Pieces, and sees his bonus raised to +2.

When spending a Fellowship phase in Lake-town, choose this undertaking and spend 4 Gold Pieces to gain a bonus to one of the following:

- *Find a goldsmith to have precious stones set into your weapon's hilt. Gain a bonus to hit OR damage.*

- *Visit an ironmonger or a woodwright to buy fine tools appropriate to your favourite trade. Gain a bonus to rolls made using that tool kit.*

- *Buy a musical instrument of superior make, be it a fiddle, a flute, a drum or a viol, or visit a master luthier to build you a new harp or lyre. Gain a bonus to any roll made when using the instrument.*

- *Learn the basics of how to prepare salves and healing herbs and acquire the necessary materials from a hospital healer. Gain a bonus to stabilize a wounded creature, and to Hit Points regained through expenditure of Hit Dice.*

- *Buy robust rope, good quality map, walking staves, comfortable sleeping cots and a regular supply of cram from a baker (biscuits the Lake-men prepare for long journeys). Gain a bonus to Embarkation OR Arrival Rolls during Journeys.*

- *Visit the shop of a tailor or shoemaker to have a rich dress or a pair of quality shoes made. Gain a bonus to to skills that use your Charisma modifier.*

- *Search the market to find a rare book or parchment, quills and ink for you to write. Gain a bonus to Intelligence skill checks.*

- See a master hunter to get all you need for your hunting exploits. Gain a bonus to rolls made when you are the hunter on a journey.

Secure a Supply of Marsh Herbs

...everywhere there was a wealth of sweet-smelling herbs and shrubs.

Herbs and curative plants may be found along the Forest River banks, where many ponds and pools signal the slow encroachment of the marshes. Companions may wander the countryside in search of such useful plants. But the undertaking is not devoid of risks...

Rather than buying herbs in the Lake-town markets, Player-heroes may chose to spend the Fellowship phase securing their own supply of healing herbs from the surrounding area, and have them made into salves and potions by a Lake-town herbalist.

After completing this undertaking, once during any Fellowship or Adventuring Phase where the Player-hero can credibly make a visit to Lake-town, they receive a supply of salves and potions.

Each time the Player-hero collects their herbs they may make a roll 1d6 on the table below. A hero proficient with the Medicine or Nature Skill gains Advantage on this roll.

The full properties of the different herbs, salves and potions can be found on page 154 of the *Adventures in Middle-earth Player's Guide*.

1: Traveller's Boon
3 x Hagweed potion (Advantage on saves against Corruption for 1 week)
1 x Kingcup flower necklace or bracelet (Luck for 1d4+1 days)
1 x Reedmace salve (recover 2 Hit Dice)

2: Prodigious Recovery
2 x Reedmace salve (recover 2 Hit Dice)
1 x White Water-lily potion (Regain full Hit Dice value when Hit Dice are used to recover hit points)
1 x Kingcup flower necklace or bracelet (Luck for 1d4+1 days)

3: Healer's Hands
4 x Hagweed potion (Advantage on saves against Corruption for 1 week)
3 x White Water-lily potion (Regain full Hit Dice value when Hit Dice are used to recover hit points)

4: Joyful Wanderer
1 x Kingcup flower necklace or bracelet (Luck for 1d4+1 days)
3 x Hagweed potion (Advantage on saves against Corruption for 1 week)

5: Warrior's Aid
2 x Reedmace salve (recover 2 Hit Dice)
3 x White Water-lily potion (Regain full Hit Dice value when Hit Dice are used to recover hit points)
1 x Red Water-lily potion (+2 damage for the next hour)

6: A Bountiful Harvest
2 x Reedmace salve (recover 2 Hit Dice)
1 x Kingcup flower necklace or bracelet (Luck for 1d4+1 days)
3 x Hagweed potion (Advantage on saves against Corruption for 1 week)
2 x White Water-lily potion (Regain full Hit Dice value when Hit Dice are used to recover hit points)
1 x Red Water-lily potion (+2 damage for the next hour)

The Long Marshes Adventure Seed

◈ A merchant returns from the Stair of Girion to report her vessel was dropped by the porters and wrecked at the falls. She is seeking brave and sturdy folk to help her recover her goods, at least those that were not ruined. Besides those trapped at the bottom of the falls, many barrels likely floated downstream into the marshes. Worst of all, amongst these goods were some especially marvellous Dwarven toys. These now wander the marshes, singing, dancing and finding their way into the sodden caves of Marsh Ogres.

BEFORE THE GAME

home is behind, the world ahead

Dearest Bilbo,

I hope you do not mind me writing to you again so soon. I have met such companions on the road, that I couldn't help but tell you. It was two days ago, and I awoke a little way from the road, wrapped in my blanket. I awoke abruptly, having been deep in such a dream of first breakfast, when what should I see just a few yards away but a camp fire, with bacon sizzling in a pan! It was poorly tended by a giant of a big person. Beran, I now know him to be named, and he is one of Beorn's people, just like you told me about! Beorn is gathering a great many like-minded folk since the Battle. It seems he is building a kingdom of his own here in the Wild!

Mustering all of my courage I made my presence known - the bacon was burning, and this fellow clearly needed my help. As I introduced myself as politely as I could, another big person appeared, carrying firewood and accompanied by a great grey hound. A fierce lady of the Woodmen is she, named only "The Bride". She at first seemed terrifying to me, and I almost ran, but while her countenance is quite fierce, she spoke kindly.

Cutting a long story short for now, it turned out we were all heading to Lake-town, to heed the summons of the new King Bard, and so we have resolved to travel together.

I will write again soon.

Yours in good spirits,

Celandine Took

Before the Game

"Sorry! I don't want any adventures, thank you. Not Today. Good morning!"

The Road goes ever on and on, and many different feet walk upon it. The Road that runs past Bag End's front door is the same that crosses Mirkwood to Esgaroth on the Long Lake, and could even carry you to the land of Gondor where the king once ruled.

Before starting a game of *Adventures in Middle-Earth*, discuss the questions below with your players. Also, ensure that the players are familiar with the Map of Wilderland, with the various cultures and regions where the game begins, and with the current situation in Middle-earth in the years between the death of Smaug and the return of the Dark Lord to his Dark Tower in Mordor. Middle-earth is rooted in places and tongues, in roads and woods.

Who Are the Heroes? What sort of player characters does the group want to play? Are they, like the Fellowship, a mix of peoples – Elves and Men and Dwarves, strangers to one another but united by common cause? Are they all from one culture – all Dwarves? All Woodmen? Are they *mostly* from one culture, but with a few unusual additions (say, a dozen Dwarves and one Hobbit)?

Even if the whole Fellowship comes from a single culture, players can choose different classes to distinguish their characters from one another. Three Woodmen with different character classes are as distinct as three Warriors from different cultures.

Having the majority of the group come from a single culture makes the game about the lands and fate of that culture; having a group from many different cultures implies a wider view of the world. Both offer plenty of opportunities for adventure; the former is better for lengthy serialised tales where every adventure is another year in the history of that culture, while the latter is better suited to episodic tales exploring the different stories of Middle-earth.

What Brings Them Together? What is the origin and purpose of the group? There are bands of heroes and treasure-hunters who wander from one side of Wilderland to the other, and each hero might have individual reasons for travelling, but your players may prefer a more coherent purpose. Do they share a quest or dream that will define the whole campaign, like retaking some ancestral hall from enemies, or striking a blow against the Shadow? Has their purpose been forced upon them? Or is theirs a chance meeting – did they all meet in the tap-room of some inn in Lake-town?

Who Might Their Patrons Be? One of the core assumptions of play in Middle-earth is that the player characters have a patron, a wise mentor or ally who helps advise the company and directs them on quests. Gandalf brought the Dwarves to Bilbo's door, and sent Frodo to Rivendell where Elrond gathered the Fellowship of the Ring. King Bard has called for heroes to help aid and rebuild Dale; Radagast has long aided the Woodmen against the dark forces in Mirkwood. Having a patron at the start of the game is not obligatory – the characters might adventure for a while before finding a patron. Other groups, especially if they already have a clear purpose or quest, might never need the guidance and direction of a patron. However, if a group plans on a series of loosely connected adventures, having a patron is a good idea, and the players should agree in advance on some suitable candidates.

What Sort of Game Is This? Review the list of precepts below that discuss how Middle-earth differs from other fantasy settings. Decide which precepts are most important to your group. It's your Middle-earth now.

Precepts of Middle-earth Play

Miles Are Miles

Going There and Back Again: all of Tolkien's heroes undertake great journeys and must overcome peril and hardship on the way. Middle-earth is wide and little-travelled. Most people never stray far from where they were born, and there is little communication between North and South, East and West. Hobbits were seen as figures out of legends in Rohan and Gondor; the Nazgûl had to search the length and breadth of the North to find the Shire.

In your games, take time to describe how the Player-heroes go There. Lavishing time and attention on Journeys – including incidents and encounters along the way – makes the distance travelled feel more significant. Impatience and skipping over important journeys diminishes the game ("more haste less speed", as Gollum might say). Travel is almost always a key part of a Middle-earth adventure.

Even in games where all the action centres around a single place, remember that it takes considerable time for news to travel in Middle-earth.

Years Are Long

Nearly three thousand years have passed since the Last Alliance defeated Sauron; and almost 900 have gone by since the last King sat on the throne of Gondor. Orcs drove the Dwarves out of Moria a thousand years ago, and Smaug drove them out of Erebor two centuries ago.

To the Elves, these passing years are a trifle, for they are immortal and recall the Elder Days. All others, though, are mortal and have short lives; the deeds of their ancestors have passed into legend and are mostly forgotten, save in the stories and songs that are a key part of Middle-earth lore.

Players should try to see the world from the perspective of their characters – most people in Middle-earth have heard little of Hobbits, or Ring-Wraiths, or the wars of three thousand years ago. Certainly, they have never heard of the *Ring*.

This emphasis on *time* has two important effects on the game. First, it means there's plenty of room for Loremasters and players to add their own historical events and cultures as needed. There is room enough for great deeds in Middle-earth that don't conflict with Tolkien's annals.

Second, and more importantly, games in Middle-Earth take place over extended periods of time. The usual rule of thumb is one adventure per year. A great quest, like the Quest of the Ring, might play out over only a few short months, but in general, games should unfold slowly, with time to breathe. Remember to count the passing seasons.

ALL ENEMIES OF THE ONE ENEMY

"It is not the strength of the body that counts, but the strength of the spirit."

Absolute good and absolute evil exist in Middle-earth. Sauron is irredeemable, a fallen angel who has chosen a ruinous path. The Orcs and other monsters created by the Enemy are similarly evil; they are a monstrous plague, and deserve only a merciful death. Between these two poles, though, are many shades of grey.

Mortals may serve the Enemy out of greed, or fear, or having beeen deluded by his lies. The Free People may act unwisely out of pride, or mistrust of others – any stranger might be a spy or servant of the Enemy. When the heroes visit unfamiliar lands, they must introduce themselves and prove that they are trustworthy.

In Middle-earth, there is an *expectation* of heroism, mechanised in the Shadow rules. Some characters may rise to this expectation and do great good. Others – like Boromir, like Thorin – may fail, and redeem themselves only in death. The right path may not always be clear, nor easy. It may not even be achievable – Frodo, for example, did his best, but still failed at the climax of the Quest of the Ring – but there is always a moral choice to be made.

There is also a single Enemy: the Lord of the Rings. There are other dark forces at work in the world, but there is only one Dark Lord.

THE LONG DEFEAT IN A FALLEN WORLD

The Player-heroes will not be the ones to defeat Sauron in the end. Nor, for that matter, will Frodo. The Enemy cannot be destroyed by any force in Middle-earth. All the Free Peoples are fighting a long defeat; they drive back the darkness, but cannot triumph over it. They can preserve and rebuild what they love, but the enemy will come back again and again.

So much has already been lost – the Elder Days were more glorious than the present darkness, and evil has conquered most of the world. The Elves are fleeing West, and the remaining Free Peoples are islands in a sea of darkness. While there is joy and humour in places in Middle-earth, these places must be protected and cherished. The Shire is free because the Rangers defend it, and other places of hope need strong defenders as well.

The Player-heroes cannot achieve victory – at best, they can win a watchful peace. There will always be more battles to fight, and most of them will be lost. Adventures are *more likely* to be about defending a place and thwarting a growing evil, not exploring new lands or intrigue between the Free Peoples.

For a lighter, less melancholy game (one more like *The Hobbit* than *The Lord of the Rings*) step back from this precept.

DELIVERANCE ARRIVES AS ALL SEEMS LOST

He found himself wondering at times, especially in the autumn, about the wild lands, and strange visions of mountains that he had never seen came into his dreams.

A recurring theme we see in Middle-earth is the joyful turning of the tide at the darkest of hours. The intervention of the Eagles in both the Battle of Five Armies and the Battle of the Black Gate, the arrival of the Rohirrim, even Gollum's treachery at Mount Doom – in every case, the heroes could not triumph on their own, but were saved at the last moment by divine intervention.

The Player-heroes are part of a larger story, and while their deeds are important, they are but one thread in a tapestry, one voice in a chorus. The game is about their deeds, but their deeds are not the only force shaping the world.

If you want to include this trope in your games, don't use it as a *deus ex machina* that solves everything for the Player-heroes. Instead, use it to reward their heroism – place them up against overwhelming odds and, if they stand and fight when all seems hopeless, then perhaps they too will cry, "The Eagles are coming! The Eagles are coming!"

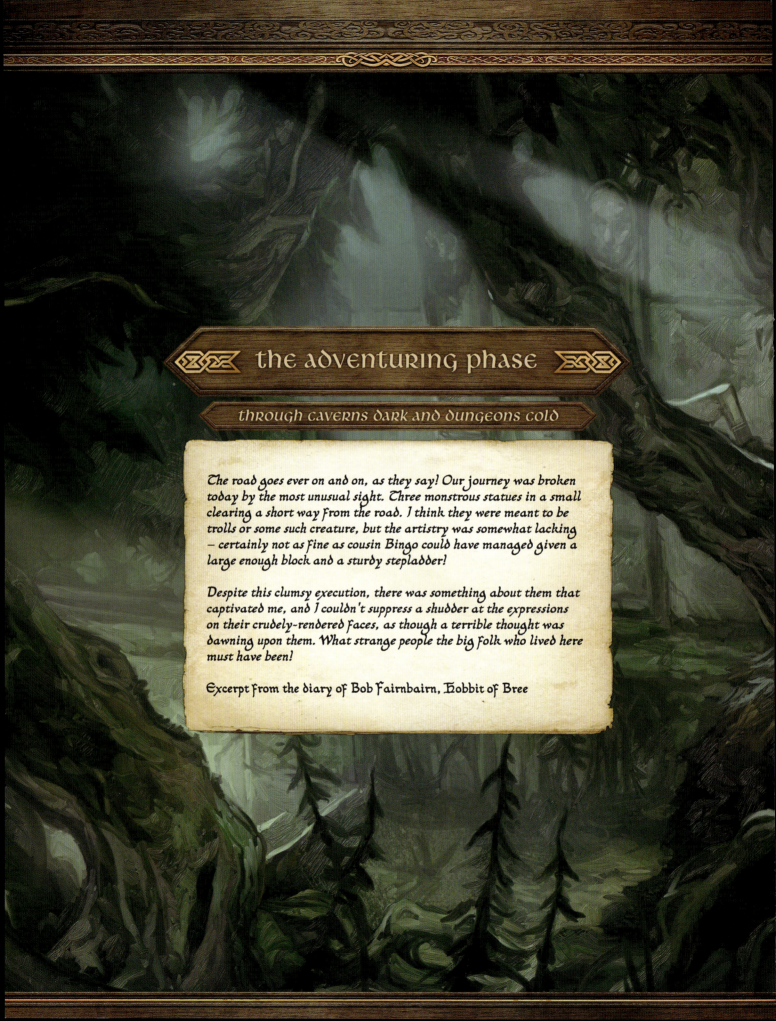

the adventuring phase

through caverns dark and dungeons cold

The road goes ever on and on, as they say! Our journey was broken today by the most unusual sight. Three monstrous statues in a small clearing a short way from the road. I think they were meant to be trolls or some such creature, but the artistry was somewhat lacking – certainly not as fine as cousin Bingo could have managed given a large enough block and a sturdy stepladder!

Despite this clumsy execution, there was something about them that captivated me, and I couldn't suppress a shudder at the expressions on their crudely-rendered faces, as though a terrible thought was dawning upon them. What strange people the big folk who lived here must have been!

Excerpt from the diary of Bob Fairnbairn, Hobbit of Bree

the
- Loremaster -

Then a minstrel and loremaster stood up and named all the names of the Lords of the Mark in their order...

The Loremaster has a more complicated role during the Adventuring phase than the players. While they are in control of their characters, the Loremaster is responsible for the entire game world: the description of locations; the actions of the people and creatures encountered; and the chain of events in the ongoing adventure.

It is the Loremaster's responsibility to introduce players who are new to roleplaying to the basics of the game. They will organise and oversee all gaming sessions, and must juggle the roles of storyteller and impartial judge, all the while playing the parts of the multitude of characters that the players encounter. In practice, during a game session, the role of the Loremaster goes a little like this:

1. Set the scene:
At the start of a game session, the Loremaster gives a short summary of what happened in the previous session, then describes where the characters are and what is happening around them. This should provide some immediate prompts to action, making sure that the game gets off to a quick and involving start.

2. Listen to the players:
The players react to the scene setting, possibly deciding on a new goal for their company or reminding themselves of their current goal. The Loremaster plays the parts of the other people present, who the players interact with.

3. Describe the consequences of the players' actions:
The Loremaster responds to the players' interactions with people, calls for dice rolls for any necessary tasks or tests and describes the outcomes of the players' actions.

4. Describe events from the ongoing plot:
The Loremaster incorporates elements of the adventure's plot as appropriate. These can be triggered either by the players' actions – such as confronting a thief might lead to the villain revealing information that leads the players to the next part of the adventure – or by a timeline of events – such as the Loremaster deciding that Orcs will raid the settlement the players are staying in just after midnight on the third night of their stay. The episode then proceeds using a combination of the last three steps, until it is resolved. After the resolution of the episode, the players may begin a journey or the

Loremaster may quickly skim over a period of time when not much happens or there are no significant opportunities for players to take action.

The Middle-earth Loremaster

...he wished to go and see the great mountains, and hear the pine-trees and the waterfalls, and explore the caves, and wear a sword instead of a walking-stick.

Arguably the most important task of a Loremaster is to act as the interface between the players and Middle-earth. Getting the Middle-earth "mood" right is essential to giving the players the feeling that they are a part of the unfolding events at the end of the Third Age. Many players will not be strangers to this much-loved setting, so familiarity with the source material is important for the Loremaster.

In addition to helping create an authentic Middle-earth experience, taking another look at Tolkien's books will remind Loremaster of many small details which can provide the seed of an adventure plot.

When choosing who will take the role of Loremaster, it is sensible to choose the individual whose 'Tolkien lore' runs the deepest, as nothing ruins a good session of play as much as a player questioning the Loremaster's knowledge of the source material.

It can seem a daunting prospect at first, but being the Loremaster is an immensely satisfying role through which a Tolkien enthusiast can truly experience the world of Middle-earth as its own creator did: by orchestrating all the elements of the setting to produce their very own epic tales.

The Qualities of a Good Loremaster

One of the most enjoyable features of all roleplaying games is the creative collaboration between the Loremaster and their players, but it is also true that the Loremaster has much more to do than anyone else. They are in charge of setting the atmosphere and tone of the game, describing what is happening and helping the players resolve their characters' actions.

The Loremaster's duties can be broken down into three roles: Director, Referee and Narrator.

The Loremaster as Director

While setting up an Adventuring phase for their group of players, the Loremaster's job can be likened to that of a theatre or movie director, choosing and arranging the basic elements of the 'stage' on which the characters act during the next session of play. By selecting the locales where the action will take place and determining the nature of the problem that the characters will endeavour to solve, including the personalities and opponents that will try to hinder (or help) them, the Loremaster provides their players with the rough outlines of a plot, ready to be turned into a full-blown narrative by the chosen actions of the players.

The Loremaster must be a flexible director, ready to follow the players' improvisations when they take a route that the Loremaster didn't anticipate. Loremasters who create their plots around a series of loose events that can be approached in a wide variety of ways are well placed to deal with the tangents that players often embark on. The last thing a Loremaster should do is restrict their players unreasonably to make them conform to a fixed idea of how the game should progress. Players must feel that their characters can attempt any action, no matter how limited the chances of a successful outcome.

Consistency

A Loremaster makes for a good director when they are able to weave a consistent storytelling experience out of a great number of elements, including the members of a company, their goals and ambitions, the places they visit and the people they meet. It is best not to plan to the smallest detail in advance, but to let the plot develop naturally, session after session. It is in fact easier, and probably wiser, to set each session up as if it was a separate episode of a longer story, with each new one building upon the consequences of the previous ones, using the prepared plot outline as a general guide.

The Loremaster as Referee

Roleplaying games are composed of rules combined with a set of social and storytelling conventions. While these conventions place roleplaying games outside the constraints of traditional board or card games (which are defined solely by their rules), the fundamental game mechanics used to regulate most of the situations encountered by players require the presence of an impartial moderator: the Loremaster. The Loremaster must be ready to adjudicate the rules at all times, whether testing the mettle of the characters during battle, or helping the players determine the outcome of their choices during the Fellowship phase.

Behavioural issues amongst the players may also be handled by the Loremaster. Everyone involved in the game is there to have fun, but sometimes one person's sense of fun can impact other people's enjoyment. This could include a player who is working against the interests of the company, or a player who tries to argue with the Loremaster's interpretation of Middle-earth. In most cases, a quiet and friendly word in private explaining the issue will sort things out, especially if the issue is raised quickly and courteously.

Fairness
When acting as a referee, the Loremaster should strive to be fair and to apply the rules properly and impartially. Events are meant to provide players with a challenge. The rules governing them are there to judge whether a character was up to the test or not, and to reward them with success if they were, or to enthrall them with the consequences of failure if they weren't. A partial Loremaster can easily ruin a game, as an unfair call when applying a rule brings the rules themselves to the players' attention and their immersion in the game is interrupted. Conversely, the Loremaster shouldn't spoil the fun of the game by relying excessively on the rules alone. Making players roll the dice for every action their character makes becomes boring and also takes some of the drama out of the tests that really matter. Moreover, structuring an adventure so that key discoveries or achievements depend on the result of a single roll is a recipe for frustration. There should always be another way of making progress.

The Loremaster as Narrator
A large part of the Loremaster's role is that of a storyteller, using words to portray what is happening to the group of heroes. They are the eyes and ears of their players, the main source of information to be fed to the collective imagination of the group. Luckily, the Loremaster is far from being alone in this task, as the entire group will have some knowledge of the source material, and the Loremaster can draw on a range of images and details that the players are already familiar with: often, a few well-chosen words are enough to give a vivid picture of what is going on, as the situation reminds the players of a scene from the books.

Creativity
A quick and rich imagination is a precious quality for a Loremaster, especially when coupled with strong communication skills. Evocative descriptions focus the attention of all players and encourage their interaction, and the ability to build the players' reactions and plans into the ongoing adventure will lead to the most involved and enjoyable games.

Tolkien's Canon
"His old life lay behind in the mists, dark adventure lay in front."

For many years, fans of the literary works of J.R.R. Tolkien have debated the existence of a consistent canon that firmly defines the world and history of Middle-earth as described in *The Hobbit, The Lord of the Rings* and later publications. This has often been cited as one of the major hurdles to roleplaying games set in Middle-earth, as it is very likely that the characters' adventures will 'interfere' with the actions of the saga's known protagonists and 'break' the canon's consistency. While a quick and easy answer to such concerns might well be that 'there is no such thing as an established Tolkien's canon,' it is interesting to delve into the subject a little bit more, as there is a lot that a Loremaster may learn from tackling this apparently insurmountable obstacle.

Subjective Sources
When facing the dilemma of altering facts perceived as being part of canon, a Loremaster could consider the information that Tolkien related in his stories not as ascribed to an infallible, all-knowing narrator, but to *witnesses* of the times, individuals who are subject to errors and personal bias (for example, *The Hobbit* relates the content of Bilbo Baggins' memoirs). This literary device served Tolkien well in his effort to create a believable 'ancient history' which includes the inevitable inconsistencies that might come from it being composed by different chroniclers, and there is no reason why a Loremaster cannot do the same, especially if they need to change an 'established' date or the details behind a known 'fact' or 'historical' figure.

To get an idea of how much the writer's perspective can distort perceptions, and possibly facts, one need look no further than the books: for example, readers of *The Lord of the Rings* can find it difficult to reconcile their image of Gimli as the redoubtable axe-wielding warrior of Erebor, with the Dwarven companions of Bilbo, who, captured by Trolls, Goblins, Spiders and Wood-elves, more often than not end up being saved by their Hobbit burglar, Bilbo...

Filling the Blanks

Tolkien wove an incredibly rich narrative tapestry, composed of believable characters set against a vivid landscape and moved by motivations firmly grounded in myth and tradition. But even such an extensive and intricate chronicle does not explore thoroughly every nook and cranny of this imagined world and period; far from it.

As the narrative focus in the books shifts from one region to another, many locations and the events related to them are left in the dark, or are only briefly touched upon.

This approach is aimed to give a subjective perspective to the protagonists of the stories, who are not familiar with every corner of Middle-earth, and it gives the Loremaster the freedom to create their own stories. The setting provided in this guide is an example of this – the Wilderland area is introduced in *The Hobbit* but is then virtually unmentioned when the narrative advances to Frodo's days. Armed with the knowledge from the stories, and supported by the many hints and notes found in the appendices, a Loremaster has everything they need to create a credible and exciting setting for their own chronicles.

It is all about Characters

Another interesting view on the canon comes from the author himself. While certainly very protective of his own creations in general, Tolkien stressed several times that what was ultimately dear to him was the integrity of his characters and their motivations, more than the preservation of his plots or other details. By applying this perspective to a chronicle in *Adventures in Middle-earth*, it would be probably not far from the mark to say that the game will remain true to its literary sources if the Loremaster pays due attention to the treatment of the canonical characters, and if its players strive to create and play plausible heroes.

Last, but Not Least…

When approached today, the bulk of Tolkien's Middle-earth-related publications give the impression of an immutable and consistent corpus. But when the author was alive, he was constantly rewriting and rearranging his own material, even to the point of making substantial changes to existing publications to be inserted in new, revised editions. These changes were sometimes aimed at correcting inconsistencies, but more often than not they were introduced to accommodate later plot changes and alterations.

It is thus possible to assume that not even Tolkien looked at his own work as being bound by any sort of established canon, and that even the chronologies he carefully created were to be considered provisional at best. In light of these considerations, Loremasters are encouraged not to feel intimidated, and simply go ahead and add their own storytelling thread to the Professor's wonderful and epic narrative tapestry.

- Adventuring - Rules

"Why O why did I ever leave my hobbit-hole?"

The **Adventuring phase** refers to events happening in your game in the most commonly encountered traditional roleplaying game 'mode' – where Player-heroes are responding directly to their surroundings, exploring an adventure location, battling their enemies and roleplaying their way through encounters with non-player characters. Other modes found in *Adventures in Middle-earth* are the **Fellowship phase** and **Journeys**, which each operate on a different, more abstract sense of passing time. See page 148 for more about the **Fellowship phase** and page 56 for **Journeys**.

An Adventuring phase usually begins when the company gather at or near a Sanctuary they have open to them (see page 152 for more detail on opening a Sanctuary). This isn't a hard and fast rule, but does reinforce the importance of Sanctuaries, and therefore the themes of the setting. Almost all the actions that occur in an Adventuring phase are covered by the core rules.

An Adventuring phase comes to a close when the Loremaster decides the current adventure is over or needs to be punctuated with a Fellowship phase. This may simply be because the adventure takes the company to a Sanctuary, or there is a natural pause in events. It may be declared because the company are wounded and unlikely to survive any more action.

The following section presents some more information on aspects of the core rules that are particularly relevant to *Adventures in Middle-earth*.

Rests

Rests in *Adventures in Middle-earth* work as they do in the core rules with one exception: during journeys, when the Player-heroes may not take a long rest. See the section on Journeys, page 57, for more information.

A long rest can be a fuzzy thing to define as the Loremaster. You may choose to rule that only a night in a bed, in a safe place can offer a long rest. A more generous interpretation requires a few needs to be met to enjoy a long rest during

---

Two Guiding Lights

In *Adventures in Middle-earth*, there are two guiding lights to help you make your decisions during the Adventuring phase. The first is the core rules, as you would expect. These ensure that things are relatively fair to everyone, that all players can expect to be able to achieve something, and that battles aren't too difficult to enjoy. They also provide a common expectation and point of reference for resolving tasks, challenges, combat and so on. The second guiding light that should help direct your journey as a Loremaster is the spirit of the setting in the books these rules seek to emulate – Middle-earth.

The setting should have a strong impact on your decisions on what happens during an Adventuring phase. Things that make sense in other settings might not make sense in Middle-earth and vice versa.

This is a heroic setting, where Player-heroes are generally good. This means certain behaviours commonly found in other games are out of place in *Adventures in Middle-earth*. The company don't steal from one another, or try to get the biggest slice of pie: they pro-actively help and care for one another. Whereas player characters in other games may choose to intimidate, steal, murder, rob and hoard gold, eventually becoming a tyrant. These aren't things we would see from the equivalent of a Player-hero in a Middle-earth story. They are bonded by a common enemy that represents all that is evil, and actively strive to not receive Shadow points that will see their character become less playable. Similarly, your NPCs and the happenings in your adventures should feel like something that would fit in *The Lord of the Rings* or *The Hobbit*.

Unsuccessful Journeys

A journey that ends at an adventure location – for example, a Goblin cave – could have gone very badly for the company. This shouldn't be considered a failure out of character: the rules are specifically meant to generate atmospheric and perilous situations just like this. The long march, accompanied by endless perils and damning exhaustion, is a feature of the books that *Adventures in Middle-earth* aims to emulate.

However, it is not unheard of for a company of Player-heroes, beleaguered by their difficult journey, to demand a long rest on arrival as the time for an Adventuring phase begins. The choice here is yours. If you want the company to have to struggle through and face a tough challenge, then stick to your plans. Underline the difficulty of travelling long distances, remind them of Frodo's travails and offer advice on the need to open Sanctuaries as soon as possible.

However, as in all things, you must be fair. It simply isn't fun as a *player* to be presented with a challenge that you *know* is impossible to overcome. Or, perhaps more importantly, *feel* is impossible. You can compromise in these situations. Allow some negotiation on how the company find a place to have a suitable rest, and reward creativity.

Some appropriate skill checks could allow for the recovery of a proportion of Hit Dice. Alternatively you could allow the recovery of 'once per long rest' abilities without the recovery of Hit Dice. If the company have to work for it, then it encourages them to be better prepared next time, or at least recognise the ever present danger in travel, to take shorter journeys by opening more Sanctuaries across Wilderland and beyond, and to generally be wary. But it also means they are not being unduly punished for being brave adventurers.

---

the Adventuring phase (remember, a company cannot take a long rest during journeys):

- **Safety from threat of attack**
  This could mean a thorough watch is posted – for example, a well guarded Elf camp in Mirkwood would allow a long rest. Arguably lying rolled in your cloak in a ditch just off the Forest Road, with your Hobbit friend trying to stay awake and watch for Spiders, would not.

- **Comfort**
  Sleeping in a Dwarf hall carved from the heart of a mountain is a very different experience than sleeping in a Goblin tunnel. Comfort might mean a bed. It might mean good food. It might mean good company that allows for proper rest.

- **Tranquility**
  Some locations may simply provide an air of peace that means good rest is available to a company. This could be an ancient Elf ruin that has held onto some of its former glow of goodness. It could be a campsite next to a bright river that raises the spirits. This is very much in line with building the feeling of Middle-earth, where characters can find peace in the wildest of places.

As the Loremaster, it is up to you when you allow access to such a location. You may keep a couple of flexible options in reserve at all times to allow the company some respite if things go unexpectedly badly for them, or they make a gamble that doesn't pay off. Middle-earth does not offer quite the same access to magical healing as can be found in some other settings, and remember that players may need some time to adjust to this. Indeed some will test the boundaries with the lives of their Player-heroes, and come to regret their choices to the detriment of the game.

One of your hidden tasks is to manage the pressure you apply to your company. It is possible, and entirely valid, to play a game where 'the dice fall where they may', and the battle against the Shadow is long and grim and very difficult. This style of play has many rewards for those brave enough to undertake it, though some will doubtless perish along the way.

Alternatively you may want your company to explore the adventure you have written with a feeling of peril, but little genuine risk to their Player-heroes. This allows players to fully commit to roleplaying their Player-heroes without having to pay too much attention to minutely managing their resources. Most groups find their own level somewhere in between. The core rules are happily set up very much to empower the Loremaster's rulings on this.

Exhaustion

Exhaustion plays a big part in *Adventures in Middle-earth* – more so than in the core rules. It is something to be carefully monitored by the players, but also by the Loremaster. Don't forget it is possible to kill a Player-hero with Exhaustion. Such a fate should be an ever-present threat, but one that rarely comes to pass. Player-heroes should certainly seek to avoid higher levels of Exhaustion and be wary of it, but actual death by Exhaustion can be a deeply unsatisfying end for a hero. In an ideal world, it is a constant, fearful threat that is never realised.

That said, a foolhardy company who rush out into the wild in the wrong roles, without help, and who are terribly unlucky may find some of their number suffer a terrible end to their adventuring careers. It is important as the Loremaster to call attention when quieter members of the company are reaching the higher levels of Exhaustion – it is possible they could die, and the company should consider breaking a journey or finding a place to properly rest during an Adventuring phase.

Exhaustion is measured in six levels.

Level	Effect
1	Disadvantage on ability checks
2	Speed halved
3	Disadvantage on attack rolls and saving throws
4	Hit point maximum halved
5	Speed reduced to 0
6	Death

A level of Exhaustion can be removed with a long rest, various Player-hero or NPC abilities, and some forms of wondrous healing. The reward of the removal of a level of Exhaustion by thematic means is a valuable tool in the Loremaster's armoury.

Inspiration
"Farewell we call to hearth and hall!"

Inspiration is a tool the Loremaster can use to reward players for playing their character in a way that's true to the hero's personality traits, the setting, their culture and background.

Gaining Inspiration
As the Loremaster you can choose to give Inspiration for a variety of reasons. Typically, Loremasters award it when players live up to their hero's personality traits; give in to the drawbacks presented by a distinctive quality, speciality, hope or despair; and otherwise portray their character in a compelling way. Players either have Inspiration or they don't – they can't stockpile multiple 'Inspirations' for later use.

Using Inspiration
If a player has Inspiration, they can expend it when they make an attack roll, saving throw, or ability check. It can also be used to power certain abilities. Spending their Inspiration gives them Advantage on that roll. Also, if they have Inspiration, they can reward another player for good roleplaying, clever thinking, or simply doing something exciting in the game. When another Player-hero does something that really contributes to the story in a fun and interesting way, a player can give up their Inspiration to give that other Player-hero Inspiration.

Inspiration as a Tool for Guiding your Game
Loremasters are encouraged to be generous with Inspiration. Since it's a one time bonus that is readily spent, it is an ideal tool for steering players towards the things you agree you all want to see play out in the game. Since it can't be stacked up or hoarded, it is preferable if your players are given plenty of opportunity to regain it. Having a discussion with your players about what will be rewarded with Inspiration during the game is a very useful thing to do – it's a perfect way to open the conversation about everyone's expectations. The Loremaster also has Shadow points to use to guide behaviour, but that can be a much more punitive and negative approach.

About Inspiration in Middle-earth

Inspiration as a mechanic reflects the themes of Middle-earth. Hand in hand with Shadow points it allows Player-heroes to derive mechanical benefit from the setting around them, and by acting in concert with its themes.

In addition to the established methods of awarding Inspiration for good roleplaying, a Loremaster might also choose to give Inspiration for sights seen in Middle-earth, and interactions with characters met along the way. Gandalf can certainly hand out Inspiration, and is seen to do so on many occasions in the books. But so too can a beautiful sunrise, or breath-taking view. Indeed, even at their lowest ebb, characters in Middle-earth dig deep and find courage from somewhere. This can be modelled, in part at least, by the rules for Inspiration.

Don't forget too that Inspiration is fun to get, and fun to spend. And that is what we are all here for.

Starting Inspiration

As an option, and as a reminder that they have access to Inspiration, it can be worthwhile to give your Player-heroes Inspiration at the beginning of the game. You can discuss with your players where this inspired state came from – for instance, it could be awarded at the start of the campaign for the company meeting for the first time. Awarding Inspiration at the start of each session opens the game on a high note.

Multiclassing

Many of the classes in *Adventures in Middle-earth* already contain a mixture of heroic archetypes, and some multiclassing combinations might feel counter-intuitive. As ever, permission to multiclass rests with the Loremaster. If you feel it benefits your game and improves your players' experience, then by all means allow it. When first taking a level in a new class, a player selects two proficiencies from the new class.

To choose more than one class, Player-heroes must meet the following prerequisites:

Class	Ability Score Minimum
Scholar	Intelligence 13
Slayer	Strength 13
Treasure Hunter	Dexterity 13
Wanderer	Constitution 13
Warden	Charisma 13
Warrior	Strength or Dexterity 13

Optional Rules

The following options are presented for the Loremaster's consideration:

Barding Swordsman Cultural Virtue
(page 101, *Player's Guide*)
Optional version: This cultural virtue may not be used with a shield.

Beorning's Great Strength
(page 102, *Player's Guide*)
Optional version: Increase your Strength score by 1. As long as you can move freely while fighting, you may profit from your great strength and nimbleness. Your lifting and carrying capacities increase as if you were one size category larger. So long as you are carrying less than half of your full capacity (or are unencumbered if using the variant Encumbrance rules) you have a +1 bonus to your AC.

The Men of Bree Cultural Virtue Desperate Courage (page 109, *Player's Guide*)
Optional version: Once per long rest, when facing an adversary with Hit Dice greater than your level, you make invoke the sheer force of your stubborn Breeland will. You gain a bonus to your armour class equal to the difference between that adversary's Hit Dice and your level. This bonus lasts for the duration of the combat, and counts only against that single adversary. Against all other opponents use your regular armour class.

Journeys Expanded
The Road Goes Ever On

The first is sitting down and never gets up,
The second eats all that is given him,
Yet is always hungry,
The third goes away,
Never to return,
Leave behind stove, fire and smoke.

The more of the fourth you take,
The more you shall leave behind:
Your footsteps on the road.

- JOURNEYS -

"There are no safe paths in this part of the world. Remember you are over the Edge of the Wild now, and in for all sorts of fun wherever you go."

Anyone who has read *The Lord of the Rings* or *The Hobbit* is familiar with extended periods of travel that present dangerous challenges and opportunities for characters to test their mettle. *Adventures in Middle-earth* seizes the opportunity to make meaningful and eventful travel part of the adventure. A key part of understanding how journeys fit into *Adventures in Middle-earth* is to consider the three different modes of play in the game. These span a spectrum: from direct action of combat and exploration of an adventure location; to the zoomed out view of journeys; to the much more abstract, shared story of the Fellowship phase.

Journeys do involve making decisions and ability checks, but these exist in what might be considered 'Journey time'. This allows a game to progress through weeks, potentially months, of travel without the need to describe every single step along the Road. Players can experience the feeling of having made an epic journey while also still enjoying a fast moving adventure. The aim of a journey is to reflect the character of travel in Middle-earth, to give the Loremaster an opportunity to further impart the feel of the setting, while allowing the players to take part in a number of exciting and decision-filled challenges to determine how well they fare on the way.

Journey events are key moments that characterise Middle-earth and the Player-heroes' journey toward their destination, both geographical and spiritual. Across the three charts that make up the journey's rules, there are only a handful of opportunities to engage foes in what we might call 'Adventuring phase time'. Most interactions occur at more of a remove, allowing speedy and engaging encounters with key aspects of the setting, without bogging down in too much rules detail. They are intended as a tool to set the scene, and to bring a little gravity to the idea of traversing the vast distances we see in *The Hobbit* and *The Lord of the Rings*.

There is intended to be peril on the Road, but not so much so that players are discouraged from travel all together. It's important that their characters, that hopefully become prized creations, don't arrive at the adventure-proper unable to swing a sword or perform the heroic actions expected of them. So it is that there are rewards, as well as punishment, to be gained from venturing beyond the threshold.

Similarly, rolling up strings of random monster encounters doesn't necessarily feel like Middle-earth. When Bilbo and the Dwarves or Frodo and Sam encounter enemies, it is part of the tale. It has meaning and is intended to both reinforce the presentation of the world of Middle-earth and to further define their characters. There's no reason why the journeys that your company undertake should be any different.

Adding Wandering Monsters and Scripted Encounters

If your preferred play style includes enjoying some random combat along the way, there is no reason not to include them. There's also huge value in adding some set-piece encounters into your journeys. The players need never know that they are scripted happenings.

A canny Loremaster can conceal their set-pieces with a few rolls of the dice behind the Loremaster's screen so that the company can't separate random happenings from scripted occurrences. And that can certainly include some combat if you want it to. Middle-earth is a hazardous place, after all. Have a care to keep an eye on just how exhausted your company get. If they're too worn down and weary from battle on the Road, remember that hiding and fleeing from enemies is wholly appropriate for the setting. Even the mightiest heroes of the age engage their enemies with prudence on the Road, often choosing discretion over valour. A wise and trusted NPC can advise this kind of caution if your Player-heroes need that guidance.

If you add in direct combat, or if you feel your Player-heroes need it, consider also adding somewhere for them to take a long rest. In the other direction, not doing so can really crank up the mechanical pressure.

You should also feel perfectly entitled to add preplanned encounters with characters and events from your adventure as if they were journey events. Weaving in scripted events amongst those created by skill checks helps create the tapestry of your game, and can make it all the more effective.

You're in Charge

If you feel a journey is becoming too punishing, to the point where, out of character, your players are not having fun, then it is well within your power to tweak the results. Allow a long rest, or the return of some Hit Dice as a reward for good roleplaying on the journey. Lucky dice rolls are their own reward, but minor failures and setbacks for characters shouldn't weigh too heavily on players. If they can summon up some courage in the face of adversity or need a little encouragement, then add in a heartening sight of beautiful scenery or a chance encounter with a talking beast that bears up their spirits in the form of a little bonus. You might even choose to fix the results of a roll on the Journey Table (page 62) to provide some relief if things are not going well. This kind of 'fudging' doesn't suit all groups, and some players feel gravely offended by such practices. So make sure you're not spoiling anyone's enjoyment by tweaking hidden dice results.

Remember, you're all in the game to enjoy it.

Rests on the Road

"This is a serious journey, not a hobbit walking-party."

The *Adventures in Middle-earth* journey rules pull Player-heroes into 'journey time', and this slightly tweaks the assumptions of the core rules. While on the Road, Player-heroes may only take short rests. Long rests are only available as part of a successful journey event, or at the discretion of the Loremaster who has decided it necessary. This means that Player-heroes need to think carefully about how much they use their abilities on the Road. If they are too quick to use Virtues or features that require a long rest to recharge, they may not have access to those powers when they reach their destination.

The reasoning here is two-fold. First, journeys are dangerous, challenging and tiring. Player-heroes must make judicious choices on the Road. The peril of travel is a key part of Middle-earth and is where much of the adventure and character development occurs. Second,

> ## Don't tell me how I feel!
>
> The journey tables present some instances where suggestions are made on the mood of the company. Don't feel that these are edicts that must be obeyed. They can be used as inspiration for the prevailing conditions that individual Player-heroes may shrug off, maintaining their emotional autonomy. If your players don't want to be told that they feel downhearted due to the way the journey has gone, be prepared to describe the conditions that would make most people in Middle-earth feel that way. Overcast weather, dismal road conditions, a lack of sleep, biting insects, small disagreements on the Road weighing heavily, a feeling of pursuit by suspicious and sinister animals – all of these kinds of things can inspire the mood that the journey tables suggest.
>
> Other players will enjoy the cues for roleplaying and thoroughly enjoy exploring the results of their dice rolls. It's up to you as the Loremaster to make that judgment call to ensure everyone is having fun. It's not a failure if a character declares that no, they do not feel downcast by the journey. Let them describe how their character has shrugged off the woes of the Road despite the pressures encountered. It all adds to the atmosphere.

the inability to fully rest while travelling heightens the importance of Sanctuaries. Players will soon realise that they cannot thrive in Middle-earth without friends and allies willing to show them hospitality. This mechanical push towards Sanctuaries promotes these key themes of the setting. A company of heroes simply cannot live forever on the Road, without engaging the peoples they meet along the way.

At the beginning of a campaign, it's likely that a company will only have access to a single Sanctuary – by default, Lake-town (page 28). If they plan to regularly travel and want to reach far-flung destinations in good shape, then being able to split an epic trek into legs between Sanctuaries will be vital. You can read more about Sanctuaries on page 151.

Describing Middle-earth

In addition to using journey events, which are intended to give a flavourful taste of Middle-earth, the Loremaster can take an active role in describing a journey. Middle-earth is an awe-inspiring place full of natural wonders. A large part of the novels concerns itself with flora, fauna and the landscape around the characters, and you can do that in your games too.

A common misapprehension is that the setting is 'an empty map'. This is far from the truth. Great swathes of Middle-earth are epic wildernesses, full of breath-taking beauty, inspiring vistas, curious animals and characterful trees. Loremasters who makes full use of a journey to explore the sights, sounds and smells of the landscape will find their games all the more rewarding. Be careful, however. Players are in the game for adventure and to feel like active and engaged participants. It's wise not to make them sit through too much florid description of tree species or lonely crags. There's a balance to be struck between making your company of adventurers feel like they are inhabiting Wilderland, and being bored.

Below are some suggestions for direct description with which to pepper your Player-heroes' journeys. These are useful for imparting the feel of passing time and an epic journey through a fantastic landscape. They also provide convenient seques between journey events: while you know there will be a series of dice thrown and perhaps scripted events, you can keep the mechanics of that backstage, unfolding an engaging and delightful journey by careful use of some description.

Ideas for Things Seen on the Road

Your journey passes through a wide boulder field strewn with large grey rocks, deer running between them in the distance.

Your company hikes past a stand of great emerald ash trees, one of their number fallen years before, covered in moss, the others inclined towards their fallen comrade.

Using many fords, you cross over the various courses of a branching stream that meanders through the heather-covered hillsides.

The road passes through great copses of ancient trees, running one into another, pierced by clearings thick with bracken.

A cloud of birds high in the sky wheeling together grabs your attention. They seem to be enjoying a conversation.

The path changes through the day. In the morning it was little more than a track used by wild sheep, deer and goats. By lunchtime it is composed of great dressed slabs of grey stone, risen and broken now, but clearly carefully placed by ancient hands long ago.

With the clearing of the morning mist and a rise in the road, the landscape unfolds around you, and you can see for miles across the East Anduin Vales, towards the Great River. To the East you can make out the Eaves of Mirkwood, a fearful black smudge all along the horizon.

You pass a day of slow inclines and tiring twists to the path.

The next day you enjoy a long afternoon of downhill travel that raises your spirits. At the end of the day you catch sight of a great white stag, lifting its head from the sward before leaping away into the distance.

You pass many tumbled boulders before realising some of them are carved with ancient runes and faces. This was once a dwelling place of some ancient people. You cannot tell who.

Interrupting Journeys
"The road goes ever on and on"

Not all journeys go to plan. Sometimes the company believe they are heading to a given final destination, but as Loremaster you may have other ideas. A surprise ending to a journey can keep your players on their toes, disrupting any comfortable plans they may have made. Alternatively, your players themselves may wish to end a journey prematurely. Perhaps they are sorely wounded by combat on the Road. Perhaps they feel they need a long rest in a safe place to recharge their powers. Perhaps they've unexpectedly changed their minds about their destination.

When ending a journey unexpectedly, the key is to implement the Arrival roll at a logical moment. That may present itself very clearly, or it may require some quick thinking to maintain suspension of disbelief. Some player groups have no problem with weaving overt mechanics into their play. Others prefer the rules to remain more hidden.

If you script a surprise end to a journey, consider when the Arrival roll will be made for maximum effect. Also consider the likely results. Do you need to apply a modifier to steer that result? For example, if the company are captured, they shouldn't have access to too much of an upbeat result. The means by which the journey comes to an end should affect the Arrival roll if it deviates from a planned arrival. Consider a modifier, or even changing the die type from a d8 to a d6 or even a d4 to ensure a lower result, reflecting the overall mood of the situation. Conversely, if the journey is interrupted in an unexpected but inspiring way – perhaps the company are taken to Beorn's House, or invited to a hidden Elf hall – consider adding a bonus (1d6+2 or 1d4+4) to reflect their good fortune.

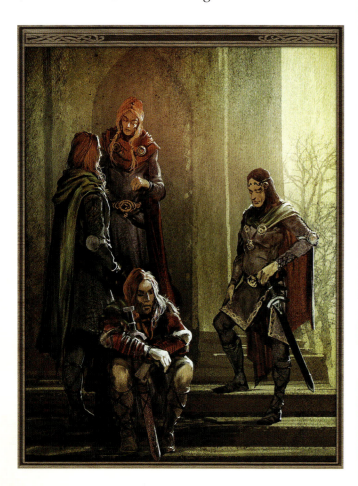

If the players call for a halt in their journey in order to rest, they will need to find somewhere suitable. As Loremaster you have some choices in how to implement this. You could simply negotiate with the players on how they plan to end the journey. This is recommended if your players are feeling especially wearied by the journey. Perhaps they look for a farmstead and earn food and lodging by means of an Audience. The simple Audience rules on page 192 of the *Player's Guide* cover this quickly and efficiently. Don't forget this could be an opportunity to add further plot hooks. Perhaps their morale as players, out of character, is so low that it is time to be kind and simply gift them a bountiful camping site with plenty of fresh water, shelter and abundant game. Think about instances from the novels where exhausted heroes received aid and took their rest.

Suggested Places to End a Journey

- An abandoned farmstead
- A lone farm inhabited by friendly locals
- A well stocked Ranger hideaway
- A bountiful nook in the landscape that offers comforts beyond those usually available
- A camp with fellow travellers who are well stocked with provisions, and perhaps wagons in which to rest
- The comfortable, if a little cramped for Big Folk, river barge of a family of River Hobbits
- An ancient cache of supplies stored away in a dry cave by a forgotten king of old
- The house of a wild hermit, curiously safe in the depths of Mirkwood
- A magical encounter with a character like jolly Tom Bombadil or fierce Beorn, who arrives at the perfect time to offer hospitality in his hidden and wondrous house.
- An encampment of Wayward Elves, wandering the wild. They can supply hospitality unheard of by Mannish folk even far from home. Elven wine and waybread restore body and spirit as quickly as a night in a feather bed!
- A meeting with an old Ent, who has slept for an age and is keen to hear of events in the world. He has a supply of Ent-draught, which although weakened in its long storage, can still reinvigorate the exhausted.

By giving up a journey and initiating an Arrival roll, a company must begin their journey anew once they have rested, with a new Embarkation roll and new journey events. They also suffer any potential ill effects of a botched Arrival roll. Things may not go as favourably as they did on the journey now coming to an end. They may be losing key bonuses earned, and there could be disagreement within the company on whether to end a journey or not. This is perfectly in keeping with the flavour of Middle-earth.

When a journey ends and play enters the Adventuring phase, there are some specifics to consider. See page 50 of this volume for further guidance.

Experience on the Road
"The road must be trod, but it will be very hard. And neither strength nor wisdom will carry us far upon it."

A Loremaster has the choice to offer a reward of Experience Points or Hit Dice whenever they see fit. Remember this when your company complete particularly difficult journey events or long journeys. If the company sail through a journey with ease, that too may warrant a reward of Experience Points, or even Hit Dice.

If your campaign uses alternative means of awarding experience, a journey shouldn't be overlooked as a venue where characters can grow. While journey events may be randomly generated, they are all part of your company's story. Levelling up on the Road is entirely in keeping with the character of the setting.

Journeys should feel perilous, but should also be rewarding and entertaining.

Making Your own Journey Events Tables
"Short cuts make long delays."

Loremasters may wish to devise their own travel tables, and published Adventures will profile additional options. Below you will find the mechanical underpinnings of journey events. These can be re-skinned as the Loremaster sees fit. The journey events presented in the *Player's Guide* work well for a wide variety of locations within Middle-earth, but if your campaign takes your company to persistently different locales, you may wish to invest some time in creating your own events that reflect the differences in setting. Future supplements will offer alternate journey events tables.

Embarkation Table: Raw

1 (or less): +2 to journey rolls and initial tests on each encounter made with Disadvantage. 1pt of Shadow.

2: 1pt of Shadow. All rolls made by each character at Disadvantage until they succeed in a roll.

3: +1 to all rolls on Journey Events table. The first roll of each event is made with Disadvantage.

4: All terrain types classed as 1 grade harder.

5: 1 level of Exhaustion.

6: -1 to all skill checks.

7: +1 to all skill checks.

8: Ignore first level of Exhaustion.

9: All terrain types classed as 1 grade easier.

10: +1 to all rolls on Journey Events table. First roll in each event is made with Advantage.

11: All characters have Advantage until they fail an ability check..

12 (or more): +2 to the rolls on the Journey Events rolls and initial tests made to determine the initial outcome of these encounters should be made with Advantage.

Journey Events Table: Raw

1 (or less): Scout: Stealth test to avoid, or Persuasion test. If Persuasion is used, success results in Advantage on the first roll of the next event. Fail results in Disadvantage.

2: Hunter: Survival test. Success results in either food (which removes 1 level of Exhaustion or restores 1 Hit Dice) or herbs chosen by the LM. Failure results in -1 to Arrival roll.

- The test is subject to Disadvantage/Advantage if Embarkation roll was 6 or 7.

3: Guide: Survival. All others Survival or Athletics (+ Animal Handling if the party has ponies or horses) Disadvantage/Advantage on these rolls if the Embarkation roll was 4 or 9.

- All succeed: +1 to Arrival roll.
- Half or more succeed: No modifiers.
- Less than half succeed: 1 level of Exhaustion.
- All fail: 1 level of Exhaustion and Arrival roll is -1.

4: Stricken folk, if they choose not to help: Wisdom saving throw to avoid gaining a point of Shadow.

- If they help: 3 tests, split between the party, against Survival, Traditions, Insight, Persuade, Animal Handling, Medicine or Nature.
- All succeed: Each character is Inspired and the party receives +1 to Arrival roll.
- Half or more succeed: 1 character is Inspired and the party receive +1 to the Arrival roll.
- 1 succeeds: +1 to Arrival roll.
- All fail: -1 to Arrival roll.

5: Look-out: Perception. Disadvantage/Advantage if Embarkation roll was 3 or 10

- Success: Party may avoid or set an ambush. If they ambush they benefit from a round of surprise.
- Failure: The enemy benefit from a round of surprise.

6: All check Wisdom or Investigation. Any succeeding may remove a level of Exhaustion. Any failing receive a level of Exhaustion. The rolls are subject to Disadvantage/Advantage if Embarkation roll was 5 or 8.

- All succeed: The party receive +1 to Arrival roll.
- All fail: They receive -1 to Arrival roll.

7: Hunter: Survival: Subject to Disadvantage/Advantage if the Embarkation roll was 6 or 7.

- Success by 5 or more: All characters may remove 1 level of Exhaustion and the party receive +1 to the Arrival roll.
- Success: All may remove 1 level of Exhaustion.
- Fail: All receive 1 level of Exhaustion.
- Fail by 5 or more: All receive 1 level of Exhaustion and the Arrival roll is at -1.

8: Scout: Investigation.

- Success by 5 or more: As a long rest, plus remove 1 level of Exhaustion and receive +1 to Arrival roll.
- Success: Remove 1 level of Exhaustion.
- Fail: Receive 1 level of Exhaustion.
- Fail by 5 or more: -1 to Arrival roll and must fight a combat.

9: All must roll a Wisdom check. If more than half succeed: +1 to Arrival roll. If more than half fail, -1 to Arrival roll.

- Success by 5 or more: gain Inspiration and remove 1 level of Exhaustion.
- Success: Inspiration.
- Failure: Corruption check or receive 2 points of Shadow.
- Failure by 5 or more: receive 1 level of Exhaustion and must make the Corruption roll to avoid 2 points of Shadow.

10: Scout: Investigation.

- Success by 5 or more: All gain Inspiration, may remove 1 point of Shadow and the Guide's Arrival roll gains a +1 bonus.
- Success: +1 to the Arrival roll.
- Fail: All must make a Corruption check to avoid gaining 1 point of Shadow.
- Fail by 5 or more: Combat with something dark and powerful.

11: If the Embarkation roll was a 3, there will be a combat.

Look-out: Perception. If successful, the party gain a round of surprise.

If the Embarkation roll was a 10: Look-out tests Perception or Stealth. If successful, the party avoid the enemy.

- If the roll fails, there will be combat but the party gain a round of surprise.

If the Embarkation was neither 3 nor 10: Each member of the party may test Stealth. If all are successful they may avoid the combat (If the party have horses or ponies, one of the characters must also make an Animal Handling roll).

- If any of these rolls fail, combat ensues, with no bonus to either side.

12 (or more): If the Embarkation roll was 1: A Servant of the Enemy is encountered.

If the Embarkation roll was a 12, a major (good) NPC is encountered.

If neither 1 nor 12 was rolled on the Embarkation roll: The Look-out makes a Perception check.

- If this succeeds by 5 or more: The party have met a major NPC and recognise them as such. Each member of the party may remove 1 point of Shadow. The party may also seek an Audience. If successful, they gain Advantage on initial rolls on the next encounter and +1 to the Arrival roll. They may also gain a Patron.
- If the roll succeeds: Insight rolls will reveal the nature of the NPC. Or a demonstration that the company is good and true will cause the NPC to show his nature.
- If the Look-out's roll fails: Each must make a Corruption check to avoid gaining 2 points of Shadow and must make Stealth (+ Animal Handling if horses or ponies are present) to sneak away. If more than half fail they gain 1 level of Exhaustion and -1 to the Arrival roll.
- If the Look-out's roll fails by 5 or more: Each gains 2 points of Shadow, 1 level of Exhaustion and -1 to the Arrival roll.

Arrival Table: Raw

Arrival:
- Easy terrain: +1
- Moderate terrain: No modifiers
- Hard or Severe terrain: -1
- Daunting terrain: -2

1 (or less): Wisdom check to avoid 2 points of Shadow.
2: 1 level of Exhaustion.
3: Disadvantage to Social rolls until they succeed at one. Advantage on Initiative.
4: An Audience, or various checks to arrive at destination successfully.
5: Remove 1 level of Exhaustion.
6: +1 to next Embarkation roll.
7: Advantage on Social rolls until they fail one.
8 (or more): Gain Inspiration and remove 2 points of Shadow.

Non-Player Characters and Audiences Expanded

Folk Along the Way

Greetings Friends,

I have sent several of these letters with travellers heading towards The Shire and I sincerely hope against hope one manages to reach you. We have made our way safely across the Misty Mountains, though I was sure on more than one occasion that we were doomed during that perilous journey. But here we are. Several days travel beyond those peaks we have found a place to build our inn! A short walk from the road we have found the perfect site, and we have begun building. Our first task is to excavate the Hobbit Holes in which we will make our new homes. While the Shire is far behind us we have brought our manners and habits with us. The inn itself will be above ground, with two storeys, as the big people prefer. But we will live in the lap of cosy luxury beneath ground as we should!

I will write again soon. I am sure that we have made the right choice to travel beyond the borders of our homeland, and I cannot wait to tell you more of our adventures. Perhaps one day you will all be able to visit us here at the Easterly Inn!

Your friend,

Dodinas

Folk
- along the way -

"Fair speech may hide a foul heart."

Wilderland is wide and strange. Long gone are the days of the kings, when the roads were safe and people travelled without fear. For many years, only the brave and desperate risked travel through the wild. Now that the dragon is dead and King Bard rules again in Dale, there is hope again in the north – a hope that will soon be endangered by the rising Shadow.

Most folk in Middle-earth, therefore, know little of the ways of others. Take the Hobbits, for example. The Shire-folk consider the people of Bree to be strange and foreign, even though they live almost next door to them. Wilderland is a distant rumour, known only through stories brought by the Dwarves who pass along the road to the Blue Mountains, and the occasional company of Elves travelling west to the Havens. The Rangers protect the Shire from outside dangers, so the Hobbits do not even know how perilous the wider world can be.

Others are not so lucky. Elsewhere in Wilderland, the Free Folk dwell in small, fortified villages and towns, like the Beornings and Woodmen, or have withdrawn into their own ancient kingdoms and are rarely seen, like the Elves. Only in the lands around Esgaroth and in the south-lands of Gondor and Rohan is there anything like regular trade and travel on the roads, where the ways of old are remembered and the king's peace is kept.

So, most folk that the adventurers encounter along the way are likely to be suspicious and mistrustful of outsiders at first. They may know the adventurers' homelands as places out of myth (*"Halflings! But they are only a little people in*

old songs and children's tales out of the North! Do we walk in legends or on the green earth in the daylight?"). If they are able to prove their trustworthiness, the adventurers are likely to find their new friends welcoming and kind.

Playing Members of the Free Folk

Men

This is a darkening time in the Third Age of Middle-earth. Men and women are worried, fearful and serious-minded. In the north, there is hope, for King Bard has reclaimed his throne and the dragon is dead, but that is just one firebrand burning as the night closes in. Still, if their spirits can be kindled and their fear turned to courage, Men can do great deeds, and the Fourth Age belongs to them. Remember, too, that the Third Age is a fallen one. The knowledge and skill of the Second Age is mostly lost, preserved only in Gondor. The great works of the past cannot be made, nor do folk remember their lore save in fragments.

When playing Men and Women of the Free Folk, measure your words carefully. Either be very insular and focus only on your own local affairs (to quote Butterbur: *"We're a bit suspicious of anything out of the way – uncanny, if you understand me; and we don't take to it all of a sudden."*) or be aware of the danger of the Shadow, even if you do not yet know how to fight it.

Elves

The Elves are fading. They are either flighty and love only merrymaking, or else wise and sorrowful, knowing that they no longer have the strength to fight the Shadow. The greatest of the Elves are still among the most powerful and dangerous beings to walk in Middle-earth, but their time is ending, and they all sense this. Young Elves encountered in one of their refuges (Northern Mirkwood, Lórien, Rivendell) may be frustratingly heedless and merry; others may be more sober-minded and focused on the threat of the Shadow, but they know that this is no longer their fight.

Dwarves

Stoic and serious-minded, the Dwarves love the physical world and its treasures. They delight in things, especially things they have made – and resent those who have taken things from them. Their hatred is strongest for the Orcs, but they have old grudges with the Elves, too. When playing a Dwarf, then, focus mainly on practical matters – couch everything in legal terms, talk about places and objects instead of peoples and ideals.

Other Folk

There are many strange creatures in Middle-earth that are not Elf nor Man nor Dwarf. Hobbits and Ents, talking beasts, unquiet spirits and mysterious beings like Tom Bombadil. The Loremaster should invent speech patterns and demeanours for such folk that are very different from those of Elves or Men or Dwarves.

Playing Characters from the Book

"I was talking aloud to myself. A habit of the old: they choose the wisest person present to speak to"

Meeting Gandalf and other heroes from Tolkien's stories is one of the wonderful opportunities of playing in Middle-earth. It is much more fun to speak to Beorn or Radagast or Galadriel than to meet a similar character of the Loremaster's invention that fills the same role. These are names to conjure with.

The players have no doubt read Tolkien's books and have their own images of these characters, so the character's presence takes on extra potency. Players sit up and pay attention when a character from the novels shows up in the game. This is a double-edged sword for the Loremaster – there is a large difference between words on a page (or an actor on screen), and the improvised, unpolished portrayal in a roleplaying game. It's fun to meet Gandalf, but the longer that the Loremaster plays Gandalf, the more likely it is that something will happen to undermine the wizard – a bad dice roll, a tongue-tied verbal slip.

The best approach for playing 'canon' characters is to refer to them often, but use them sparingly. Have many people speak of the Grey Wizard, or of King Bard, or Bilbo Baggins, but only have such heroes play a direct part in the game for brief periods.

Characters of Middle-earth

The following nonplayer characters are typical of the Free Folk of Middle-earth. For those that the Player-heroes are likely to encounter in an Audience, we have included Motivations and Expectations (see page 80) to aid in roleplaying.

Chieftain

A king will have his way in his own hall, be it folly or wisdom.

The leader of a village or tribe of Men – one of Beorn's followers, perhaps, or a Woodman chief, or the Master of one of the new settlements that have arisen around Dale. Is the chieftain old, or did they win the trust of their followers through great deeds? Do they rule wisely or foolishly? Is their reign marked by peace, or by trouble? In any case, they likely mistrust strangers from distant lands, but will welcome their kinsfolk or those known to them, and offer shelter from the wild.

Motivation: Preserve her people's fortunes
Expectations:
- This land is ours; the bones of our ancestors are buried here. None shall take it from us. +2 if the Player-heroes warn of a threat to the settlement.
- Strangers must show respect to our ways. +1 if the Player-heroes display respect.
- Everyone just does what they must to survive. -1 if the Player-heroes confirm the chieftain's natural mistrust and pessimism.
- I reject your trickery! -2 if the chieftain discovers the Player-heroes are lying.

Chieftain
Medium Human

STR	DEX	CON	INT	WIS	CHA
13 (+1)	10 (+0)	12 (+1)	13 (+1)	14 (+2)	14 (+2)

Armour Class 13 (corselet of mail)
Hit Points 33 (6d8+6)
Speed 30 ft

Skills Insight +5, Riddle +4, Perception +5
Senses passive Perception 15
Languages Westron
Challenge 1/2 (100 XP)

Special Traits

Commanding: Allies of the chieftain gain Advantage on attack rolls against enemies engaged with the chieftain.

Actions

Broad sword: *Melee Weapon Attack:* +3 to hit, reach 5 ft, one target. *Hit:* 5 (1d8+1) slashing damage.

Town Guard

"Your business is your own, no doubt," said the man; "but it's my business to ask questions after nightfall."

Few towns in Wilderland are large enough to have a formal guard, but even a small village might have a gatekeeper or night watchman. The role of the guard is to deal with troublemakers and nuisances, and in time of danger, to sound the alarm and hold the door until help arrives.

Motivation: Protect the gate
Expectations:
- A coin or two is always welcome. +2 if the Player-heroes offer a bribe and aren't otherwise dangerous.
- Weapons by the door. +1 if the Player-heroes agree to leave their weapons in the guard's keeping.

- Blame always falls on those that deserve it least. -1 if the gatekeeper fears something strange is afoot that will end up causing trouble for him.
- Unexpected travellers are an annoyance, and sometimes are dangerous. -2 if the Player-heroes appear dangerous or threatening.

Town Guard
Medium Human

STR	DEX	CON	INT	WIS	CHA
13 (+1)	10 (+0)	12 (+1)	10 (+0)	11 (+0)	11 (+0)

Armour Class 14 (hide armour, shield)
Hit Points 11 (2d8+2)
Speed 30 ft

Skills Traditions +2, Perception +2
Senses passive Perception 12
Languages Westron
Challenge 1/4 (50 XP)

Special Traits

Raise the alarm: A town guard who has not yet attacked in this combat has 5 temporary hit points. These hit points are lost as soon as the town guard attacks or one of the town guards raises the alarm.

Actions

Spear: *Melee or Ranged Weapon Attack:* +3 to hit, reach 5 ft or range 20/60 ft, one target. *Hit:* 4 (1d6+1) piercing damage or 5 (1d8+1) piercing damage if used with two hands to make a melee attack.
Or
Club: *Melee Weapon Attack:* +3 to hit, reach 5 ft, one target. *Hit:* 3 (1d4+1) bludgeoning damage.

Merchant
The next day carts rolled up the Hill, and still more carts.

Before the death of the dragon, the only merchants regularly encountered on the Road were Dwarves, exiled from their ancestral halls and reduced to being tin-smiths and traders. Now that there is a king in Dale again and the Beornings guard the crossings of the River and the Mountains, there are more traders risking the Wild again. Toys from Dale, wine from Dorwinion, weapons and tools from the forges under the Mountain, furs and hide from the hills – there is a fortune to be made by merchants brave enough to travel and canny enough to get a good deal. A merchant always has a smile and a friendly word for a fellow traveller – or is that smile plastered on to fool an unwary mark?

Motivation: To make a fortune
Expectations:
- Almost everybody else is a fool to be cheated. +2 if the Player-heroes agree to buy from the merchant.
- Wealth is a sign of worthiness. +1 if the Player-heroes have any Prosperous or Rich characters in their company.

- Beware of those who are not fools. -1 if the Player-heroes prove worryingly insightful.
- Begone, beggars! -2 if all the Player-heroes have a Martial or lower standard of living.
- There's always peril in the wild, and it is best to avoid confronting it. -2 if the Player-heroes advocate leaving the Road or doing something dangerous.

Merchant
Medium Human

STR	DEX	CON	INT	WIS	CHA
10 (+0)	13 (+1)	13 (+1)	11 (+0)	11 (+0)	14 (+2)

Armour Class 11
Hit Points 11 (2d8+2)
Speed 30 ft

Skills Persuasion +4, Traditions +2
Senses passive Perception 10
Languages Westron, one or two other dialects
Challenge 1/8 (25 XP)

Actions

Club: *Melee Weapon Attack:* +2 to hit, reach 5 ft, one target. *Hit:* 2 (1d4) bludgeoning damage.

Messenger

"A man is here, lord," he said, "an errand-rider of Gondor."

The only way for news to travel in Middle-earth is for someone to bring it. Usually, news travels slowly, carried by merchants or wandering Dwarves or other wanderers on the Road, trading gossip from the far side of Wilderland for a spot by the fire and a crust of bread. Certain messages, though, are urgent, and must be carried by a courier. Such swift travellers criss-cross the ways of Middle-earth, carrying letters or secret messages on behalf of their masters.

Motivation: Bring the message to its recipient
Expectations:
- News from afar. +2 if the Player-heroes bring interesting information.
- It's good to have company on the road, but they must not slow you down. +1 if the Player-heroes offer protection and company.
- Those who refuse to share news have something to hide. -1 if the Player-heroes refuse to speak of themselves.

Messenger
Medium Human

STR	DEX	CON	INT	WIS	CHA
10 (+0)	15 (+2)	14 (+2)	10 (+0)	14 (+2)	11 (+0)

Armour Class 14 (leather corselet)
Hit Points 26 (4d8+8)
Speed 30 ft

Skills Traditions +2, Survival +4, Perception +4
Senses passive Perception 14
Languages Westron
Challenge 1/2 (100 XP)

Special Traits

Well-Travelled: The messenger has Advantage on all Survival tests related to travelling along the Road or in familiar lands. This Advantage is lost if the messenger is trying to reach an unfamiliar destination.

Actions

Short sword: *Melee Weapon Attack:* +4 to hit, reach 5 ft, one target. *Hit:* 5 (1d6+2) slashing damage.

Farmer

They went into the farmer's kitchen, and sat by the wide fire-place. Mrs. Maggot brought out beer in a huge jug, and filled four large mugs.

Small farmsteads support most of the folk of Wilderland. These farmsteads might be clustered together near a village, like Bree-land, or they might be isolated farmsteads like Beorn's house, out in the Wilderness and beholden to no lord or master. A farmer might have a dozen neighbours, or there might not be another living soul within a hundred leagues. In either case, a farmer's home is a good place to find shelter in the wild – assuming he does not set his dogs on trespassers!

- Strangers are suspect. -1 if the Player-heroes include at least one Unknown culture.
- A man is a king under his own roof, no matter how humble it is. -2 if the Player-heroes are disrespectful.

Farmer
Medium Human

STR	DEX	CON	INT	WIS	CHA
10 (+0)	10 (+0)	10 (+0)	10 (+0)	14 (+2)	11 (+0)

Armour Class 12 (hide armour)
Hit Points 9 (2d8)
Speed 30 ft

Skills Nature +4
Senses passive Perception 12
Languages Westron or the local dialect
Challenge 1/4 (50 XP)

Special Traits

Call the Dogs: Once per short or long rest, the farmer may whistle for his dogs, calling 1d4 Mastiffs to aid him. They arrive at the end of the farmer's next turn.

Actions

Club: *Melee Weapon Attack:* +2 to hit, reach 5 ft, one target. *Hit:* 2 (1d4) bludgeoning damage.

Motivation: Mind your own business.
Expectations:
- There's evil in the world. +2 if the Player-heroes prove they have recently struck a blow against the Shadow by slaying Orcs, Wargs or other such foes.
- Things will get worse; dig in for a long winter. +1 if the Player-heroes honestly ask for help.

Warrior

Behind him marched proudly a dusty line of men, well-armed and bearing great battle-axes.

Though some fortunate lands have been left in peace for long years (or shielded from woe by the Rangers and other unseen friends), most of Middle-earth is a perilous place. Orcs and worse things lurk in the mountains and the dark woods, and there are outlaws and cruel men aplenty. Sometimes, it is necessary to set axe to flesh instead of wood, and to take shelter behind a warrior's shield. This particular warrior is typical of most warriors of the North, the sort that might be found in the Vales of Anduin or in the vanguard of the armies of Dale. Only a few warriors – those in the service of wealthy kings, or Dwarf-Lords – can afford heavy armour and weapons. Most make do with axes and lighter protection.

Sage

Elrond knew about runes of every kind. That day he looked at the sword they had brought from the troll's lair, and he said, "These are not troll-make. They are old swords, very old swords of the High Elves of the West."

Sages remember the old lore of their people, and advise kings and chieftains on what to do. A sage might be wise, like Elrond, or puffed-up with ego and foolish pride, like the herb-master of Gondor, or even malicious and deceitful, like Wormtongue. Learning is a mark of wisdom, but it is not the only one, and a fellow may know all the lore of the world and still not be counted among the Wise. While the lore of elder days is preserved only in places like Rivendell and Gondor, each of the Free Peoples have their own sages and scholars. The Woodmen know secrets of herb-lore and wood-lore, the Dwarves have no equal when it comes to smithing and building, and even the Shire-Hobbits have great expertise in certain obscure branches of scholarship.

Warrior
Medium Human

STR	DEX	CON	INT	WIS	CHA
14 (+2)	11 (+0)	14 (+2)	10 (+0)	11 (+0)	11 (+0)

Armour Class 14 (hide armour, shield)
Hit Points 19 (3d8+6)
Speed 30 ft

Skills Intimidation +2, Traditions +2
Senses passive Perception 12
Languages Westron
Challenge 1/2 (100 XP)

Special Traits

Warrior's Charge: The warrior gains Advantage on all attacks made in the first round of combat.

Actions

Multiattack: The warrior makes two melee attacks.
Axe: *Melee Weapon Attack:* +4 to hit, reach 5 ft, one target. *Hit:* 6 (1d8+2) slashing damage.

Sage
Medium Human

STR	DEX	CON	INT	WIS	CHA
6 (-2)	10 (+0)	10 (+0)	16 (+3)	14 (+2)	13 (+1)

Armour Class 10
Hit Points 9 (2d8)
Speed 30 ft

Skills Traditions +5, Lore +5
Senses passive Perception 12
Languages Westron, Sindarin, a little Quenya, one or two other obscure tongues
Challenge 1/8 (25 XP)

Special Traits

Cunning Speech: If the sage has a chance to speak, then any intelligent foes within earshot must make a Wisdom saving throw (DC13) or suffer Disadvantage when attacking the sage.

Actions

Staff: *Melee Weapon Attack:* +0 to hit, reach 5 ft, one target. *Hit:* 1 (1d6-2) bludgeoning damage or 2 (1d8-2) bludgeoning damage if wielded with two hands.

Motivation: Accumulate lore, so that one may know the correct thing to do.

Expectations:
- Most people are simple-minded and lack perspective. Speak only to the Wise. If none here are among the Wise, speak to yourself. +2 if the Player-heroes demonstrate a mastery of lore.
- Debate is the fire in which knowledge is forged. +1 if the Player-heroes argue openly and are not hidebound by custom and propriety.
- Only the lessons of the past matter. The present age is a fallen one, and there is little or nothing to learn from it. -1 if the Player-heroes focus on current events.
- Violence is the last refuge of fools. -2 if the Player-heroes try intimidation.

foreshadow events to come or to underline the importance of a place or concept.

Motivation: Entertain and earn a coin or two.

Expectations:
- To raise spirits. +2 if the Player-heroes are inspired or especially interested in the song.
- To have an attentive and appreciative audience. +1 if the Player-heroes appreciate the song.

Singer
Medium Human

STR	DEX	CON	INT	WIS	CHA
10 (+0)	12 (+1)	12 (+1)	13 (+1)	11 (+0)	15 (+2)

Armour Class 11
Hit Points 11 (2d8+2)
Speed 30 ft

Skills Traditions +3, Lore +3, Performance +3
Senses passive Perception 10
Languages Westron, Dalish, a little Sindarin
Challenge 1/8 (25 XP)

Special Traits

Inspiring Song: Once per combat, the singer may grant a Singer's Inspiration die (d6) to one ally. That ally may roll that d6 and add the result to an attack roll or saving throw.

Actions

Dagger: *Melee Weapon Attack:* +3 to hit, reach 5 ft, one target. *Hit:* 3 (1d4+1) piercing damage.

Singer

Often they heard nearby Elvish voices singing, and knew that they were making songs of lamentation for his fall, for they caught his name among the sweet sad words they could not understand.

All folk in Middle-earth delight in singing. A singer might make merry in an inn, leading the company in a lively dance or drinking-song, or sing a lament for the fallen, or beat the drum on a march to war, or recall long-lost memories and forgotten secrets that have been preserved in old lays. Songs have power and meaning in Middle-earth; Loremasters might use singers and their songs to

Thug

"If you pick up with a horse-thief, and bring him to my house," said Butterbur angrily, "you ought to pay for all the damage yourselves and not come shouting to me. Go and ask Ferny where your handsome friend is!"

Thugs and thieves like this are opportunists, preying on the weak and vulnerable. They are not servants of the Shadow by any means – they are simply greedy and cruel. Their ilk lurks around the alleyways of Lake-town and Dale, and even Gondor. Anywhere there is coin to be made from mugging passers-by, these folk can be found.

Thug
Medium Human

STR	DEX	CON	INT	WIS	CHA
14 (+2)	10 (+0)	14 (+2)	10 (+0)	8 (-1)	8 (-1)

Armour Class 14 (Hide armour, shield)
Hit Points 13 (2d8+4)
Speed 30 ft

Skills Intimidation +1
Senses passive Perception 9
Languages any one language (usually Westron)
Challenge 1/4 (50 XP)

Special Traits

Coward: When injured, the thug suffers Disadvantage on all combat rolls.

Actions

Club: *Melee Weapon Attack:* +4 to hit, reach 5 ft, one target. *Hit:* 4 (1d4+2) bludgeoning damage.

Outlaw
"These lands are dangerous, full of foul rebels and brigands."

Outlaws lie in wait along the Road, in greater numbers now that there is more traffic and trade to be robbed. They make their lairs in Northern Mirkwood, in the Grey Mountains, along the river Running, and – despite the watchful Beornings – near the crossings of the Anduin.

Outlaw Chief
Medium Human

STR	DEX	CON	INT	WIS	CHA
15 (+2)	13 (+1)	15 (+2)	13 (+1)	13 (+1)	14 (+2)

Armour Class 15 (Hide Armour, Shield)
Hit Points 65 (10d8+20)
Speed 30 ft

Skills Intimidate +5, Perception +4, Stealth +4, Survival +4
Senses passive Perception 15
Languages any one language (usually Weston)
Challenge 4 (1,100 XP)

Special Traits

Ambush: During their first turn, the outlaw chief has Advantage on attack rolls against any creature that hasn't taken a turn. If the outlaw chief scores a melee critical hit on a target in this turn, that target is knocked Prone.

Actions

Multiattack: The outlaw chief makes two spear attacks.

Spear: *Melee or Ranged Weapon Attack:* +5 to hit, reach 5 ft or range 20/60 ft, one target. *Hit:* 5 (1d6+2) piercing damage or 6 (1d8+2) piercing damage if used with two hands to make a melee attack.

Volley: The outlaw chief makes a bow attack, and any outlaws who make a bow attack this round have Advantage on their attacks.

Bow: *Ranged Weapon Attack:* +4 to hit, range 80/320, one target. *Hit:* 4 (1d6+1) piercing damage.

Terrorise: The outlaw chief targets up to three intelligent creatures they can see within 30 feet. If there are more outlaws present than targets of this ability, then those targets must succeed on a DC 16 Wisdom saving throw or become Frightened until the end of the outlaw chief's next turn.

Non-player Characters and Audiences Expanded

Outlaw
Medium Human

STR	DEX	CON	INT	WIS	CHA
13 (+1)	13 (+1)	13 (+1)	10 (+0)	11 (+0)	11 (+0)

Armour Class 15 (Hide Armour, Shield)
Hit Points 33 (6d8+6)
Speed 30 ft

Skills Perception +2, Stealth +3, Survival +2
Senses passive Perception 12
Languages any one language (usually Westron)
Challenge 2 (450 XP)

Special Traits

Ambush: During its first turn, the outlaw has Advantage on attack rolls against any creature that hasn't taken a turn. If the outlaw scores a melee critical hit on a target in this turn, that target is knocked Prone.

Actions

Multiattack: The outlaw makes two spear attacks.
Spear: *Melee or Ranged Weapon Attack:* +3 to hit, reach 5 ft or range 20/60 ft, one target. *Hit:* 4 (1d6+1) piercing damage or 5 (1d8+1) piercing damage if used with two hands to make a melee attack.
Bow: *Ranged Weapon Attack:* +3 to hit, range 80/320, one target. *Hit:* 4 (1d6+1) piercing damage.

their number, or have the blessing of a Wizard.
- Most people cannot understand the peril they are in; it would freeze their souls. Better they be kept ignorant. +1 if the Player-heroes avoid speaking openly of danger.
- There is strength in secrecy; exposure to the Enemy brings peril. Do not speak openly of important matters. -1 if the Player-heroes blurt out secrets.
- Cowardice is giving in to the Enemy. -2 if the Player-heroes advocate selfishness or undue caution, and do not act like heroes.

Ranger

Stout men and lordly they are, and the Riders of Rohan look almost as boys beside them; for they are grim men of face, worn like weathered rocks for the most part.

The Rangers guard Rivendell and the North from the depredations of the Enemy, and patrol the boundaries of the vanished kingdom of Arnor. At times, too, they cross over the Misty Mountains to travel through Wilderland and the south. They disguise themselves and their lordly heritage, appearing as nothing more than weather-beaten nomads and vagabonds.

Motivation: Defend the Free People against the Enemy.
Expectations:
- The Rangers remember. +2 if the Player-heroes have visited Rivendell, include Rangers or High Elves among

Ranger
Medium Human (Dúnedain)

STR	DEX	CON	INT	WIS	CHA
14 (+2)	13 (+1)	16 (+3)	12 (+1)	16 (+3)	11 (+0)

Armour Class 14 (leather corselet, Defence)
Hit Points 72 (16d8)
Speed 30 ft

Saving Throws: Strength +7, Constitution +8
Skills History +6, Survival +8, Stealth +6
Senses passive Perception 18 (23 in the wild)
Languages Westron, Sindarin, Quenya
Challenge 5 (1,800 XP)

Special Traits

Endurance of the Dúnedain: The Ranger may continue to act normally for one round after being reduced to 0 hit points.

Actions

Multiattack: The Ranger makes a sword and knife attack, or two bow attacks.
Long Sword: *Melee Weapon Attack:* +5 to hit, reach 5 ft, one target. *Hit:* 6 (1d8+2) slashing damage.
Knife: *Melee Weapon Attack:* +5 to hit, reach 5 ft, one target. *Hit:* 4 (1d4+2) slashing damage.
Bow: *Ranged Weapon Attack:* +4 to hit, range 150/600 ft, one target. *Hit:* 5 (1d8+1) piercing damage.
Númenórean Arrow: Instead of making a normal bow attack, the Ranger may fire a Númenórean arrow. *Ranged Weapon Attack:* +6 to hit, range 150/600 ft, one target. *Hit:* 7 (1d8+3) piercing damage, and the target has Disadvantage on all attack rolls next turn.

Elf
Eldest of all, the Elf-children.

Elves still linger in Middle-earth in a few blessed places. Those of Mirkwood are mostly Elves of the Twilight – they never visited the Blessed Realm in the far west, but they are stalwart foes of the Shadow. The days of their greatness are behind them; now, they fade, and in their fading become more childlike and wayward, concerned only with their own amusements and distractions.

Elf
Medium Elf

STR	DEX	CON	INT	WIS	CHA
12 (+1)	16 (+3)	12 (+1)	12 (+1)	14 (+2)	13 (+1)

Armour Class 15 (leather corselet)
Hit Points 33 (6d8+6)
Speed 30 ft

Skills Lore +3, Perception +4, Stealth +5
Senses passive Perception 14
Languages Westron, Sindarin, Silvan
Challenge 1 (200 XP)

Special Traits

Shadow Bane: The Elf gains a +1 bonus to attacks against servants of the Shadow.

Actions

Broadsword: *Melee Weapon Attack:* +5 to hit, reach 5 ft, one target. *Hit:* 7 (1d8+3) slashing damage.
Bow: *Ranged Weapon Attack:* +5 to hit, range 80/120 ft, one target. *Hit:* 6 (1d6+3) piercing damage.

Elf-Lord

But the king, when he received the prayers of Bard, had pity, for he was the lord of a good and kindly people.

This is not one of the great Elf-Lords like Galadriel or Elrond, nor any one of their households like Glorfindel or Celeborn. This is a lesser Elf-Lord, the leader of a travelling company of Elves or a courtier or emissary in the Woodland Realm.

Like the rest of his kin, the Elf-Lord has seen many hundreds of years roll by in Middle-earth, and knows that the Shadow always returns. In time, the Elf-Lord knows, he must go to the Havens and seek the safety of the Blessed Realm across the sea where the Shadow cannot go, but he loves the forests of Middle-earth too much to leave so soon.

Elf-Lord
Medium Elf

STR	DEX	CON	INT	WIS	CHA
14 (+2)	14 (+2)	15 (+2)	16 (+3)	15 (+2)	15 (+2)

Armour Class 12
Hit Points 78 (12d8+24)
Speed 30 ft

Saving Throws Dexterity +5, Charisma +5
Skills Lore +6, Perception +5, Persuasion +5, Traditions +6
Senses passive Perception 15
Languages Westron, Sindarin, Silvan, Quenya
Challenge 4 (1,100 XP)

Special Traits

Stargazer: The Elf-Lord's ancient wisdom and insight aids her when dealing with impatient mortals. Wisdom (Insight) checks to discern the Elf-Lord's thoughts have Disadvantage.

Actions

Multiattack: The Elf-Lord makes two bitter spear attacks.
Bitter Spear: *Melee Weapon Attack:* +6 to hit, reach 5 ft, one target. *Hit:* 7 (1d8+3) piercing damage. On a critical hit, the Elf-Lord deals an additional 7 (2d6) damage.

Motivation: Protect the Woodland Realm or the travelling company from all threats.

Expectations:
- Remember old friendships. +2 if the Player-heroes remind the Elf-Lord of ancient alliances between the Elves and the other Free Peoples.
- Flattery works wonders. +1 if the Player-heroes appeal to the Elf-Lord's ego.
- Courtesy will be met with courtesy. -1 if the Player-heroes insult the Elf-Lord.
- The forest is ours. -2 if the Player-heroes have hunted, trespassed or damaged the trees in the Elf-Lord's domain.

Dwarf

"We have done well," he said, "but in metal-work we cannot rival our fathers, many of whose secrets are lost. We make good armour and keen blades, but we cannot again make mail or blade to match those that were made before the dragon came. Only in mining and building have we surpassed the old days."

Now that there is a King Under The Mountain again, the Dwarves of the north have rallied under the banner of Dáin. Their wealth and influence grow with each passing year. The statistics here are typical of a Dwarven guard; a wandering pot-smith or traveller on the way back from the Blue Mountains might wear lighter armour and carry a mattock instead of an axe.

Dwarf
Medium Dwarf

STR	DEX	CON	INT	WIS	CHA
13 (+1)	10 (+0)	14 (+2)	13 (+1)	8 (-1)	8 (-1)

Armour Class 18 (Ring-mail, Great Shield)
Hit Points 26 (4d8+8)
Speed 25 ft

Skills Athletics +3, Survival +1
Senses passive Perception 9
Languages Westron, Dwarven
Challenge 1/2 (100 XP)

Special Traits

Old Hatred: When you are fighting Orc-kind using a melee weapon, whenever you roll for damage, you can re-roll your weapon's damage die and use either total.

Actions

Dwarf-Forged Axe: *Melee Weapon Attack:* +4 to hit, reach 5 ft, one target. *Hit:* 6 (1d8+2) slashing damage.

Dwarf-Lord

Hood and cloak were gone; they were in shining armour, and red light leapt from their eyes. In the gloom the great dwarf gleamed like gold in a dying fire.

The descendants of Durin – the cousins and relatives of Thorin Oakenshield, like Dáin Ironfoot, and those kin to his trusted companions, like Gimli son of Gloin – have reclaimed much of the wealth and power of their ancestors. Dwarven kingdoms like Erebor, the Iron Hills and the Blue Mountains are once again linked by bonds of trade and kinship, and efforts are underway to reclaim other lost kingdoms, including the fabled Dwarrowdelf, known in the common tongue as Moria. This Dwarf-Lord looks to the future and sees a brighter age.

Motivation: Ensure that his followers are safe and prosperous.

Expectations:
- Tribute or profit. +2 if the Player-heroes can make the Dwarf-Lord wealthier, or promise the return of lost treasures of old.
- Great is the work of the Dwarves. +1 if the Player-heroes praise the craftsmanship and architecture of his hall.
- Flattery is for fools. -1 if the Player-heroes try to trick the Dwarf-Lord with honeyed words.
- No compromise, no forgiveness. -2 if old grudges and hatreds are recalled by the words of the Player-heroes.

Dwarf-Lord
Medium Dwarf

STR	DEX	CON	INT	WIS	CHA
16 (+3)	11 (+0)	16 (+3)	15 (+2)	13 (+1)	14 (+2)

Armour Class 16 (Heavy mail)
Hit Points 90 (12d8 + 36)
Speed 30 ft

Skills Athletics +6, Survival +4, Traditions +5
Senses passive Perception 11
Languages Westron, Dwarven
Challenge 4 (1,100 XP)

Special Traits

Old Hatred: When you are fighting Orc-kind using a melee weapon, whenever you roll for damage, you can re-roll your weapon's damage dice and use either total.

Dwarf-Forged Armour: Critical hits on the Dwarf-Lord become normal hits.

Actions

Multiattack: The Dwarf-Lord makes two melee attacks.

Dwarf-Forged Mattock: *Melee Weapon Attack:* +7 to hit, reach 5 ft, one target. *Hit:* 11 (2d6+4) piercing damage.

Non-player Characters and Audiences Expanded

- Audiences -

"Pay heed to the tales of old wives. It may well be that they alone keep in memory what it was once needful for the wise to know."

The Audience rules in the *Adventures in Middle-earth Player's Guide* offer a firm foundation for structuring meetings with important NPCs. They establish the idea that, while pure roleplaying is rewarding and a lot of fun, sometimes the Loremaster needs more structure to fairly adjudicate what happens when a company meets someone important. They also afford the player whose personal charisma doesn't match their character's score a chance to sway a social encounter, and have some limelight at the table.

The scenario that the *Player's Guide* presents is a straightforward one – Player-heroes arrive at the hearth of a significant NPC seeking help. The results of the interaction determine how much help they receive.

But there are many different ways in which Player-heroes might encounter a significant NPC. What about a situation where the NPC in question wants something from the Player-heroes?

This section provides expanded rules for just such an occurrence, building on the established rules.

The Loremaster should use their personal judgment when deciding if a meeting with an NPC warrants the use of these rules. They aren't intended to replace interpersonal roleplaying, and they should never be deployed to hamper creativity or damage the atmosphere of your game. If a scene is progressing nicely without the application of any rules, then the Loremaster should feel able to simply let it take its course.

In other instances, setting some goals can help the Loremaster achieve a consistent and characterful feeling to their NPCs, and make sure that they have all their bases covered.

Planning Audiences

Before a company of Player-heroes run through an Audience, it's important for the Loremaster to make some decisions. It is quite likely that the Loremaster knows what the Player-heroes want from the Audience, but it is worth taking the time to prepare a little more widely just in case.

The Loremaster must also be aware of what the NPC in question wants, or is likely to want in a given situation. This is an expansion to the basic rules in the *Player's Guide* and it covers more intertwining situations. There are two things to decide for any NPC involved in an Audience: their Motivation and their Expectations.

Motivation

First the Loremaster decides on the main Motivation of the NPC at the heart of the Audience. This will guide their roleplaying and prompt their reactions within the Audience. A crotchety village elder might have the immediate Motivation of just wanting the company to leave her village. Gandalf the Grey might have the broader Motivation of wanting to gather anyone of good heart to his cause. Defining an NPC's Motivation is never all encompassing, but should be considered a guiding principle around which their behaviour revolves.

Example Motivations:
- To lead a quiet life
- To preserve the peace that their people enjoy
- To defend their people from harm
- To recruit agents to their cause
- To extend their influence
- To cause harm to the people in the next valley
- To make money

Expectations

Next the Loremaster needs to consider the Expectations of an NPC. A crotchety village elder might consider being shown deference and respect as their main Expectation. Gandalf the Grey is far less concerned with that, but may well be judging all interactions in order to find helpers of stout heart.

The Loremaster should write out a list of these Expectations in advance when planning an Audience. Consider things that will make the NPC like and trust the company, and things that will make them more likely to dislike and oppose the company.

Items on the list are then grouped together into groups of the same level of intensity, ranging from the most preferred Expectation of the NPC to the most unfavourable Expectation. Each of these groups is assigned a bonus, usually ranging from +2 to -2. There's no need to include an Expectation in every group, but a broad catch-all like "Being disrespected" is a common negative Expectation, and "To be respected" is a common positive Expectation for NPCs worthy of an Audience.

The more favourable behaviours the company exhibit, the more likely the NPC is to be friendly toward them and offer a positive outcome. If the company repeatedly display unfavourable behaviours from the list, the chances of an agreement being struck diminish accordingly.

Example of Positive Expectations:
- To be flattered
- To be shown honesty
- To be left alone
- To be reminded of home
- To be shown generosity
- To find other good people in the world

Example of Negative Expectations:
- To be disrespected
- To suffer rudeness
- To see evil in those around them
- To suffer requests for aid
- To be falsely flattered

Outcomes

In the last part of the planning stage, the Loremaster should consider the available results of the Audience. What are the best things that can happen for the Player-heroes and the NPC? What are the worst? Knowing ahead of time what is at stake helps provide a structure to the whole Audience and allows you to order the results from best – success on the final check by +6 or more – to worst. You can add any level of detail you want at this stage. Because these rules are about both parties wanting something from the other, there's plenty of scope for a wide range of options in the results. Perhaps on a very high margin of success, everyone gets what they want, and the company get an unexpected bonus. On a moderate failure, perhaps the company are simply dismissed. Perhaps if they fail tremendously badly they are incarcerated or even attacked.

The Loremaster can use the results of an Audience to add optional or improvised side quests at both ends of the spectrum. Escaping incarceration after a failed Audience is arguably how Bilbo ended up clinging to a barrel. At the other end of the scale, huge success could result in a new Patron for the company or the opening of a Sanctuary, if you are an especially kind Loremaster.

It also provides an excellent opportunity to offer forks in the road, where a company's actions determine the choices available to them. Not every Audience must be with a noble, manners-obsessed Elf-lord who rewards those who respect her hospitality to encourage your Player-heroes to adopt a noble bearing worthy of an Aragorn or a Boromir. But many an encounter can be.

With such vast distances to travel, making friends in Middle-earth should be a very important aspect of your game. Much is written about 'typical adventuring parties' and how they don't fit into Middle-earth. With the mechanics of Audiences, you can strongly encourage more wayward players to understand why it's not a good idea to roam from place to place murdering and stealing.

Example: Gella, the Village Elder

The company find themselves in a Woodman village. They're looking for a bed for the night and some supplies for the road. They request an Audience with the crotchety village elder, Gella. If there is no more to the story, the basic rules from the *Player's Guide* work just fine – the company must impress her, and if they do they get a bed for the night and perhaps some more help.

But in this instance, Gella the village elder has a problem – some Goblins in a nearby cave have been stealing the village livestock. She also wants to bring in some coin to supplement the loss of income from the livestock and preserve her position.

Because this NPC wants something from the company, as well as the company wanting something from her, the Loremaster opts to use these more advanced rules.

In their notes for this adventure, the Loremaster has written down the following information about Gella, the Village Elder.

Her Motivation:
- To have a quiet life, without troubles from strangers.
- To find someone to deal with Goblins holed up in a nearby cave.

Her Expectations:
+2: Made to look good in front of her people (This means deference is a good strategy to win her over) Offers of coin from strangers (This means making an offer of a monetary gift is a good strategy too)
+1: Politeness (she can be in part won over by simple manners)
-1: Rudeness (the opposite of politeness! She can't stand rude travellers, and has many problems to consider without rude strangers at her door.)
-2: Open disrespect (Those who seek hospitality must respect her position or they get nothing!)
Harm to her people (Under all her gruffness she cares deeply about her folk)

Possible outcomes:
- Success by 6+: Gella trusts the company enough to give them the quest of slaying the Goblins.
- Success by 3-4: Gella gets some gold from the company and/or is impressed by their manners, and in return gives the company a bed for the night and provisions (possible mechanical benefit).
- Success by 0 -2: Gella offers the company a bed for the night.
- Failure: Gella dismisses the company without any help at all.

RUNNING AUDIENCES

Once the planning is done and the game is underway, the first step in any Audience falls to the Loremaster – you need to describe the scene, both in general terms and in more detail, presenting to the players their surroundings and who they will be speaking to. This is a chance to impart some clues about the NPC's Motivation to the players, build up the Middle-earth atmosphere by having Audiences occur in locations that invoke both the mood and stature of whomever they seek an Audience with. Successful Audiences are built together with your players, and that starts with a good atmospheric description of the place in which the Audience occurs and some clues as to the NPC's demeanour.

You can do a great deal to steer the tone of an Audience – the way you set the stage is key. For a grand and demure NPC like Elrond, you need an appropriate build up to set the scene and give the company clues as to how they might favourably win over this character. The Player-heroes should see guards, members of a wealthy household and noble-looking Elf-lords and ladies as they go on their way to Elrond himself. Soaring pillars, melodious laughter through open doors and bright harp music all add to the tone.

Alternatively, if the company seek an Audience with local Bree bandit chief Crooked Ted, they may see some less salubrious sights on their way to Ted's grotty den...

> ### Meeting Strangers
>
> On one hand it can be tempting to hide the true nature of an NPC and surprise the company with it. Using the Player-heroes' preconceptions against them can be an effective way of building in some fun and atmosphere. Don't forget though, as the eyes and ears of the players in Middle-earth, it's also easy to cheat them this way. And that just isn't enjoyable.
>
> It is a lot more fun to figure out the best way to approach an important person, read the clues, make a plan, and then attempt to execute that plan. To be fair to your players, consider giving them those clues to guide their approach as well as building the Middle-earth feel. Of course, in order to faithfully play their chosen characters, they may wish to deliberately go against any cues you give. A cheeky young Hobbit Wanderer may have no time for grumpy old big folk trying to run a nasty, dirty village! It's fun to allow this, with a little steering from convenient NPCs to prevent one flavourful character from ruining everyone's chances in an Audience. That's all part of the game.

The Introduction

Once the stage is set, the company must decide who among their number will introduce them to the NPC. The NPC may ask for an introduction, or it may be for the Player-heroes to speak up unannounced. This varies as the situation demands.

The Player-hero chosen to make the introduction must make an Intelligence (Traditions) check at a base difficulty DC 15 to introduce the group.

The Loremaster may choose to offer bonuses or minuses to this Introduction Check as appropriate to the given situation. Carefully consider how difficult you wish to make the Audience for the players. Will it be possible for them to convince the NPC that they should be treated well? Should it actually be impossible for some types of characters to succeed? What frame of mind is the NPC in? If they're extremely unreceptive, or the company have already taken actions that may sway the NPCs initial attitude, then a bonus or minus may be appropriate. The result of this check influences how the NPC will view the company in the ensuing Audience, potentially modifying the final check.

If the Introduction Check is a success, the company use the DC indicated by the Final Audience Check Table overleaf. If they fail their Introduction Check, they are considered one step lower on the table.

> ### Example: Introduction to Gella
>
> Our company has reached Gella's hall. The Loremaster describes its smoky atmosphere, with chunks of peat smouldering in the warm dark. Gella appears, hobbling out of the bedchamber behind her dais. "What? What is it that you want? Who are you?"
>
> The company confers. They judge that The Bride is the best character to make the introduction. Despite her lower Intelligence, she is of the Woodmen, so offers the best chance of success with a favourable DC for the final Audience roll. The Bride's player makes her introduction in character, and rolls the die for a DC 15 Intelligence check. The Loremaster sees no reason in this instance to modify the roll.
>
> She passes! She will use the "Generally Favoured" result for the final roll. It's now up to the company to make the best case they can, hoping they can ascertain what will make them appear trustworthy to Gella, the poor and crotchety village elder.

Roleplaying the Audience

Once the introduction is made, the rules step back and roleplaying is the order of the day. Playing through an Audience is an ideal time to bring lots of Middle-earth flavour to your game, as well as being an entertaining chance for players to meet characters they've only previously read about. There's lots of advice for playing NPCs elsewhere in this guide. Remember to use your NPC's Motivation as the centre of their character – it's there to help you.

As the Audience progresses, the Loremaster should keep note of what the Player-heroes are saying and doing. If their behaviour corresponds to any of the NPC's stated Expectations, positive or negative, make note of the relevant bonus. Crucially though, the players can only gain a given bonus ONCE. So if there are three different Expectations listed under +1, they only qualify for a single +1 bonus, no matter how many of those three Expectations they trigger. They can, however, gain multiple bonuses, both positive and negative. It's possible for the company to dip deep into negative total bonuses, and then recover with a change of tack.

As the Loremaster, you have final say on any additional bonus you believe the company deserves. If their behaviour heads off on a wild and unexpected tangent, you are free to award them modifiers as you see fit. The Expectations list is a tool to aid consistency of character and to give an Audience a clear and fair structure. But it is not a straight jacket. You are the Loremaster! Optionally you may choose to tell the company when they are scoring bonuses, to help steer them in the right direction. Whether this suits your play style, or is seen as an interruption to the roleplaying is something only you can judge.

The Final Audience Check

When the push and pull of the roleplaying reaches a natural place to decide the result of the Audience, all bonuses should be totalled up by the Loremaster. A single Player-hero must now make a Final Audience Roll, modified by any bonuses won during the Audience, and their proficiency or skill bonus, if an appropriate skill or ability is relevant – your players may make suggestions for which skill or ability might qualify for such a bonus. By including a proficiency or skill bonus, the Player-hero's level has an influence on the outcome, which can be highly appropriate – mighty heroes are more often welcomed than turned away. The DC for this check was determined by the Introduction Check and the culture of the Player-hero who made it.

The Cultural Attitudes table on page 192 of the *Adventures in Middle-earth Player's Guide* determines which row of the table to use. A failed Introduction Check pushes the Player-hero one row lower, giving a higher DC.

Final Audience Check DC Chart

Culture of the Player-hero introducing the company	DC for final check
Generally Favoured	DC 10
Generally Friendly	DC 11
Generally Neutral	DC 12
Unknown	DC 13
Askance	DC 13
Mistrustful	DC 14

Outcomes

The Final Audience Check determines the outcome, in line with what the Loremaster has prepared for the NPC.

How you use these rules depends very much on your group's preferred play style. They might all occur behind a Loremaster's Screen, with only the rolls at the beginning and end breaking up pure conversational roleplaying. You might choose to put the rules more out in the open, giving clear clues as to which approaches are winning bonuses, and which are not.

Example: Audience with Gella

Having made a good impression, the company decide that each of them will make a case for why they should be welcome in Gella's hall. She responds in line with her Motivation of wanting a quiet life. Pretty words do not sway her, though Trotter impresses her with his manners, gaining the company a +1. When Lifstan, ever the one with an eye on the treasure, pats his coin purse, the deal looks sealed with another +2. Beran makes an offer to help with any problems the village might have – on the way to the Audience he noticed there seems to be a problem with Goblins. But the +2 has already been won by Lifstan's purse pat. So no additional bonus is gained. Once everyone has spoken, and by and large suffered the rough tongue of the irascible Gella, the Audience draws to a natural end. It is time to make that Final Audience Check.

Example: Final Audience Check with Gella

With their solid introduction, and some wise choices in what they said, the Company have a very good bonus (+3) for a low target number (DC 10) – The Bride, as a Woodman qualified for the "Generally Favoured" DC of 10. Due to her successful introduction she stayed as "Generally Favoured", not being able to get any higher. If she had failed her introduction roll she would have dropped to "Generally Friendly". The Loremaster decides that The Bride can use her skill modifier due to her high Intimidate skill. It's not so much that Gella is intimidated, but rather that she respects The Bride's fierce countenance. The Bride's player rolls a d20, getting a 13. Adding their bonuses of +1 and +2, and her skill bonus of +3 takes the company well over the success level needed to get Gella's maximum assistance. Gella is swayed to their cause, and in addition to putting them up for the night is so impressed that she offers them the side quest of tackling the Goblins.

In an alternate scenario, let's imagine Beli the Dwarf of the Lonely Mountain attempts the introduction, and fails his roll. Let's also imagine the company don't realise that they have a lot of ground to make up due to this failure, and are very brusque in demanding hospitality (-1), and speak down to Gella in her own hall (-2). The Final Audience Check should have been at "Unknown" for a Dwarf, but the failure at the introduction took this one step lower, to "Mistrustful". This gives a DC of 14.

The Final Audience Check is made at -3. Despite his poor performance, the Loremaster decides that Gella still has some admiration for the gruff nature of the Dwarf, and allows him to use his Intimidation skill modifier of +3. The modifiers cancel out, so Beli's player must roll 14 to get a bed for the night. He rolls a 4. The company will be sleeping under the stars this night, despite their players being desperate for a long rest... Perhaps they will learn that the next time they seek hospitality they need to choose their spokesperson a little more carefully, and show some manners!

Audiences Summary

1. The Loremaster plans the Audience, setting Motivation, Expectations, and outcomes (or uses those in a published scenario).
2. The Loremaster sets the scene.
3. A chosen Player-hero introduces the company, thereby setting the DC of the Final Audience Check.
4. Players and the Loremaster roleplay the encounter; the Loremaster notes down bonuses and minuses indicated on the NPC's Expectations list as the roleplaying proceeds.
5. Once the Audience reaches a natural climax or conclusion, one of the company must make the Final Audience Check, suggesting any ability or skill that might allow a bonus.
6. The Loremaster assesses by how much the check was passed or failed, and compares this to the list of outcomes.
7. The outcome is roleplayed out.

Adversaries and Battle

Dark Things from the Houseless Hills

Spears splintered and shields shivered,
A field of dead men,
Hooped and hasped the shieldwall waits,
No hope to stint in hard handplay.
Butcher birds fly and find their mark in broken boards
As long as hand can round shield tightly hold,
Our boasts yet to perform.
The brave hearth-band stoutly stood,
Arrayed in hard helms and fey-handed.
Singing hard-filed words of battle
As the slaughter wolves came
Not so softly shall you carry off our lives.

- Adversaries -

Before you could get round Mirkwood in the North you would be right among the slopes of the Grey Mountains, and they are simply stiff with Goblins, Hobgoblins, and Orcs of the worst description."

The Free Folk of the North have long been beset by many enemies. Numerous wars have been fought in the lands between the Misty Mountains and the Running River, and the Free Peoples have celebrated many victories, but to no avail: the shadowy corners of Wilderland hide countless cunning creatures, endlessly scheming for their own dark purposes or waiting for the return of their Master. This chapter presents a selection of foes to freeze the heart, both the servants of the Enemy and other foul things that populate Middle-earth, along with rules and advice on how to use them to best effect in your games.

Battle in Middle-earth

In both *The Hobbit* and *The Lord Of the Rings* we as readers are witness to many battles. The ones that interest us the most as gamers are perhaps not the huge conflicts at Pelennor Fields or The Battle of Five Armies, but more the smaller scale "company-sized" battles. These exemplify the idea of an adventuring party encountering foes during a quest. Examples of this type of combat are the battle against the orcs and troll in Moria; the conflict on Weathertop with the Nazgûl, and the battle against the Goblins and Wargs in *The Hobbit*.

So how does a Loremaster create the feel of Middle-earth for their players during combat? What is special about The fights in *The Lord of the Rings* and *The Hobbit*, and what makes them so absorbing?

First and foremost each of them occurs in an interesting location, which tells us something about Middle-earth. Characters rarely square up to the enemy on a flat piece of ground and trade blows. The scenery gets in the way, or is used by one side or another.

The locations also often favour the enemy - whether it's dark cave tunnels or an isolated ruin where no help will come, the setting for the battle is often chosen to hinder the characters and help their enemies.

The company are often prevented from escape, making the fight all the more desperate - they can't run away from Balin's Tomb, Helm's Deep or Weathertop. Once our characters are engaged, they have to fight for survival.

The fighting is often defensive, right until the very end of *The Lord of the Rings*. Discovery by the Enemy is always a hazard to be avoided. It seems the Wise are aware that if you are spotted by Orcs, word will soon get back to their master, and so even mighty heroes are wary of engaging agents of the Shadow.

Battles often involve a fate larger than merely the survival of the heroes. While Bilbo's journey is very much about him learning to care for more than his own skin, Frodo, Aragorn and Gandalf are aware early on that they must survive not merely to avoid death, but to save the very world itself.

Heroes avoid combat when possible: a persistent theme of Middle-earth is that great power can cause great harm, or can fall from grace all the more easily.

The monsters encountered are genuinely frightening - be they an unstoppable horde of orcs, always increasing in number, ancient and evil, or the terrifyingly weird Barrow-wights. Characters never encounter monsters they regard as routine, and their lives are always at risk.

However, very few characters actually die in battle in *The Lord of the Rings* or *The Hobbit*, unless it is a part of the plot, and heavy with meaning. While the characters always feel in very real peril, it is rare they actually die.

How much all this is taken into account by the Loremaster and their players is a matter of personal preference. You may be using Middle-earth simply as a backdrop to your regular gaming adventures, or you may be trying very hard indeed to recreate the feel of the novels.

Battle in Middle-earth

- The setting appears to favour the enemy to increase a feeling of peril.
- In set-piece battles characters are often locked in to the location.
- Combat is often defensive.
- There are consequences beyond injury or death to engaging the enemy.
- Opponents are frightening - in appearance, numbers and/or threats and powers.
- Few characters die, and injury is meaningful for the story.

In order to promote some of these themes at the table, *Adventures in Middle-earth* offers some additional special rules and extra detail to standard rules for combat. These are entirely optional, and should be only used if you as the Loremaster feel they will improve your games.

Scenery in - Combat -

"Towards danger; but not too rashly, nor too straight."

In *The Hobbit* and *The Lord of the Rings*, every tale of battle takes the scenery into account, and often that scenery tells a story. The following rules provide a quick and easy reference for a Loremaster wishing to provide interesting battlefields for their games. Sometimes you want to run a quick and dirty skirmish against a band of Goblins in a flat clearing. But that can be spiced up with a piece of interesting scenery that provides cover or allows some tweak on attack rolls.

In addition to offering ideas for suitable scenery that your company of Player-heroes might see, modifiers to combat checks are included so the scenery can take a more active role in battle. Scenery is divided up by location type, but this should not be considered a barrier to mixing whatever scenery feels appropriate and adds interest to a battlefield. It is recommended that you add only a few such details into each combat location so that you do not have to slow down the action to account for every tiny detail. The scenery should be a feature, not an encumbrance.

The Wild
"Fly you fools"

Bog
Deeper than simple mud, a bog – whether formed of marshy peat, a flooded river or torrential rain – presents a challenging battleground.
- Boggy areas count as difficult terrain (halve movement).
- Creatures gain one level of Exhaustion for every three rounds they fight in a bog.

Cliffs
A vertical or nearly vertical rocky incline, a cliff is 10 feet high or more.
In combat, a cliff takes an entire movement action to climb per 10 feet of height. Climbers have a -2 to AC when suffering a ranged attack.
- Creatures at the top may use a shove action to push another creature off the cliff.

Crags, rocky outcrops (defensible rocks), huge boulders
Whether brought here by giants in ancient days, or simply the tip of a subterranean mountain, boulders and craggy outcrops can provide a vital combat Advantage.
- Using an entire movement action to climb up onto these pieces of scenery gives defenders Advantage on attack rolls against creatures below them. The uncertain footing means no more than this can be gained.

- Crags and rocky outcrops can also be used for total cover from ground level – creatures behind a huge boulder, crag or rocky outcrop cannot be targeted.
- Creatures can hide among or behind them.

Lone trees, boulders

A lone tree makes a significant metaphor as well as a place to take cover from Orc arrows. Medium sized boulders covered with moss or spattered with lichen can also provide cover.
- Creatures can hide among or behind them.
- They offer three-quarters cover (+5 bonus to AC and Dexterity saving throws).

Nettle bank or briar patch

A significant bank of nettles or a briar patch can pose a serious obstacle to movement. While the stinging rash or tearing thorns are merely an inconvenience in the face of injury in combat, nettles and briars slow movement.
- Nettles and briars can be crossed, but count as difficult terrain.

Mud

Thick mud underfoot can cause problems to combatants.
- Creatures fighting in thick mud suffer -1 to attack rolls.

Scattered rocks, moorland heather, small streams

Uncertain and uneven footing, dense plants that obscure the ground, and small rivulets crossing the scene of a battle can all present challenges.
- These count as difficult terrain (half move through the area).

Sloping terrain

A simple incline to the battlefield provides a tactical consideration as well as making the world feel a bit less like a flat battle map. Whether it's part of a rolling grassy hill, a tussocked ridge, or a stony promontory, a slope might affect the whole battlefield or just a part of it. Different slopes might occur in different directions.
- A shallow slope provides creatures on the higher ground with Advantage on attack rolls.
- A steep slope additionally inflicts Disadvantage on attack rolls to creatures on the lower ground.

Ravines

Ravines might be deep cracks in rocky ground or channels in peaty soil carved out by now-sunken streams.
- Movement is prevented across them unless a successful Dexterity check (DC 13 or more) is made.
- Creatures can hide within a ravine.

River shallows, stream, flood water

Broadly speaking, water flowing up to knee deep. These present difficult footing, and impedes movement.
- These count as difficult terrain (half move through the watery terrain).

Rock edges

One or a series of rocky ledges, one to three feet high.
- Moving up them halves movement; moving down imparts no penalty.
- Attacking from a higher position gives Advantage on attack rolls.

Thicket

Close-growing stands of trees, a thicket is typically dominated by birch or hawthorn, or younger trees like larch or elm.
- Ranged attacks through a thicket are made at Disadvantage, even at close range. Long range attacks cannot be made through a thicket.
- This counts as difficult terrain (half move through the thicket).

WOODLAND

"The world is indeed full of peril and in it there are many dark places."

Bog

Deeper than simple mud, a bog – whether formed of marshy peat, a flooded river or torrential rain – presents a difficult battleground.
- This counts as difficult terrain (half move through the bog).
- Creatures gain one level of Exhaustion for every three rounds they fight in a bog.

Bracken

Bracken grows in prodigious quantities in woodland climes, forming thick banks of foliage that are difficult, but not impossible, to cross.
- Bracken areas count as difficult terrain.

Thick trunked trees

Thick trunked trees provide excellent cover and their twisted root masses can provide hiding places for the stealthy.

- These can provide total cover – a creature behind a thick trunked tree cannot be targeted.
- Creatures can hide behind or within the branches or roots of a thick trunked tree.

Fallen tree, pile of timber

A large fallen tree can provide cover from Orkish darts, as well as an elevated position from which to attack.

- A fallen tree provides total cover from ground level.
- Use of a full movement action allows a creature to climb onto a fallen tree, allowing Advantage on attack rolls as long as they stay on the tree. Jumping down is considered normal movement.
- Creatures on a tree trunk gain a +2 modifier to a shove action on opponents below.

Mossy masonry, root-covered wall

Damp from long years under the canopy of leaves or needles, this ancient stonework is crumbling and water logged, or burdened with the slow creep of mighty roots.

- Crouching behind an old wall provides half cover (+2 to AC and Dexterity saving throws).
- Crumbling masonry is unsuitable for climbing on.

Mud

Thick mud underfoot can cause problems to combatants.

- Creatures fighting in thick mud suffer -1 to attack rolls.

Nettle bank or briar patch

A significant bank of nettles or a briar patch can pose a serious obstacle to movement. While the stinging rash or tearing thorns are merely an inconvenience in the face of injury in combat, nettles and briars slow movement.

- Nettles and briars can be crossed, but count as difficult terrain.

Path, deer track

A path cutting through other obstacles or terrain features offers free movement, but channels creatures in certain directions.

- The path allows normal movement through other obstacles.

Impenetrable hedge of tree limbs

It can be completely impractical to move through particularly thick woodland growth. Sharp twigs stab at the face, ivy binds boughs together, undergrowth piles up in a thick tangle between roots, and low hanging branches bar the way.

- This area cannot be passed through during combat.

Passable hedge of tree limbs

Dried and brittle, or composed of thin limbs easily broken, this kind of foliage can be pushed through with a struggle. It offers protection from ranged attacks, and can be somewhere to disappear.

- The hedge counts as difficult terrain (halves movement).
- The hedge provides half cover (+2 to AC and Dexterity saving throws).
- The tangle of branches can be used to hide.

Low boughs

The great limbs of ancient trees curve close to the ground.

- Ranged attacks through low boughs are made at Disadvantage, even at close range. Long range attacks cannot be made through low boughs.
- Areas with low boughs can be crossed, but count as difficult terrain.

Sloping terrain

A simple incline to the battlefield provides a tactical consideration as well as making the world feel a bit less like a flat battle map. Whether it's part of a rolling grassy hill, a tussocked ridge, or a stony promontory, a slope might affect the whole battlefield or just a part of it. Different slopes might occur in different directions.

- A shallow slope provides creatures on the higher ground with Advantage on attack rolls.
- A steep slope additionally inflicts Disadvantage on attack rolls to creatures on the lower ground.

Thicket

A close-growing stand of trees, a thicket is typically dominated by birch or hawthorn, or younger trees like larch or elm.

- Ranged attacks through a thicket are made at Disadvantage, even at close range. Long range attacks cannot be made through a thicket.
- This counts as difficult terrain (half move through the thicket).

Mirkwood

"There are older and fouler things than Orcs in the deep places of the world."

Black toadstools
Growing in clumps on the ground, these toadstools release poisonous spores if kicked.
- Any creature crossing an area of these toadstools must make a DC 10 Dexterity check. If they fail they are considered Poisoned.
- Alternatively, another species of toadstool inflicts the Blinded condition for ten minutes.

Flooded pit
A deep pit full of brackish water is covered in a blanket of fallen leaves, rendering it invisible.
- Any creature falling into the pit must make a DC 10 Constitution saving throw or gain one level of Exhaustion.

Impenetrable hedge of tree limbs
It can be completely impractical to move through areas where Mirkwood grows particularly thick. Sharp twigs stab at the face, ivy binds boughs together, undergrowth piles up in a thick tangle between roots, and low hanging branches bar the way.
- This area cannot be passed through during combat.

Sucking bog
A deep slimy expanse of rotted black leaf mould lies over deep, shifting, greasy soil.
- Any creature crossing the bog must make a DC 12 Dexterity or Strength check. If they fail, they are considered Grappled every round until they can make the same check successfully, at which point they may exit the bog on any side.
- A shove action can be used to push a creature adjacent to the sucking bog into it.

Poison nettles, black briars
A swathe of evil-looking nettles or brambles.
- Any creature attempting to cross must make a DC 10 Constitution saving throw or suffer 5 (1d10) slashing damage. Optionally, these may also inflict the Poisoned condition.

Poisonous fumes
Air so stagnant, so filled with the miasma of toadstools and rotting leaf mould, that it is dangerous to breathe in.
- Creatures moving through the fume are considered Poisoned while in it, and for 1d6 rounds after they leave the fume.

Rotten trees
For long ages the great black trees in Mirkwood can stand dead, rotting away from the inside. If disturbed they fall, bringing their sodden weight of branches down on any not quick enough to leap aside.
- If combat comes within 10 feet of a rotten tree, there is a 1 in 6 chance each round that it will fall, showering everyone within a 10-foot radius of the trunk with heavy branches or the trunk itself. Creatures within this radius suffer 5 (1d10) bludgeoning damage.

Roots
Great tangles of roots cover the forest floor in parts of Mirkwood.
- To cross the roots, creatures must make a DC 10 Dexterity check. If they fail, they are considered Prone.

Sloping terrain
A simple incline to the battlefield provides a tactical consideration as well as making the world feel a bit less like a flat battle map. Whether it's part of a great ridge through the forest, a hummock covered in black pine needles, or an ivy choked promontory, a slope might affect the whole battlefield or just a part of it. Different slopes might occur in different directions.
- A shallow slope provides creatures on the higher ground with Advantage on attack rolls.
- A steep slope additionally inflicts Disadvantage on attack rolls to creatures on the lower ground.

Webs
Great limp curtains of ancient Spider webs hang in the air in the silent depths of Mirkwood.
- Any creature crossing the webs must make a DC 12 Dexterity or Strength check. If they fail, they are considered Grappled every round until they can make the same check successfully, at which point they may exit the web on any side.

Ruins

Ancient dyke
Long overgrown, this ancient fortification still stands as an obstacle or a useful defensive feature.
- A shallow sloping dyke provides creatures on the higher ground with Advantage on attack rolls.
- A steep sloping dyke additionally inflicts Disadvantage on attack rolls to creatures on the lower ground.

Bracken
Bracken grows in prodigious quantities in the shade of ruins, forming thick banks of foliage that are difficult, but not impossible, to cross.
- Bracken can be crossed, but at half movement.

Covered pit
A stone-lined cistern or subterranean room whose ceiling has collapsed, leaving a pit in the ground. The pit is invisible through a growth of foliage.
- Falling into the covered pit inflicts 2d10 damage and requires a successful DC 10 Dexterity check to climb out.
- Creatures can hide in the covered pit.
- The pit provides total cover to creatures inside it.
- Once it has been uncovered, a shove action can be used to push adjacent creatures into the pit.

Dust
Long ages of mouldering stone work, gnawed by frost and wind, can be reduced to a powder. If disturbed, a cloud of dust fills the air.
- Creatures who cross the area of the dust who fail to make a DC 10 Dexterity check suffer the Blinded condition until the end of their next turn.

Fallen statue, old walls, statue, giant fallen statue head
A large statue, or sturdy old walls, or fallen pieces of monumental masonry can provide cover from ranged attacks, as well as an elevated position from which to attack.
- These ruins can provide total cover at ground level.
- Use of a full movement action allows a creature to climb onto a fallen statue, allowing Advantage on attack rolls as long as they stay on the statue. Jumping down is considered normal movement.
- Creatures on a fallen statue gain +2 modifier to a shove action on opponents below.

Foundations
Barely clearing the ground cover, these stone blocks can make movement difficult. They usually form linear features, with some spread of tumbled masonry.
- Moving through foundations counts as difficult terrain (half move through the foundations).

Nettle bank or briar patch
A significant bank of nettles or a briar patch can pose a serious obstacle to movement. While the stinging rash or tearing thorns are merely an inconvenience in the face of injury in combat, nettles and briars slow movement.
- Nettles and briars can be crossed, but at half movement.

Old floors
Flagstone laid in ages long past create uncertain and uneven footing – poor ground on which to make a stand.
- Old floors count as difficult terrain (half move across the old floors).

Partial and collapsed floors, stairs, broken stairs
One or more masonry ledges, each one to three feet high.
- Moving up them halves movement; moving down has no penalty.
- Attacking from a higher position gives Advantage on attack rolls.

Pillar
A carved stone pillar stands long after its fellows have fallen.
- Creatures can hide behind a stone pillar.
- Stone pillars offer three-quarters cover (+5 bonus to AC and Dexterity saving throws).

Pit
A simple hole in the ground marks where some ancient cellar has collapsed.
- Creatures can hide in a pit.
- Being inside the pit offers total cover.
- A shove action can be used to push adjacent creatures into the pit.
- Falling into the pit inflicts 2d10 damage and requires a successful DC 10 Dexterity check to climb out.

Rubble

Creating uncertain and uneven footing, rubble flung across the battlefield can make movement difficult.

- Rubble counts as difficult terrain (half move through the rubble).
- Creatures can hide among large enough rubble.

Unstable walls

Long years and the passing seasons have taken their toll on this once fine stonework. It is ready to topple at any moment.

- Unstable walls provide half cover (+2 to AC and Dexterity saving throws).
- These unstable structures are unsuitable for climbing.
- A shove action allows a creature to push the wall onto other creatures on the other side. They must make a DC 13 Dexterity saving throw or suffer 11 (2d10) bludgeoning damage from falling masonry.

Webs

Giant Spiders haunt ancient ruins, making the most of the opportunities to weave their webs.

- Any creature crossing the webs must make a DC 12 Dexterity or Strength check. If they fail, the character becomes Restrained. On their turn they may use their action to make a DC 12 Dexterity or Strength check to break free. They may then exit the web on any side.

Windowed walls

The remains of a wall may contain many small windows or a single large aperture.

- Windowed walls provide half cover (+2 to AC and Dexterity saving throws).
- These unstable structures are unsuitable for climbing.

CAVES

Cliffs

A subterranean vertical or nearly vertical rocky incline, a cliff is 10 feet high or more.

- In combat, an entire movement action is required to climb 10 foot of cliff. Climbers have a -2 to AC when suffering a ranged attack.
- Creatures at the top may use a shove action to push another creature off the cliff.

Crags, rocky outcrops (defensible rocks), huge boulders

Whether brought here by giants in ancient days, or thrust up by the earth's shudders, boulders and craggy outcrops can provide a vital combat Advantage.

- Using an entire movement action to climb onto these pieces of scenery gives defenders Advantage on attack rolls against creatures below them. The uncertain footing means no more than this can be gained.
- Crags and rocky outcrops can also be used for total cover from ground level – creatures behind a huge boulder, crag or rocky outcrop cannot be targeted.
- Creatures can hide among or behind them.

Freezing pool

Never warmed by the sun, a deep rock pool of frigid water is a dangerous place to fall.

- Any creature crossing the pool must make a DC 10 Constitution save. If they fail, they gain a level of Exhaustion.
- A shove action can be used to push a creature adjacent to the pool into it.

Low ceilings

The cavern was not formed with Big Folk in mind.

- All creatures of medium size or larger must crouch, suffering Disadvantage on all ability checks and attack rolls.

Narrow walls

The walls of the cavern squeeze tightly together.

- Two-handed weapons impose Disadvantage.

Puddles, slimy floor, slippery floor

Whether the rock floor is polished to a shine by centuries of water flow, or still runs wet with muddy condensation, movement is difficult in this part of the cavern..

- Slippery floors count as difficult terrain (half move across the wet area).
- When creatures move onto the slippery floor, they must make a DC 9 Dexterity check. If they fail, they fall Prone.

Rock edges

One or a series of rocky ledges, one to three feet high.

- Moving up them halves movement; moving down them has no penalty.

- Attacking from a higher position gives Advantage on attack rolls.

Rocky floor, tiny stalagmites, pool, rubbish-strewn floor, shale floor

These various obstacles make movement difficult.
- They count as difficult terrain (half move through the affected area).

Rock pillar

A fused stalactite and stalagmite forms a large rocky pillar standing alone in a cavern.
- Creatures can hide behind a rock pillar.
- Rock pillars offer three-quarters cover (+5 bonus to AC and Dexterity saving throws).

Slope

A simple incline to the battlefield provides a tactical consideration as well as making the world feel a bit less like a flat battle map. Whether it's part of a huge cavern with its own landscape, a tight pothole steeply angled into the ground, or upwardly winding passages, a slope might affect the whole battlefield, or just a part of it. Different slopes might occur in different directions.
- A shallow slope provides creatures on the higher ground with Advantage on attack rolls.
- A steep slope additionally inflicts Disadvantage on attack rolls to creatures on the lower ground.

Unstable stalactites

Grown slowly in the dark over thousands of years, these stalactites are fractured and ready to collapse.
- If combat comes within 10 feet of the unstable stalactites, there is a 1 in 6 chance each round that they will fall, showering everyone within a 10-foot radius with pieces of rock. Creatures within this radius suffer 5 (1d10) bludgeoning damage.

Atmosphere

Queer sounds, dead silence, an unsettling atmosphere, an eerie humming sound, disturbing echoes

- Creatures considered good who fail a DC 10 Wisdom save have Disadvantage on ability checks and attack rolls. They may attempt another save at the end of their next turn.

Roar of water

- Any creature in the affected area is considered to have the Deafened condition.

Terrible stench, the scent of death

- Creatures considered good who are affected have Disadvantage on ability checks and attack rolls.

The incessant buzzing of insects

- Creatures affected have Disadvantage on ability checks and attack rolls until the insects are dealt with.

Birdsong

The singing of thrushes or blackbirds can lighten the most burdened heart.
- Creatures considered good are heartened in the presence of birdsong. They gain Inspiration.

Weather

Freezing cold, torrential downpour, blizzard

- These invasive weather conditions mean that creatures without shelter from them suffer Disadvantage to their attack rolls and ability checks.

Gale, strong wind

- Ranged attacks are made at Disadvantage.

Thick fog, smoke, eerie mist

- Creatures trying to navigate their way through these atmospheric conditions are considered to have the Blinded condition.

The warm golden sun, slanting rays of golden light, the sun breaks through the clouds

Creatures considered good are heartened by the appearance of the sun.
- They gain Advantage on ability checks and attack rolls the next round, and Inspiration.

A Wilderland
- Bestiary -

Here is a selection of creatures for the Loremaster to pit against their company of heroes. They are grouped by creature type, with geographical subdivisions where appropriate.

Orcs

Bred by the first Dark Power in the early years of the world to serve him in many wars, Orcs are an evil race of intelligent creatures. Their malicious spirit is full of hatred for all living things including their own kind, and when left to their own devices they often end up quarrelling fiercely over futile questions. They are usually strong and agile, quick and robust, and ready to learn or devise new methods or instruments of torment. Their appearance and size differs from tribe to tribe, but many prominent features are common to all Orcs, such as swarthy skin, short legs, and broad, slanted eyes, wide mouths and long fangs.

Great Orcs

Great Orcs are a powerful breed of Orc often encountered as leaders and chieftains of their weaker-blooded relatives. Legends hint at the possibility that they descend from servant spirits that once took an Orkish shape to serve the Dark Power's purposes. King Golfimbul, the Great Goblin, Azog and his son Bolg were Great Orcs.

Great Orc
Medium humanoid (Orc-kind)

STR	DEX	CON	INT	WIS	CHA
18 (+4)	14 (+2)	17 (+3)	10 (+0)	14 (+2)	14 (+2)

Armour Class 20 (Orc-Mail and Huge Hide-Shield)
Hit Points 75 (10d8+30)
Speed 30 ft

Saving Throws Strength +7, Constitution +6, Wisdom +5
Skills Intimidation +4
Senses darkvision 60 ft, passive Perception 12
Languages: Orkish, Westron
Challenge 4 (1,100 XP)

Bulky Armour. The Great Orc has Disadvantage on Dexterity checks.
Fell Speed. The Great Orc may take a bonus action to Disengage from one opponent and engage another without provoking an opportunity attack. The new opponent must be within its regular movement rate.
Sunlight Sensitivity. While in sunlight, the Great Orc has Disadvantage on attack rolls, as well as on Wisdom (Perception) checks that rely on sight.

Actions

Multiattack. The Great Orc makes two attacks with its orcish scimitar, orc-axe or heavy orc-spear.
Orcish Scimitar. *Melee Weapon Attack:* +7 to hit, reach 5 ft, one target. *Hit:* 9 (2d4+4) slashing damage.
Orc-axe. *Melee Weapon Attack:* +7 to hit, reach 5 ft, one target. *Hit:* 7 (1d6+4) slashing damage or 8 (1d8+4) slashing damage if used with two hands.
Heavy Orc-Spear. *Melee Weapon Attack:* +7 to hit, reach 5 ft, one target. *Hit:* 9 (1d10+4) piercing damage. Two-handed.

Reaction

Commanding Voice. The Great Orc can inspire its allies with barked commands and horrible threats. It may use its reaction to utter a command or shout a warning when a non-hostile creature, that it can see within 30 feet of it, is about to make an attack roll or a saving throw. The target can add a d6 Command Die to that roll, provided it can hear and understand the message. A creature can benefit from only one Command Die at a time, and creatures that possess Commanding Voice cannot benefit from this effect.

Hobgoblin

Hobgoblins are an especially malevolent race of Orcs bred in the North in ages past. They are tall and gaunt, with long limbs and flat, almost noseless faces. Only a few members of that fell race survive today, in dark caverns beneath the Grey Mountains and under the Mountains of Mirkwood. Like the smaller Goblins of the mountains, they hate the light of the sun and rarely venture far from their lairs, but they are exceedingly powerful at night or when prowling in darkness (their small but acute eyes and extraordinary sense of smell let them see perfectly even in total darkness). Cruel and cannibalistic, Hobgoblins are never encountered with other breeds of Orcs. They also barely tolerate the company of Trolls, and prefer to conduct their raids with the help of Wolves and Great Bats.

Hobgoblin Aventure Seeds

- The hobgoblins of the Long Marsh benefit greatly from the miasma that lingers above those fetid fens, and can be found hunting and prowling about by day when the mists are particularly thick. Tales told in Lake-town claim that the goblins know some devilish method of conjuring mists by pouring noxious potions into the water.

- While camped for the night or travelling in the dark, the company hears a grinding noise and the guttural sounds of Hobgoblin speech. A hidden door has opened nearby and a band of these foul creatures has ventured forth from their tunnels. Where are the hobgoblins headed, and can their prey be warned in time?

Hobgoblin
Medium humanoid (Orc-kind)

STR	DEX	CON	INT	WIS	CHA
14 (+2)	15 (+2)	12 (+1)	10 (+0)	10 (+0)	7 (-2)

Armour Class 14 (Unarmoured, Shield)
Hit Points 33 (6d8+6)
Speed 30 ft

Skills Perception +2, Stealth +4
Senses blindsight 30 ft, darkvision 60 ft, passive Perception 12
Languages Orkish, Westron
Challenge 1 (200 XP)

Aggressive. As a bonus action, the Hobgoblin can move up to its speed toward a hostile creature that it can see.
No Quarter. When the Hobgoblin reduces an enemy to 0 hit points that enemy is considered to already have failed one death save.
Sunlight Sensitivity. While in sunlight, the Hobgoblin has Disadvantage on attack rolls, as well as on Wisdom (Perception) checks that rely on sight.

Actions
Multiattack. The Hobgoblin makes two attacks: one with its bite and one with its orc-axe.
Foul Bite. *Melee Weapon Attack:* +4 to hit, reach 5 ft, one target. *Hit:* 5 (1d6+2) piercing damage, and the target must make a DC 13 Constitution saving throw. It it fails, it becomes Poisoned until it takes a short rest.
Orc-axe. *Melee Weapon Attack:* +4 to hit, reach 5 ft, one target. *Hit:* 5 (1d6+2) slashing damage or 6 (1d8+2) slashing damage if used with two hands.

Marsh-Hag

These solitary monsters appear to be large, twisted Water-goblins, with long arms and iron-hard claws. They are called hags as their heads seem covered by thick tresses of green hair, giving them the appearance of horrible, wicked crones. Marsh-hags hide in watery chambers beneath deep stagnant pools, waiting for an unfortunate traveller to stumble upon their hiding place. When a victim is within its reach, the Marsh-hag emerges to drown and devour its victim, and then retreats to its subaqueous haunts. When faced by a serious threat, like a group of men-at-arms or well-prepared adventurers, several Marsh-hags emerge together and confront the menace: while one hag seizes an opponent, another slashes at the victim with its claws.

Marsh-hag Adventure Seeds

- Recently, people have been disappearing from the River Running near where boats put out for portage down the Stairs of Girion. Their bodies are never found, and the men of Lake-town who work the portage are beginning to desert their posts. Someone needs to find the foul creature, most likely a Marsh-hag, before its depredations shut down the Stairs.

- There is a place on the Long Lake that none go, for all know it is the lair of a Marsh-hag known as Old Meg. However, this spot, close upon the margins between the Long Marshes and the Long Lake, is rich in the herbs and plants that healers need, such as reedmace and hagweed. If Old Meg can be defeated or driven off, a bounty in herbs will go to the victor.

Marsh-Hag
Medium humanoid (Orc-kind)

STR	DEX	CON	INT	WIS	CHA
15 (+2)	17 (+3)	12 (+1)	9 (-1)	10 (+0)	7 (-2)

Armour Class 13
Hit Points 22 (4d8+4)
Speed 30 ft

Skills Athletics +4, Stealth +5, Perception +2
Senses darkvision 60 ft, passive Perception 12
Languages Orkish, Westron
Challenge ½ (100 XP)

Amphibious. The Marsh-hag can hold its breath for such long periods that it is effectively a water-breather in combat situations.
Nimble Escape. The Marsh-hag can take the Disengage or Hide action as a bonus action on each of its turns.
Pack Tactics. The Marsh-hag has Advantage on an attack roll against a creature if at least one of the Marsh-hag's allies is within 5 feet of the creature and that ally isn't Incapacitated.

Actions

Grasping Claws. *Melee Weapon Attack:* +5 to hit, reach 5 ft, one target. *Hit:* 4 (1d4+2)) slashing damage. If the Marsh-Hag is not already Grappling a creature, the target becomes Grappled (escape DC 15). Until the Grapple ends, the target is Restrained. If there is a body of water within 5 ft of the Marsh-Hag, it can spend an action to drown a Grappled creature. The creature takes 7 (2d4+2) bludgeoning damage as the Marsh-hag chokes it.

Mordor-Orcs

Several different breeds of Orc comprise the growing armies in the service of Mordor, from the small but deft Snaga to the large Black Uruk. Broad, with crooked legs and long arms, Mordor-Orcs differ greatly in size and capabilities but are all cruel and cunning, often directly subject to the will of their Dark Lord. In the years following the Battle of Five Armies, Orcs bearing the Red Eye have started once again to issue from Mordor, agents spreading the taint of the Shadow and bearing orders for all malevolent creatures with hate for the Free Peoples.

Black Uruk

Large, evil Orcs of great strength, picked from among the fiercest to act as lieutenants, bodyguards or chosen warriors, they are sent to reinforce a colony of lesser Orcs.

Black Uruk
Medium humanoid (Orc-kind)

STR	DEX	CON	INT	WIS	CHA
16 (+3)	12 (+1)	15 (+2)	8 (-1)	12 (+1)	10 (+0)

Armour Class 18 (Orc-Mail, Shield)
Hit Points 39 (6d8+12)
Speed 30 ft

Saving Throws Strength +6, Wisdom +3
Skills Intimidation +3
Senses darkvision 60 ft, passive Perception 13
Languages Orkish, Westron
Challenge 2 (450 XP)

Aggressive. As a bonus action, the Black Uruk can move up to its speed toward a hostile creature that it can see.
Bulky Armour. The Black Uruk has Disadvantage on Dexterity checks.

Actions
Orcish Scimitar. *Melee Weapon Attack:* +5 to hit, reach 5 ft, one target. *Hit:* 8 (2d4+3) slashing damage.
Spear. *Melee or Ranged Weapon Attack:* +5 to hit, reach 5 ft or range 20/60 ft, one target. *Hit:* 6 (1d6+3) piercing damage or 7 (1d8+3) piercing damage if used with two hands to make a melee attack.

Reaction
Parry. The Black Uruk adds 2 to its AC against one melee attack that would hit it. To do so, the orc must see the attacker and be wielding a melee weapon.

Messenger of Lugbúrz

An emissary of the Shadow, a Messenger of Lugbúrz is always on an errand for his Master, be it to spy upon Men, Elves or Dwarves, or to rouse all creatures with evil intent in an area.

Messenger of Lugbúrz
Medium humanoid (Orc-kind)

STR	DEX	CON	INT	WIS	CHA
14 (+2)	16 (+3)	15 (+2)	12 (+1)	11 (+0)	15 (+2)

Armour Class 16 (cobbled-together Orc armour)
Hit Points 13 (2d8+4)
Speed 30 ft

Skills Deception +4, Intimidation +4, Perception +2, Persuasion +4, Stealth +5
Senses darkvision 60 ft, passive Perception 12
Languages Orkish, Westron, Silvan
Challenge ½ (100 XP)

Bandolier of Knives (Recharge 4-6). As a bonus action, the Messenger can hurl a cluster of small blades at any opponent within 10 feet. The target must make a DC 15 Dexterity saving throw or suffer 6 (1d6+3) slashing damage.
Nimble Escape. The Messenger of Lugbúrz can take the Disengage or Hide action as a bonus action on each of its turns.
Sunlight Sensitivity. While in sunlight, the Messenger has Disadvantage on attack rolls, as well as on Wisdom (Perception) checks that rely on sight.

Actions
Broad-Bladed Sword. *Melee Weapon Attack:* +4 to hit, reach 5 ft, one target. *Hit:* 9 (2d6+2) slashing damage. Heavy, two-handed.

Reaction
Commanding Voice. The Messenger can inspire its allies with veiled threats of the Dark Lord's attention. It may use its reaction to utter a command or shout a warning when a non-hostile creature, that it can see within 30 feet of it, is about to make an attack roll or a saving throw. The target can add a d6 Command Die to that roll, provided it can hear and understand the message. A creature can benefit from only one Command Die at a time, and creatures that possess Commanding Voice cannot benefit from this effect.

Snaga Tracker

Snaga trackers are a smaller breed gifted with wide, snuffling nostrils, able to catch the scent of enemies from a distance, even after a prolonged period of time has passed. Trackers are a weak and lazy lot, but quick and clever.

Snaga Tracker
Small humanoid (Orc-kind)

STR	DEX	CON	INT	WIS	CHA
10 (+0)	12 (+1)	11 (+0)	12 (+1)	10 (+0)	13 (+1)

Armour Class 12 (Orcish Leathers)
Hit Points 7 (2d6)
Speed 30 ft

Skills Perception +2, Stealth +5
Senses darkvision 60 ft, passive Perception 12
Languages Orkish, Westron
Challenge 1/8 (25 XP)

Coward. Once injured, the Snaga Tracker suffers Disadvantage on all combat rolls.
Sneak Attack. Once per turn, the Snaga Tracker deals an extra 3 (1d6) damage when it hits a target with a weapon attack and has Advantage on the attack roll, or when the target is within 5 feet of an ally of the Snaga Tracker that isn't Incapacitated and the Snaga Tracker doesn't have Disadvantage on the attack roll.
Sunlight Sensitivity. While in sunlight, the Snaga Tracker has Disadvantage on attack rolls, as well as on Wisdom (Perception) checks that rely on sight.

Actions

Jagged Knife. *Melee Weapon Attack:* +3 to hit, reach 5 ft, one target. *Hit:* 3 (1d4+1) piercing damage.
Bow of Horn. *Ranged Weapon Attack:* +3 to hit, range 80/320 ft, one target. *Hit:* 4 (1d6+1) piercing damage. The victim must also make a DC 11 Constitution saving throw or be Poisoned for 1 minute.

Orcs of the Misty Mountains

...near the Gladden Fields he was waylaid by the Orcs of the Mountains, and almost all his folk were slain.

Among the most numerous of the malicious creatures serving the Shadow, the Orcs of the Misty Mountains are used to living and making war in the deep places beneath the earth, where their sight is keener than any other Orc. When they are encountered in their mines, they are savage fighters and reckless in assault, but they leave the dark under the mountains only when marching to war or to avenge their fallen kind, as they badly suffer the light of the sun.

The Orcs of the Misty Mountains are a wild and independent lot, bent on their own purposes and aims when the Shadow's influence is weak, but ready to obey the will of their Master when directly subject to it. The smallest among them are often referred to as Goblins.

Misty Mountain Goblin
Small humanoid (Orc-kind)

STR	DEX	CON	INT	WIS	CHA
11 (+0)	12 (+1)	8 (-1)	10 (+0)	8 (-1)	8 (-1)

Armour Class 14 (Orcish Leathers, Shield)
Hit Points 5 (2d6-2)
Speed 30 ft

Skills Stealth +5
Senses darkvision 60 ft, passive Perception 9
Languages Orkish, Westron
Challenge ¼ (50 XP)

Nimble Escape. The Misty Mountain Goblin can take the Disengage or Hide action as a bonus action on each of its turns.

Sunlight Sensitivity. While in sunlight, the Misty Mountain Goblin has Disadvantage on attack rolls, as well as on Wisdom (Perception) checks that rely on sight.

Actions

Bent Sword. *Melee Weapon Attack:* +3 to hit, reach 5 ft, one target. *Hit:* 4 (1d6+1) slashing damage.

Spear. *Melee or Ranged Weapon Attack:* +2 to hit, reach 5 ft or range 20/60 ft, one target. *Hit:* 3 (1d6) piercing damage or 4 (1d8) piercing damage if used with two hands to make a melee attack.

Reaction

Parry. The Misty Mountain Goblin adds 2 to its AC against one melee attack that would hit it. To do so, the goblin must see the attacker and be wielding a melee weapon.

Orc of Goblin-town

The Orcs and Goblins of Goblin-town hate Dwarves, and will attack a company that includes Dwarves with blind fury. In addition to the regular Misty Mountain Goblin statistics, an Orc of Goblin-town also gets Advantage on Wisdom (Survival) checks to track Dwarves as well as on Intelligence checks to recall information about them. If they discover a Dwarf, they pursue that Dwarf, and anyone accompanying them, until they are dead.

Orc of Mount Gram

The Orcs of Mount Gram fiercely hate all Hobbits, and will relentlessly attack a company that includes Hobbits with blind fury. In addition to the regular Misty Mountain Goblin statistics, an Orc of Mount Gram also gets Advantage on Wisdom (Survival) checks to track Hobbits as well as on Intelligence checks to recall information about them. If they discover a Hobbit, they pursue that Hobbit, and anyone accompanying them, until they are dead.

Orc-Chieftain

Only the most wicked and cruel of Orcs live long enough to become chieftains and lead their tribe or war band to battle. An Orc-chieftain is easy to recognise, as it is usually the largest in a group, wielding the keenest weapons and donning superior armour. Often, tell-tale scars or mutilations mark a chieftain's long service under the Shadow.

Orc Adventure Seed

◈ While on other business, the party spots a lone Orc, small of stature and hurrying quickly yet stealthily along. This creature is a messenger carrying instructions from one evil chieftain to his lieutenants. Where is he heading? What will he lead the company into?

Orc-Chieftain
Medium humanoid (Orc-kind)

STR	DEX	CON	INT	WIS	CHA
15 (+2)	14 (+2)	14 (+2)	10 (+0)	12 (+1)	12 (+1)

Armour Class 16 (Orc Mail)
Hit Points 52 (8d8+16)
Speed 30 ft

Saving Throws Constitution +4, Wisdom +3
Skills Intimidation +3, Perception +3
Senses darkvision 60 ft, passive Perception 13
Languages Orkish, Westron
Challenge 3 (700 XP)

Bulky Armour. The Orc-Chieftain has Disadvantage on Dexterity checks.
Sunlight Sensitivity. While in sunlight, the Orc-Chieftain has Disadvantage on attack rolls, as well as on Wisdom (Perception) checks that rely on sight.

Actions

Multiattack. The Orc-Chieftain makes two attacks with either its Heavy Orc-Spear or Whip.
Heavy Orc-Spear. *Melee Weapon Attack:* +4 to hit, reach 5 ft, one target. *Hit:* 7 (1d10+2) piercing damage. Two-handed.
Whip. *Melee Weapon Attack:* +4 to hit, reach 10 ft, one target. *Hit:* 4 (1d4+2) slashing damage.

Reaction

Parry. The Orc-Chieftain adds 2 to its AC against one melee attack that would hit it. To do so, the goblin must see the attacker and be wielding a melee weapon.
Commanding Voice. The Orc-Chieftain can inspire its allies with its imposing presence and authoritative voice. It may use its reaction to utter a command or shout a warning when a non-hostile creature, that it can see within 30 feet of it, is about to make an attack roll or a saving throw. The target can add a d6 Command Die to that roll, provided it can hear and understand the message. A creature can benefit from only one Command Die at a time, and creatures that possess Commanding Voice cannot benefit from this effect.

Orc Soldier

Often armed with characteristic bent swords, Orc Soldiers are a loud, undisciplined lot. Only a forceful chieftain with a cruel whip and a sharp blade can keep them in line...

Orc Soldier
Medium humanoid (Orc-kind)

STR	DEX	CON	INT	WIS	CHA
15 (+2)	10 (+0)	14 (+2)	7 (-2)	11 (+0)	10 (+0)

Armour Class 13 (Orcish Leathers, Shield)
Hit Points 19 (3d8+6)
Speed 30 ft

Skills Intimidation +2
Senses darkvision 60 ft, passive Perception 10
Languages Orkish, Westron
Challenge ½ (100 XP)

Aggressive. As a bonus action, the Orc Soldier can move up to its speed toward a hostile creature that it can see.
Sunlight Sensitivity. While in sunlight, the Orc Soldier has Disadvantage on attack rolls, as well as on Wisdom (Perception) checks that rely on sight.

Actions

Bent Sword. *Melee Weapon Attack:* +4 to hit, reach 5 ft, one target. *Hit:* 5 (1d6+2) slashing damage.
Spear. *Melee or Ranged Weapon Attack:* +4 to hit, reach 5 ft or range 20/60 ft, one target. *Hit:* 5 (1d6+2) piercing damage or 6 (1d8+2) piercing damage if used with two hands to make a melee attack.

Goblin Archer

A Goblin Archer is an Orc chosen for his keen eyes. His ability to see in the dark, coupled with a steady hand, lets him shoot arrows with precision by night or day.

Goblin Archer
Small humanoid (Orc-kind)

STR	DEX	CON	INT	WIS	CHA
11 (+0)	14 (+2)	13 (+1)	9 (-1)	14 (+2)	10 (+0)

Armour Class 13 (Orcish Leathers)
Hit Points 9 (2d6+2)
Speed 30 ft

Skills Perception +4
Senses blindsight 30 ft, darkvision 60 ft, passive Perception 14
Languages Orkish, Westron
Challenge ¼ (50 XP)

Aggressive. As a bonus action, the Goblin Archer can move up to its speed toward a hostile creature that it can see.
Hawk's Eye (Recharge 4-6). The Goblin Archer may use this ability as a bonus action. It does not suffer Disadvantage on attack rolls due to being at long range this turn.
Sunlight Sensitivity. While in sunlight, the Goblin Archer has Disadvantage on attack rolls, as well as on Wisdom (Perception) checks that rely on sight.

Actions

Jagged Knife. *Melee Weapon Attack:* +4 to hit, reach 5 ft, one target. *Hit:* 4 (1d6+2) piercing damage.
Bow of Horn. *Ranged Weapon Attack:* +4 to hit, range 80/320 ft, one target. *Hit:* 5 (1d6+2) piercing damage. The victim must also make a DC 13 Constitution saving throw or be poisoned for 1 minute.

Orc Guard

The strongest and boldest Orcs are equipped with the toughest armour they can put together. Wielding a sword and sturdy shield, they are placed to keep watch on an area.

Orc Guard
Medium humanoid (Orc-kind)

STR	DEX	CON	INT	WIS	CHA
16 (+3)	12 (+1)	15 (+2)	8 (-1)	12 (+1)	10 (+0)

Armour Class 18 (Orc-Mail, Shield)
Hit Points 26 (4d8+8)
Speed 30 ft

Skills Perception +3
Senses passive Perception 13
Languages Orkish, Westron
Challenge 1 (200 XP)

Aggressive. As a bonus action, the Orc Guard can move up to its speed toward a hostile creature that it can see.
Bulky Armour. The Orc Guard has Disadvantage on Dexterity checks
Sunlight Sensitivity. While in sunlight, the Orc Guard has Disadvantage on attack rolls, as well as on Wisdom (Perception) checks that rely on sight.

Actions

Orcish Scimitar. *Melee Weapon Attack:* +5 to hit, reach 5 ft, one target. *Hit:* 8 (2d4+3) slashing damage.
Spear. *Melee or Ranged Weapon Attack:* +5 to hit, reach 5 ft or range 20/60 ft, one target. *Hit:* 6 (1d6+3) piercing damage or 7 (1d8+3) piercing damage if used with two hands to make a melee attack.

Spiders of Mirkwood

These foul things belong to a very ancient race, almost as ancient as Darkness itself. Evil, intelligent creatures in spider-form, they weave hideous webs whose black threads hang across the trees of Mirkwood, waiting for any living being to be hopelessly trapped in them. The dense cobwebs seem to snare light itself, plunging their surroundings into perpetual night and earning the forest its name. For almost two thousand years, the Spiders of Mirkwood have spied upon all who dared approach the forest, watching and waiting. They have plagued the Woodmen living along the western eaves of the wood and the Elves of Thranduil's Hall with furtive assaults and ceaseless warfare. Unlike Orcs, they are not direct servants of the Shadow, but their own machinations often find them in league with it.

Attercop

...there were Spiders huge and horrible sitting in the branches above him.

Many-eyed and many-legged, Attercops are giant Spiders reaching up to the size of boars. They are crafty predators who attack unwary victims, first tying them up with their Spider-thread and then poisoning them. While a single Attercop does not pose a significant threat to any but a less-experienced adventurer, a roused Spider-colony can be a challenge even for a veteran company of heroes.

Attercop
Medium monstrosity

STR	DEX	CON	INT	WIS	CHA
12 (+1)	17 (+3)	12 (+1)	12 (+1)	11 (+0)	8 (-1)

Armour Class 13 (natural armour)
Hit Points 22 (4d8+4)
Speed 30 ft, climb 30 ft

Skills Intimidation +1, Perception +2, Stealth +5
Senses darkvision 60 ft, passive Perception 12
Languages Westron, Orkish
Challenge ½ (100 XP)

Spider Climb. The Attercop can climb difficult surfaces, including upside down on ceilings, without needing to make an ability check.
Web Sense. While the Attercop is in contact with a web, it knows the exact location of any other creature in contact with the same web.
Web Walker. An Attercop ignores movement restrictions caused by webbing.

Actions

Bite. *Melee Weapon Attack:* +5 to hit, reach 5 ft, one target. *Hit:* 6 (1d6+3) piercing damage.
Sting. *Melee Weapon Attack:* +3 to hit, reach 5 ft, one target. *Hit:* 3 (1d4+1) poison damage. The victim must make a DC 13 Constitution saving throw or be Stunned until the end of the Attercop's next turn. If this damage reduces the hero to 0 hit points, they become Poisoned until they take a short rest.
Web (Recharge 5-6). *Melee Weapon Attack:* +5 to hit, range 30/60 ft, one Large or smaller creature. *Hit:* The creature is Restrained by webbing. As an action, the Restrained creature can make a DC 13 Strength check, escaping from the webbing on a success. The effect also ends if the webbing is destroyed. The webbing has AC 10, 5 hit points, vulnerability to fire damage and immunity to bludgeoning, poison and psychic damage.

Spiders of Mirkwood Adventure Seed

◊ Some Spiders can talk. What secrets might they tell one another when they think no one is listening? How many ages of the world have they seen, and who have they eaten?

GREAT SPIDER

...he noticed a place of dense black shadow ahead of him, black even for that forest, like a patch of midnight that had never been cleared away.

Great Spiders display their dreadful heritage much more prominently than the lesser Attercops. They are gigantic in size, sometimes as big as horses or greater, but their soft, flexible bodies enable them to hide in surprisingly narrow passages. While they can always be described as monstrous Spider creatures, their features often differ from one individual to another. The number and appearance of their legs and eyes may vary, for instance – some are supported by long, thin stalks; others move about on strong, hairy limbs ending in claw-like appendages; some spy from the dark with clustered eyes; and others follow their prey with bulbous, many-windowed eyes. Regardless of the details, Great Spiders are always a terrifying sight.

GREAT SPIDER
Large monstrosity

STR	DEX	CON	INT	WIS	CHA
15 (+2)	20 (+5)	18 (+4)	13 (+1)	11 (+0)	10 (+0)

Armour Class 15 (natural armour)
Hit Points 76 (8d10+32)
Speed 40 ft, climb 40 ft

Skills Intimidation +3, Perception +3, Stealth +8
Senses darkvision 60 ft, passive Perception 13
Languages Westron, Orkish
Challenge 5 (1,800 XP)

Fear Aura. Any creature hostile to the Great Spider that starts its turn within 30 feet of the Great Spider must make a DC 15 Wisdom saving throw, unless the Great Spider is Incapacitated. On a failed save, the creature is Frightened until the start of its next turn. If a creature's saving throw is successful, the creature is immune to any Great Spider's Fear Aura for the next 24 hours.

Spider Climb. The Great Spider can climb difficult surfaces, including upside down on ceilings, without needing to make an ability check.

Web Sense. While the Great Spider is in contact with a web, it knows the exact location of any other creature in contact with the same web.

Web Walker. A Great Spider ignores movement restrictions caused by webbing.

Actions

Multiattack. The Great Spider makes two bite attacks, two sting attacks or one bite and one sting attack.

Bite. *Melee Weapon Attack:* +8 to hit, reach 5 ft, one target. *Hit:* 12 (2d6+5) piercing damage.

Sting. *Melee Weapon Attack:* +5 to hit, reach 5 ft, one target. *Hit:* 7 (2d4+2) poison damage. The victim must make a DC 15 Constitution saving throw or be Paralysed until the end of the Great Spider's next turn. If this damage reduces the hero to 0 hit points, they become Paralysed until they take a short rest.

Terrifying Gaze. The Great Spider can take an action to select a target within 20 feet and force that creature to make a DC 15 Wisdom saving throw. On a failed save, the creature gains the Paralysed condition for 1d4 rounds. If a creature succeeds on a saving throw it is immune to this ability for 24 hours.

Web (Recharge 3-6). *Melee Weapon Attack:* +8 to hit, range 30/60 ft, one Large or smaller creature. *Hit:* The creature is Restrained by webbing. As an action, the Restrained creature can make a DC 13 Strength check, escaping from the webbing on a success. The effect also ends if the webbing is destroyed. The webbing has AC 10, 15 hit points, vulnerability to fire damage and immunity to bludgeoning, poison and psychic damage.

Trolls

Trolls are one of the evil races created by the Great Enemy in the Elder Days. They were bred to fight in many bitter wars. They were created strong and powerful, yet slowwitted and dull, and appear monstrous and misshapen, as if left unfinished by their cruel maker. It is not known whether they were generated in many forms, or if they have changed since their first appearance, but by the end of the Third Age several different breeds of Trolls can be encountered.

Cave-Troll

A huge arm and shoulder, with a dark skin of greenish scales, was thrust through the widening gap.

Cave-trolls were created to fight and hunt deep under the earth. Barely more intelligent than wild beasts, they have dark skin with a greenish hue, covered with tight, robust scales. While not necessarily inferior in size to other breeds of Trolls, they appear shorter as they are extremely hunched and often advance on all fours, walking on their knuckles.

Nobody knows if Cave-trolls can endure the light of the sun, as they never leave their hunting grounds under mountains, hills and fells.

Hill-Troll Chief

A Troll-chief is a larger, meaner and more intelligent Hill-troll, a formidable opponent even for the most valorous (or reckless) heroes.

Cave-Troll
Large Giant (Troll-kind)

STR	DEX	CON	INT	WIS	CHA
15 (+2)	10 (+0)	17 (+3)	6 (-2)	7 (-2)	8 (-1)

Armour Class 12 (natural armour)
Hit Points 51 (6d10+18)
Speed 30 ft
Senses darkvision 60 ft, passive Perception 9
Languages Orkish, Westron
Challenge 4 (1,100 XP)

Stony Hide. The Cave-troll's thick scales provides resistance to non-magical piercing and slashing damage.

Actions
Multiattack. The Cave-troll makes two attacks, one bite and one slam.
Bite. *Melee Weapon Attack:* +5 to hit, reach 5 ft, one target. *Hit:* 7 (2d4+2) slashing damage.
Slam. *Melee Weapon Attack:* +5 to hit, reach 5 ft, one target. *Hit:* 13 (2d10+2) bludgeoning damage.

Hill-Troll Chief
Large Giant (Troll-kind)

STR	DEX	CON	INT	WIS	CHA
19 (+4)	8 (-1)	19 (+4)	8 (-1)	10 (+0)	10 (+0)

Armour Class 16 (bits of previous victims' armour)
Hit Points 95 (10d10+40)
Speed 30 ft
Saving Throws Strength +7, Constitution +7, Wisdom +3
Skills Intimidation +3, Perception +3
Senses darkvision 60 ft, passive Perception 11
Languages Westron, Orkish
Challenge 5 (1,800 XP)

Hideous Toughness (Recharge after a short or long rest). The Hill-troll Chief can endure enormous damage. It may spend an action to spew forth various taunts and imprecations along with a great deal of spittle. It then gains a pool of 10 (3d6) temporary hit points that last till the end of the fight if not removed by combat damage.

Actions
Multiattack. The Hill-troll Chief makes two attacks: one bite and one maul.
Bite. *Melee Weapon Attack:* +7 to hit, reach 5 ft, one target. *Hit:* 9 (2d4+4) slashing damage.
Maul. *Melee Weapon Attack:* +7 to hit, reach 5 ft, one target. *Hit:* 18 (4d6+4) bludgeoning damage.

Hill-Troll

Taller and broader than Men they were, and they were clad only in close-fitting mesh of horny scales, or maybe that was their hideous hide...

Hill-trolls are the most common breed of this cruel race, as they prowl desolate areas from the Coldfells in the north to Gorgoroth in the south. They are wild and beastly in battle, prone to bellowing and roaring to intimidate their enemies, but can be disciplined to use simple weapons and armour.

Troll Adventure Seed

◆ The tactic of stalling Stone Trolls until the sun rises and petrifies them works fine, at least unless said Trolls are encountered deep under the earth or beneath the boughs of Mirkwood. In such cases the adventurers must either use force of arms or quick thinking to find a means of getting the sun's rays into a place that has never seen them. Such a task might be much more difficult than simply facing a rampaging Troll with shield and spear. Can the company lure the beast into the light, or cut through the forest canopy so the sun can strike true?

Hill-Troll
Large Giant (Troll-kind)

STR	DEX	CON	INT	WIS	CHA
17 (+3)	8 (-1)	16 (+3)	5 (-3)	7 (-2)	7 (-2)

Armour Class 13 (natural armour)
Hit Points 59 (7d10+21)
Speed 30 ft

Senses darkvision 60 ft, passive Perception 8
Languages Westron, Orkish
Challenge 2 (450 XP)

Fearsome Bellow. As a bonus action the Hill-troll may scream at a target within 20 ft. That target must make a DC 13 Wisdom saving throw or become Frightened until the end of the Hill-troll's next turn.

Actions

Multiattack. The Hill-troll makes two attacks: one bite and one slam.
Bite. *Melee Weapon Attack:* +5 to hit, reach 5 ft, one target. *Hit:* 8 (2d4+3) slashing damage.
Slam. *Melee Weapon Attack:* +5 to hit, reach 5 ft, one target. *Hit:* 14 (2d10+3) bludgeoning damage.

Marsh-Ogre

Poor Bilbo sat in the dark thinking of all the horrible names of all the giants and ogres he had ever heard told of in tales...

Some of the more terrifying tales surviving in the North talk of horrible man-eating Giants who were said to prowl lonely moors and bogs in search of prey. The most dangerous among them are said to have once lived in the marshes to the east of Mirkwood. No one has seen an Ogre in recent times, and the old and wise among the Men of the Lake say that they retreated among the mists of the bogs when Smaug took residence under the Lonely Mountain – few monsters were a match for a great Dragon! But now Smaug is dead, and the Marsh-ogres could emerge once again from their stinking retreats to threaten Lake-town and its prospering inhabitants.

A Marsh-ogre is a huge monster, as big as a Mountain-troll, although they cannot match those beasts pure aggression and prowess at arms. Ogres are brutish and beastly, speaking no languages spoken by Men, Dwarves or Elves.

Marsh-Ogre Adventure Seed

◆ Long thought nothing much more than old tales, Marsh-ogres have begun prowling around the edges of the Long Marshes. The Master of Lake-town fears that these giants might begin to search for prey on the Long Lake, and none know if these creatures can swim. Perhaps is some stout hearted folk could find out more about the Marsh-ogres, and discern the best way that they might be driven back into their swampy lairs.

Mountain-Troll

Great beasts drew it, Orcs surrounded it, and behind walked mountain-trolls to wield it.

Mountain-trolls are the largest of all Troll-races, often twelve feet or more in height. Immensely strong and dangerous, luckily they are rarely encountered, and are dull-witted and slow.

Marsh-Ogre
Large Giant

STR	DEX	CON	INT	WIS	CHA
17 (+3)	10 (+0)	18 (+4)	5 (-3)	7 (-2)	7 (-2)

Armour Class 13 (natural armour)
Hit Points 76 (8d10+32)
Speed 30 ft

Skills Athletics +5
Senses darkvision 60 ft, passive Perception 8
Languages -
Challenge 3 (700 XP)

Savage Attack. When the Marsh-ogre scores a critical hit, it does an additional 6 (1d12) damage. This damage is not doubled by the critical hit.

Actions

Grasp. *Melee Weapon Attack:* +5 to hit, reach 5 ft, one Medium or smaller target. *Hit:* The target becomes Grappled (escape DC 15). As an action, the Marsh-ogre may inflict 14 (2d10+3) bludgeoning damage on the Grappled creature.
Slam. *Melee Weapon Attack:* +5 to hit, reach 5 ft, one target. *Hit:* 14 (2d10+3) bludgeoning damage.

Mountain-Troll
Large Giant (Troll-kind)

STR	DEX	CON	INT	WIS	CHA
22 (+6)	6 (-2)	19 (+4)	4 (-3)	6 (-2)	6 (-2)

Armour Class 15 (natural armour)
Hit Points 85 (9d10+36)
Speed 30 ft

Senses darkvision 60 ft, passive Perception 8
Languages Westron, Orkish
Challenge 5 (1,800 XP)

Fear Aura. Any creature hostile to the Mountain-troll that starts its turn within 30 feet of the troll must make a DC 15 Wisdom saving throw, unless the Mountain-troll is Incapacitated. On a failed save, the creature is Frightened until the start of its next turn. If a creature's saving throw is successful, the creature is immune to any Mountain-troll's Fear Aura for the next 24 hours.

Actions

Multiattack. The Mountain-troll makes two attacks: one crush and one slam.
Crush. *Melee Weapon Attack:* +9 to hit, reach 5 ft, one target. *Hit:* 13 (2d6+6) bludgeoning damage.
Slam. *Melee Weapon Attack:* +9 to hit, reach 5 ft, one target. *Hit:* 17 (2d10+6) bludgeoning damage.

Stone-Troll

...there were three fair-sized trolls at hand in a nasty mood, quite likely to try toasted dwarf, or even pony, for a change...

Stone-Trolls live in small groups in filthy caves strewn with the remains of unwary travellers. They seem to be more intelligent than other Troll types, maybe thanks to their habit of prowling in the proximity of populated areas. Their appearance, while always frightful, is made less monstrous by their tendency to wear simple clothes, cook their food and use tools like drinking jugs and barrels.

A very ancient breed, Stone-Trolls owe their name to the fact that they turn to stone if exposed to the light of the Sun.

Stone-Troll
Large Giant (Troll-kind)

STR	DEX	CON	INT	WIS	CHA
17 (+3)	8 (-1)	16 (+3)	8 (-1)	7 (-2)	6 (-2)

Armour Class 15 (natural armour)
Hit Points 85 (9d10+36)
Speed 30 ft

Saving Throws Dexterity +2
Senses darkvision 60 ft, passive Perception 8
Languages Westron, Orkish
Challenge 4 (1,100 XP)

Sunlight Curse. Stone-trolls become Petrified and turn into stone if they are touched by the bright light of the sun. Once the sun rises, a Stone-troll must make a DC 10 Dexterity saving throw at the beginning of its turn in order to find enough cover to avoid being turned to stone. On a failure, the Stone-troll becomes Petrified.

Actions

Multiattack. The Stone-troll makes two attacks: one with its troll-club and one slam.
Troll-club. *Melee Weapon Attack:* +5 to hit, reach 5 ft, one target. *Hit:* 12 (2d8+3) bludgeoning damage.
Slam. *Melee Weapon Attack:* +5 to hit, reach 5 ft, one target. *Hit:* 14 (2d10+3) bludgeoning damage.

Wolves of the Wild

By the time of Bilbo's adventures, Wolves, Wargs and Werewolves could be encountered at night in the eastern vales close to the Misty Mountains, where they prowled in search of prey. The Wargs and Orcs of the Mountains often help one another in raids against the Woodmen, gathering food for the Wolves and slaves to work for the Orcs.

Wargs

"How the wind howls!" he cried. "It is howling with wolf-voices. The Wargs have come west of the Mountains!"

Wargs are a particularly evil breed of Wolves living over the Edge of the Wild, displaying wicked cunning and malicious intent. They communicate using a dreadful language, foul to the ears of listeners not sharing their love for cruel and hateful deeds. Wargs generally look like lean and powerfully-built grey wolves, with eyes shining in the dark, but their size and appearance vary according to age and experience.

Wild Wolf

The average Warg, a Wild Wolf is slightly larger than an ordinary Wolf, and much more vicious. It can be encountered in packs, but also as a solitary hunter or scout, ready to howl and alert other Wargs and evil creatures for miles around. Orcs learn how to ride upon Wild Wolves like men do on horses.

Wild Wolf
Large Beast (Warg-kind)

STR	DEX	CON	INT	WIS	CHA
12 (+1)	14 (+2)	13 (+1)	5 (-3)	12 (+1)	7 (-2)

Armour Class 14 (natural armour)
Hit Points 26 (4d10+4)
Speed 50 ft

Skills Perception +3, Stealth +4
Senses darkvision 60 ft, passive Perception 13
Languages Wargspeech
Challenge ½ (100 XP)

Fear of Fire. Wild Wolves are fearful of fire. If a torch or other flame comes within 10 feet of them, the Wild Wolf suffers Disadvantage on its attack rolls. In addition, the Wild Wolf is not able to use its Pack Tactics ability.
Keen Hearing and Smell. The Wild Wolf has Advantage on Wisdom (Perception) checks that rely on hearing or smell.
Pack Tactics. The Wild Wolf has Advantage on an attack roll against a creature if at least one of the Wild Wolf's allies is within 5 feet of the creature and the ally isn't Incapacitated.

Actions

Bite. *Melee Weapon Attack:* +3 to hit, reach 5ft, one target. *Hit:* 8 (2d6+1) piercing damage. If the target is a creature, it must make a DC 13 Strength saving throw or be knocked Prone.

Wolves of the Wild Adventure Seed

◈ After the Battle of Five Armies, the wargs were scattered across the North. Some goblins fled with the wargs, and now find themselves virtual slaves to their former allies. The wargs sometimes have uses for two-legged minions with deft hands and keen eyes. Some warg packs have even considered capturing human children and raising them as servants, training them as a human might train a dog.

Wolf Leader

Greater in stature, cruelty and cunning than ordinary Wargs, a Wolf Leader is called upon by its lesser kin to deal with serious threats, like bands of travelling adventurers trespassing into Warg territory. A Wolf Leader is never encountered alone, but always surrounded by a pack of Wild Wolves.

Wolf Leader
Large Monstrosity (Warg-kind)

STR	DEX	CON	INT	WIS	CHA
14 (+2)	16 (+3)	17 (+3)	7 (-2)	12 (+1)	9 (-1)

Armour Class 14 (natural armour)
Hit Points 59 (7d10+21)
Speed 50 ft

Skills Perception +4, Stealth +6
Senses darkvision 60 ft, passive Perception 14
Languages Westron, Wargspeech
Challenge 3 (700 XP)

Fear of Fire. The Wolf Leader is fearful of fire. If a torch or other flame comes within 10 feet of them then the Wolf Leader suffers disadvantage on its attack rolls. In addition, the Wolf Leader is not able to use its Pack Tactics ability.

Keen Hearing and Smell. The Wolf Leader has Advantage on Wisdom (Perception) checks that rely on hearing or smell.

Pack Tactics. The Wolf Leader has Advantage on an attack roll against a creature if at least one of the Wolf Leader's allies is within 5 feet of the creature and the ally isn't Incapacitated.

Savage Attack. When the Wolf Leader scores a critical hit, it does an additional 5 (1d10) damage. This damage is not doubled by the critical hit.

Actions

Multiattack. The Wolf Leader makes two attacks: one bite and one claw attack.

Bite. *Melee Weapon Attack:* +4 to hit, reach 5 ft, one target. *Hit:* 9 (2d6+2) piercing damage. If the target is a creature, it must make a DC 13 Strength saving throw or be knocked Prone.

Claw. *Melee Weapon Attack:* +4 to hit, reach 5 ft, one target. *Hit:* 8 (1d12+2) piercing damage.

Werewolves

"Listen, Hound of Sauron!" he cried. "Gandalf is here. Fly, if you value your foul skin! I will shrivel you from tail to snout, if you come within this ring."

It is suspected by the most learned among the Wise that the cruelest packs of Wargs might be led by the foulest of creatures: trusted servants of the Dark Lord returned from the Ancient World to serve him once again. Devouring spirits trapped in wolf-form, they hate the very soil they walk upon, and desire only to defile and ruin in an attempt to quench the dreadful hunger that consumes their mortal bodies.

The Werewolf of Mirkwood

The Werewolf of Mirkwood is a monstrous wolf-like creature. Greater than any Wolf or Warg, its body has been twisted by the terrible power that has possessed it for uncounted centuries.

This dreadful beast has made its lair under the mountains of the Wild Wood, a complex of caves it leaves only to temporarily satisfy its thirst.

Werewolf
Large Fiend

STR	DEX	CON	INT	WIS	CHA
26 (+3)	18 (+4)	19 (+4)	12 (+1)	16 (+3)	12 (+1)

Armour Class 16 (natural armour)
Hit Points 85 (9d10+36)
Speed 50 ft
Skills Perception +6, Stealth +7
Damage Resistances bludgeoning, piercing, and slashing damage
Senses blindsight 30 ft, darkvision 60 ft, passive Perception 16
Languages Westron, Orkish, Silvan
Challenge 6 (2,300 XP)

Fell Spirit (Recharge 5-6). When the Werewolf would be reduced to 0 hit points, it may use its reaction to add 10 (3d6) temporary hit points.

Hard Eyed. The Werewolf is an ancient spirit of evil and an accomplished killer. The Werewolf scores critical hits on a 18, 19 or 20 on any attack roll.

Keen Hearing and Smell. The Werewolf has Advantage on Wisdom (Perception) checks that rely on hearing or smell.

Savage Attack. When the Werewolf scores a critical hit, it does an additional 5 (1d10) damage. This damage is not doubled by the critical hit.

Actions

Multiattack. The Werewolf makes three attacks: one with its bite and two with its claws.

Bite. *Melee Weapon Attack:* +6 to hit, reach 5ft, one target. *Hit:* 10 (2d6+3) piercing damage.

Claw. *Melee Weapon Attack:* +6 to hit, reach 5 ft, one target. *Hit:* 9 (1d12+3) piercing damage.

Hound of Sauron

Chosen for its ferocity and malicious intelligence, a Hound of Sauron is a minion of the Dark Lord, a servant sent on a precise errand, be it the gathering of forces for a coming war, the hunt for a specific individual, or spying on an area. Hidden behind the shape of an ordinary Warg, a Hound of Sauron conceals much greater powers.

Hound of Sauron
Large Monstrosity (Warg-kind)

STR	DEX	CON	INT	WIS	CHA
15 (+2)	17 (+3)	18 (+4)	10 (+0)	12 (+1)	9 (-1)

Armour Class 15 (natural armour)
Hit Points 94 (9d10+45)
Speed 50 ft

Skills Perception +4, Stealth +7
Damage Resistances bludgeoning, piercing, and slashing damage
Senses darkvision 60 ft, passive Perception 14
Languages Wargspeech
Challenge 4 (1100 XP)

Fear Aura. Any creature hostile to the Hound that starts its turn within 10 feet of the Hound must make a DC 13 Wisdom saving throw, unless the Hound is Incapacitated. On a failed save, the creature is Frightened until the start of its next turn. If a creature's saving throw is successful, the creature is immune to the Hound of Sauron's Fear Aura for the next 24 hours.

Keen Hearing and Smell. The Hound has Advantage on Wisdom (Perception) checks that rely on hearing or smell.

Savage Attack. When the Wolf Leader scores a critical hit, it does an additional 5 (1d10) damage. This damage is not doubled by the critical hit..

Actions

Multiattack. The Hound of Sauron makes one bite attack and one claw attack.

Bite. *Melee Weapon Attack:* +5 to hit, reach 5 ft, one target. *Hit:* 9 (2d6+2) piercing damage. If the target is a creature, it must make a DC 13 Strength saving throw or be knocked Prone.

Claw. *Melee Weapon Attack:* +5 to hit, reach 5 ft, one target. *Hit:* 8 (1d12+2) piercing damage.

Vampires

In the Elder Days, the Dark Lord counted among his servants a number of mysterious bat-like creatures, sometimes said to possess the power to change shape. A race of vampire-bats endures to this day: when roused, they fly in huge swarms, heralding the coming of an Orc-host by forming a dark cloud above its ranks. But a darker menace lurks among the heights of the Mountains of Mirkwood and in forgotten pits under Dol Guldur, a brooding presence that accompanied the Shadow when it first descended upon Greenwood the Great…

Great Bats

…the great bats … fastened vampire-like on the stricken.

Unusually large bats, whose taste for blood often leads them to follow when Orcs and Wargs go on raids or to war.

Great Bat
Medium Beast

STR	DEX	CON	INT	WIS	CHA
12 (+1)	16 (+3)	11 (+0)	2 (-4)	12 (+1)	6 (-2)

Armour Class 13
Hit Points 18 (4d8)
Speed 10 ft, fly 60 ft.

Senses blindsight 60 ft, passive Perception 11
Languages -
Challenge ¼ (50 XP)

Echolocation. The Great Bat can't use its blindsight while Deafened.

Keen Hearing. The Great Bat has Advantage on Wisdom (Perception) checks that rely on hearing.

Sunlight Sensitivity. While in sunlight, the Great Bat has Disadvantage on attack rolls, as well as on Wisdom (Perception) checks that rely on sight.

Actions

Bite. *Melee Weapon Attack:* +3 to hit, reach 5ft, one target. *Hit:* 4 (1d6+1) piercing damage

Secret Shadows

Taking the form of great misshapen bats, these servants of Sauron fly on their great-fingered wings to carry his dark tidings or to spy upon the land, or join a swarm of Great Bats when war or hunt has provided them with prey. These Vampires belong to an astute and patient breed, always aware of the will of their Master and ready to do his bidding. Ages ago they were able to disguise their foul appearance and appear as beautiful women. Today, they may appear as such only briefly, to confound their opponents.

Vampire Adventure Seed

◈ There was once a Great Vampire that dwelt in Mirkwood, until the Elves destroyed it. Since then, lesser vampires have quarrelled amongst themselves, trying to claim the mantle of their fallen mistress. These vampires plot against one another, and sometimes even trick mortal heroes into attacking their rivals...

Secret Shadow
Large Fiend

STR	DEX	CON	INT	WIS	CHA
12 (+1)	16 (+3)	14 (+2)	9 (-1)	14 (+2)	10 (-0)

Armour Class 16 (natural armour)
Hit Points 45 (6d10+12)
Speed 30 ft, fly 60 ft

Saving Throws Dexterity +6, Wisdom +5
Skills Perception +4, Stealth +5
Senses blindsight 60 ft, passive Perception 14
Languages Westron, Orkish, Silvan
Challenge 3 (700 XP)

Echolocation. The Secret Shadow can't use its blindsight while Deafened.
Keen Hearing. The Secret Shadow has Advantage on Wisdom (Perception) checks that rely on hearing.
Nimble Escape. The Secret Shadow can take the Disengage or Hide action as a bonus action on each of its turns.
Savage Attack. If the Secret Shadow scores a critical hit, it does an additional 5 (1d10) damage. This die is not doubled by the critical hit.
Sunlight Sensitivity. While in sunlight, the Secret Shadow has Disadvantage on attack rolls, as well as on Wisdom (Perception) checks that rely on sight.

Actions

Multiattack. The Secret Shadow makes two attacks: biting once and clawing once.
Bite. *Melee Weapon Attack:* +3 to hit, reach 5ft, one target. *Hit:* 4 (1d6+1) piercing damage
Claws. *Melee Weapon Attack:* +3 to hit, reach 5ft, one target. *Hit:* 6 (2d4+1) slashing damage
Bewilder. The Secret Shadow can briefly assume the appearance of a beautiful humanoid, confusing all around her. All creatures within 30 feet of the Secret Shadow must make a DC 13 Wisdom saving throw or be Stunned for 1d4+1 rounds. As long as the effect lasts, the Secret Shadow may then make a melee attack against a Stunned creature as a bonus action. A Secret Shadow can only use this ability once per long rest.

Creature Actions
- and Abilities -

This section presents a menu of abilities and actions that a Loremaster can use to customise and individualise their enemy encounters, making them fresh and unpredictable. Some of these abilities and actions increase a creature's abilities in combat. Others decrease it. This allows the Loremaster either to balance an encounter by adding a strengthening ability for every weakening ability or to make an encounter more difficult or easier for the company.

Most of these abilities and actions are not sufficient alterations to change the overall Challenge Rating of an enemy, except at lower ratings. For creatures with CR of less than 1, consider every action or ability that boosts the capabilities of a creature to step it up one fractional CR level until it reaches 1. Beyond CR 1 there is no change unless several abilities are added, in which case the CR should increase, to offer a greater XP reward. However resulting changes to the proficiency bonus of the creature may prove to a step in book-keeping too far. For every action or ability that lowers a creature's capabilities, step it down one fractional CR level if it begins at 1 or less.

It is worth considering whether you wish to surprise your players with some of these abilities or whether to offer them as a clearly broadcast obstacle to overcome. For example, an Orc soldier with the Bite ability may be a sudden surprise that adds to the feeling of how awful Orcs are. Conversely, making it obvious from the beginning of a battle that one of their foes, being in possession of the Mewling ability, is less committed than their fellows, may give the company a chance to plan their tactics and feel some satisfaction in doing so. When using these abilities, there is the potential to be excessively punishing to your company. By offering a wide range of options, these menus also allow "power combinations" well in excess of their intended use. Take care to ensure that everyone is enjoying the game, and that these extra actions are used to bring an enjoyable variety, rather than an excess of Player-hero death, to the table.

A strongly thematic game should certainly feel perilous, but very few characters should die in an inconsequential battle. Equally, inexperienced Loremasters should take the time to become familiar with what these actions and abilities could mean at the table.

A small sprinkling of extra abilities can make an encounter flavourful, fresh and exciting. Ladling them on will make combat drawn out and unreasonably gruelling for your company. As an optional rule, if an encounter becomes too overpowering due to an unforeseen effect of using one or more of these actions and abilities, have the creature lose access to them when wounded. It is also worth bearing in mind how much book keeping you wish to do. If you are also using the additional scenery rules, there could be a lot of extra factors to manage in a given combat. These optional rules are intended to add variety and to be used sparingly. A couple of extra abilities and a couple of scenery options are plenty to achieve that aim.

The creative Loremaster is encouraged to come up with their own additional actions based on those found here. Altering the conditions under which abilities and actions are triggered, or tying them to specific scenery options is a great starting point.

List of Creature Actions & Abilities

Big. This creature is a large specimen of its kind. Add +1 Hit Die, +2 to its strength, and thus +1 to melee damage.

Bite Attack. This creature's wide maw and menacing teeth allow it to make a bite melee weapon attack, +1 to hit, with a 5ft range, against one target. Hit: 5 (2d4) slashing damage.

Call for Aid. A creature with this ability may take an action to seek assistance from nearby allies. Orcs blow horns, Wolves howl, Trolls roar, Spiders make unusual chittering sounds. 1d4 creatures of the same type arrive in 1d6+1 rounds. If all the original opponents are slain, the allies are unable to find them and do not appear, unless the Loremaster wishes them to do so.

Clumsy. Visibly less capable and confident than its fellows, on failing an attack roll, this creature must make a Dexterity save of DC 12 or fall over, acquiring the Prone condition.

Coward. When injured, this creature suffers Disadvantage on all combat rolls.

Deeply Sinister. This creature exudes menace of a deeply unsettling kind. Attacks against this creature are made at with a -1 modifier.

Desperate. This wild-eyed creature begins attacking madly if it believes its life is in danger. When this creature reaches half its hit point total, it gains Advantage on its attack rolls.

Dirty Brawler. In addition to a fearsome countenance, this creature favours the shove action in combat, and will always attempt to use it.

Disarming Strike. This creature can aim to strike blows to knock whatever its opponent is holding out of its hand. On a successful roll to hit, their opponent must make a Dexterity save of DC 12 or drop whatever they are holding. The attack does no other damage.

Distraction Attack. This especially wily creature can take an action to feint, kick burning ash, or otherwise distract an opponent with whom it is engaged in melee. The opponent must make a Wisdom saving throw against DC 10 + the distracting creature's Dexterity modifier or the distracting creature's attacks have Advantage against the opponent until the end of its next turn.

Gimlet Eyed. This creature inflicts +2 damage on all damage rolls made at night or underground.

Great Leap. This creature is capable of jumping huge distances. This creature may make a special Dash action to go twice its normal movement in a single jump. Any opponents in melee combat with the creature when it uses Great Leap get opportunity attacks as normal.

Hatred (Subject) (Recharge 5-6). This creature hates members of a specified culture so much that it goes out of its way to do them ill. The creature has Advantage on attacks against the hated race. Such creatures often signal their dislike of a given culture with harsh insults and promises at the opening of combat.

Mewling. When this creature loses half its initial hit points, it will attempt to flee.

Multiattack. This creature can make more than one attack with a single action.

Poorly Armed. This creature's weapons or natural attacks are inferior to the average of its kind. Its damage rolls are subject to a -2 modifier.

Poorly Protected. This creature's armour or natural protection is weak. Reduce its AC by 2.

Really Big. This creature is larger than others of its kind. Increase its size category by 1. Add 2 additional Hit Dice, +4 to its Strength, and thus +2 to the melee damage it inflicts.

Rubbery Skin. This creature's rubbery flesh is immune to bludgeoning damage.

Savage Attack. If this creature scores a critical hit, it does additional damage equal to its hit die. This damage does not double due to the critical hit.

Screamer. This creature constantly yells and screams in a particularly piercing fashion, causing foes attacking it to suffer Disadvantage on their attack rolls.

Sneaking (Recharge 6). This creature inflicts an extra 2d6 damage to a target it hits with a weapon attack if its target is within 5 feet of an ally of the creature.

Starving Cannibal. This creature breaks from combat as soon as an ally is killed and attempts to move toward the fallen in order to eat them.

Stony Hide. This creature's hardened skin, unusually tough scales, or impenetrable chitin provides resistance to non-magical piercing and slashing damage.

Stupid. This creature always takes the least favourable action using scenery or hazards on a battlefield – falling into pits, triggering stalactites to fall and so on.

Tittering Laugh. This creature continually laughs or makes other disturbing and off-putting noises. Foes within 10 feet must make a Wisdom saving throw against a DC 12 or attack this creature in preference to any other enemies, including closer or more dangerous ones.

Venomous. One or more of this creature's attacks are toxic. After being successfully attacked, targets must make a Constitution saving throw against a DC 13 or acquire the Poisoned condition for the duration of the battle.

Vile (1/day). This creature is capable of horrific, disgusting or revolting acts. When it takes a vile action, its opponents must make a Wisdom saving throw against a DC 15 or be Stunned until the end of this creature's next turn.

War Paint. When creatures so marked fight in combat and outnumber their foes by more than 2 to 1, they gain a +1 to all attack and damage rolls.

Weak in Limb. This creature moves at half the speed normal for creatures of its type.

Weakling. This creature has half its normal number of hit points. It appears visibly weaker than its companions.

Weak Willed. When damaged by an attack, this creature attempts to disengage its foe and move to attack a different adversary as soon as it is able to do so.

Creature Bonus Actions

Aggressive. As a bonus action, this creature can move up to its speed toward a foe that it can see.

Bandolier of Knives (Recharge 4-6). As a bonus action, this creature can hurl a cluster of small blades at any opponent within 10 feet. The target must make a Dexterity saving throw against a DC 12 + this creature's Dexterity modifier or suffer 1d6 + the creature's Dexterity modifier in damage.

Berserk. After the first round of combat, this creature may make a single melee weapon attack as a bonus action on each of its turns.

Fell Speed. This creature may take a bonus action to Disengage from one opponent and engage another without provoking an opportunity attack. The new opponent must be within the creature's regular movement rate.

Foul Reek. This creature exudes such a horrid stink that, as a bonus action, it can force an opponent engaged in melee combat with it to make a Constitution saving throw against a DC 12 or acquire the Poisoned condition until the end of its next turn.

Long Arms. This creature's extended limbs allow it to unexpectedly lash out at unwary opponents. This creature may take a bonus action to effectively add 5 feet to its reach till its next turn. In most cases, this gives the creature a reach of 10 feet with any following melee attacks or attacks of opportunity.

Savage Assault. When this creature rolls a natural 18 or 19, it may, as a bonus action, make a single additional melee attack against the same opponent.

Creature Reactions

Biter. When wounded, this creature can, as a reaction, make a single bite melee attack against any single target at +1 to hit, with a 5ft range. Hit: 5 (2d4) slashing damage.

Reckless Hatred. When reduced to 0 hit points, this creature can, as a reaction, make a single melee attack against any target within 5 feet before succumbing to death.

Snake-like Speed (Recharge 5-6). This creature is adept at avoiding injury and can use its reaction to halve the attack damage on an attack that it is aware of.

Vicious Hiss (Recharge after a short or long rest). After this creature has taken 10 or more points of damage, it may, as a reaction, express its anger in a very threatening manner, such as a piercing hiss or a devastating bellow. All opponents engaging the creature must make a Wisdom saving throw against a DC 15 or suffer Disadvantage on ability checks and attack rolls until the creature is defeated.

Troupe Abilities, Actions and Bonus Actions

These abilities and actions apply to a group of allied creatures that the Loremaster has decided are working together as a band. They need not be of the exact same type, but some common sense should apply: while many types of Goblins and Wargs are commonly allied and could easily be considered a single troupe, Goblins and Spiders are not, and it would be most unusual for them to join forces in such a way as to qualify as a troupe. A troupe of allied creatures can have more than one troupe ability or action. This can allow them to be more fierce in one respect, and weaker in another. So a gang of Goblins with Blood Thirsty and Weak Willed Alliance will be a stronger set of foes initially, but if the company start to inflict damage upon them, the troupe soon show themselves to be less dangerous than expected.

Bloodthirsty. Each round that a member of this troupe inflicts damage upon an opponent, one of their number gains Advantage on their next attack.

Foul Alliance. As a bonus action and with suitable imprecations, these creatures can urge on a single member of their troupe to gain +1 to combat rolls by taking -1 on their own combat rolls. Up to three creatures may use this action on one of their allies in a single round, to a maxium bonus of +3.

Last One Standing. When it becomes the last survivor of the troupe, this creature gains one of the following abilities/actions: Coward, Mewling, Multiattack, Screaming or Vile.

Ill-prepared for Battle. Creatures sharing this ability suffers Disadvantage as soon as one of their number becomes injured.

The Strong Die First. Creatures sharing this ability become weaker when they lose members of their troupe. If they lose half (or optionally a quarter, or three quarters, at the Loremaster's discretion) of their allies sharing this ability, they suffer Disadvantage.

Terrifying in Aspect. This group of adversaries presents a truly horrifying enemy to be overcome. As such, they remove any and all Inspiration from their foes. However, once half of the troupe is defeated, ALL of their opponents gain Inspiration.

Vengeful Band. When one member of the troupe is killed, another member may make a single melee weapon attack as a bonus action on their next turn.

Vile Gang. These creatures redouble their attacks if they believe their allies are in peril. When the majority of its allies reach half their hit point total, they add a bonus of +1 to both their attack and damage rolls.

War Cry. During the first round of combat, the whole troupe may choose to deliver a war cry as their initial action. This gives them Advantage on their combat rolls until one of their number is wounded.

Weak Willed Alliance. As soon as one of the creatures sharing this ability is slain, all must make a DC 10 Wisdom save or attempt to flee. It is possible that, if the Loremaster decides that such an individual is present, a creature deemed the troupe leader can use a reaction to rally the troupe with a successful DC 10 Wisdom save.

Especially Strong Abilities and Actions

These actions and abilities single out a creature as being an especially dangerous foe. They are designed for leaders and creatures that the Loremaster wishes to be an extra challenge. These abilities often increase the challenge rating of the enemy. At the Loremaster's discretion, a creature surviving an encounter with a company may return later in the campaign, having gained one of these abilities.

Commanding Voice. This creature can inspire its allies with its imposing presence and authoritative voice. This creature use its reaction to utter a command or shout a warning whenever a non-hostile creature, that it can see within 30 feet of it, is about to make an attack roll or a saving throw. The target can add a d6 Command Die to its next roll, provided it can hear and understand the message. A creature can benefit from only one Command Die at a time, and creatures that possess Commanding Voice cannot benefit from this effect.

Denizen of the Dark. This creature is particularly adept at using the environment and shadows to its benefit. It may take the Hide action, even in plain sight. It makes a Dexterity (Stealth) check and any foes must make an opposed Wisdom (Perception) check to track its movements.

Excessive Strength of Arms (Recharge 5-6). This creature can deliver a blow so powerful, or so penetratingly painful, that any opponent struck must make a Dexterity save of DC 12 or fall Prone.

Hard Eyed. This creature has won many battles and knows how to kill. Increase the threat range of all of its attacks by 2, meaning it will score critical hits on a 18, 19 or 20 on an attack roll.

Hideous Toughness (Recharge after a short or long rest). This creature can endure enormous damage. By spending an action preparing in an appropriately frightening way, the creature gains a pool of 10 (3d6) temporary hit points that last till the end of the fight if not removed by combat damage.

Last Stand. This creature may take this reaction when it reaches 0 hit points. Rather than fall Unconscious and/or die, the creature may continue to act normally for one additional round and has Advantage on any actions it takes on its final round. At the conclusion of its turn, it expires.

No Quarter. When this creature reduces an enemy to 0 hit points that enemy is considered to already have failed one death save.

Rotting. This creature's diseased flesh slows it, but makes it all but immune to pain. This creature always goes last in any combat round; however, it is immune to piercing and slashing damage.

Survivor. When outnumbered by its opponents, this creature always uses the Dodge action. When an opponent misses it, it can make a single melee attack as a reaction.

Vicious Wounds (Recharge 5-6). This creature may use an Attack action to inflict bleeding wounds on its opponent. At the start of each of a wounded creature's turns, it takes 2 (1d4) damage from blood loss. This damage continues until the wounded creature or one of its allies uses an action to make a DC 15 Wisdom (Medicine) check. On a success the bleeding stops.

Creature Specific Actions and Abilities: Orcs & Goblins

Cruel Lash. An Orc with this ability can take an action to "encourage" all its allies within 10 feet. Whip-encouraged creatures gain +1 damage on their next attack.

Drums (Recharge after a short or long rest). This Orc can take an action to beat their war drum in order to break their foes' spirits. Foes hearing the drums must make a Wisdom saving throw at DC 12 or suffer Disadvantage on all their attacks against Orcs until they succeed at drawing blood from one, e.g. causing 1 or more hit points of damage. Any given foe can only be affected by Drums once per day.

Foul Liquor. This Orc carries a flask of disgusting yet invigorating brew. As an action the Orc may take a swig, regaining 3 (1d6) hit points. Typically this flask is broken when the Orc is slain, however if recovered it can be used by Player-heroes, and the flask will contain 1d4 swigs. They gain one Shadow point for each swig taken, but also recover 3 (1d6) hit points per dose.

Grim Banner (Recharge after a short or long rest). A Goblin bearing such a banner may take an action to encourage their allies. This acts as a variation of the Help action for all of the Goblin's allies within 30 feet who can see the banner, giving all of them Advantage on their next attack roll.

Creature Specific Actions and Abilities: Trolls and Ogres

Clobbering Sweep (1/day). This particularly large Troll or Ogre can use its great size to strike multiple foes at once. It can make a melee attack against any number of targets within 5 feet, with a separate attack roll for each target. Targets must also make a DC 13 Dexterity check or be knocked Prone.

Fierce Bees (Troll adversaries only – Recharge after 1/Day). A Troll with this ability keeps a hive of bees or wasps about to throw at their opponents. The Troll can take an action to hurl such a "weapon" at his foes. 1d2 Swarms of Insects pour out of the broken hive and proceed to attack random foes around the area (including the Troll).

In the Sack with You! A Troll can take an action to heave a Medium size or smaller Grappled target into a Troll bag. Targets in a Troll bag count as being Blinded and Restrained. To escape, they need to cut their way out. The inside of a Troll's larder sack has AC 12 and it takes 10 points of damage to slice free; however, anyone struggling to escape is limited to using a small piercing weapon, such as a dagger. Furthermore, a Troll not engaged in melee combat can take a bonus action to "quiet" anyone in one of their larder sacks, automatically inflicting 15 (2d8+6) damage on them.

Seize Victim (Recharge 5-6). Trolls may choose to spend an action grabbing a potential victim instead of inflicting damage upon them. Their target is automatically Grappled if the Troll succeeds on their attack roll and their target is of Medium size or smaller. To escape the Troll's grasp, the target must use an action to escape: they must succeed on a Strength (Athletics) or Dexterity (Acrobatics) check against a DC 10 + the Troll's Strength modifier. If they fail, they take 5 damage and remain Grappled.

Shield Smasher (Recharge after a short or long rest). To destroy a shield, the Troll takes an Attack action, concentrating all its damage on the shield itself. The Troll must hit AC 20 and must succeed in inflicting more than 20 hit points worth of damage in a single round. If the Troll succeeds, the targeted shield is utterly destroyed and worthless.

Thick Hide (Troll adversaries only – Recharge 4-6). The enduring toughness of some Trolls is the stuff of frightful legend. These Trolls may use their reaction when struck to give themselves resistance to all non-magical bludgeoning, piercing and slashing damage till their next turn.

Creature Specific Actions and Abilities: Spiders

Dying Frenzy. When this Spider reaches single figure hit points it becomes frenzied, gaining an extra attack per combat round.

Paralysing Attack. The sting of this Spider inflicts the Paralysed condition unless the victim can make a successful Constitution saving throw at DC 15. The effect lasts until the victim takes a short rest.

Great Spider Actions

Acidic Drool. The venom that drips from some Great Spiders' fangs is highly caustic as well as poisonous. Their bite attacks cause an additional 7 (2d6) acid damage. Additionally, if their target wears armour, it is degraded by 1 AC on each successful bite until it has been repaired by a blacksmith.

Eightfold Gaze. The Great Spider can take an action to select a target within 20 feet and force that creature to make a DC 15 Wisdom saving throw. On a failed save, the creature gains the Paralysed condition for 1d4 rounds. The Great Spider may then use any of its attacks (including webbing) as a bonus action against the Paralysed target. Once a creature succeeds in a saving throw it is immune to this ability for 24 hours.

Woven from Darkness (1/day). Some Great Spiders are capable of spinning webs that can catch and hold darkness itself, holding out all natural light. Great Spiders can take an action to spin such a web, which can fill a 30-foot radius sphere with darkness that does not abate. Creatures with night vision cannot see through the darkness and non-magical light cannot illuminate it. Such webs are immediately broken and dispelled if exposed to any sort of magical illumination.

Creature Specific Actions and Abilities: Wargs and Wolves

Blood Driven. Some Warg packs concentrate on bringing down the injured. When facing a group of opponents, they focus their attacks on a single individual that has lost 10 or more hit points. Against such a foe, they get a bonus of +1 to both their attack and damage rolls; however, they completely ignore other targets, even more dangerous ones.

Evil Maw. This Wolf or Warg can bite exceptionally hard – its bite attack does an additional 3 (1d6) points of slashing damage.

Keen Mounts. Wild Wolves that have been frequently ridden by Orcs eventually learn how to assist their riders in dispatching their foes. Wolves with this ability can use the Help action as a bonus action while being ridden.

Terrifying Howl. Wolves or Wargs with this ability can give such a howl that opponents within hearing range must make a DC 12 Constitution save or become Frightened until the end of their next turn..

Unclean Stench. A Wolf or Warg with this ability is in possession of an excessively noisome stench. Any opponent within 10 feet must make a Constitution saving throw at DC 12 or be considered Poisoned until the creature is slain.

Wondrous, Legendary and Healing Items

All That Glitters

When the Master left, I saw it all. I can't stop thinking about it. I watched him go, with the bags of gold and all the treasure he could lay his hands on. I've seen what's come back too, and I know that's not even half of what he left with. The rest must still be out there somewhere, dropped on the way or hid for safety. I know I can find it. I think of little else.

Treasure
- and Rewards -

Bilbo had heard tell and sing of dragon-hoards before, but the splendour, the lust, the glory of such treasure had never yet come home to him.

Wealth in Middle-earth is a curious beast. On one hand we see clear evidence that some of the foremost adventurers in the novels are driven by a desire for gold – take Thorin and company for instance. But more often than not, this is used as a moral example – "Dragon Sickness" is a flaw, not a strength and Smaug the Golden, hoarder of coins, is the very embodiment of greed.

Other characters from the novels seem to have little use for coin in their pockets. Gandalf might presumably pay for a pint of beer in the Prancing Pony, but largely seems to live a life without monetary wealth. It seems unlikely that Éomer carries around small change to pay for his meals, buy a new sword, or have his horse shod, yet he is a hero of great renown and feats of arms.

Conversely, it is easy to imagine merchants in Lake-town, pubs in the Shire, or a market in Dale that uses coins and supports a class of merchants, artisans and other paid workers who spend their wages.

Wealth in Middle-earth is simply more *complicated* than it is in many other fantastical settings. So it is that a great big pile of gold coins could well be the spur for a quest, but then reveals itself as a huge moral quandary. Wealth alone does not make characters important or successful. Gold is a metaphor and a device to be used to drive a plot. Piles of gold exist, are sought after, but with a kind of fairy tale logic: gold matters when it matters. When it doesn't, it doesn't. This can be sharply at odds with the common aim of most roleplaying games, which is acquisitive in nature.

This might give a Loremaster who is attempting to bring the feel of Middle-earth to their gaming table a few concerns. First, how do you structure adventures and campaigns to reflect the way wealth works in Middle-earth? Second, how do you wean players off the idea of acquiring gold coins as the core aim of an adventurer's life? Especially when they're playing a treasure hunter...

Out of Character Treasure Hunters

If your players fall into more common habits of adventurers in fantasy games – rifling through the pockets of the newly dead for small change, searching every chamber for a hidden chest of gold to inexplicably slip into the backpack, to later exchange at the magic item shop – what can you do? None of those things "work" in Middle-earth. How do you alter their perceptions and manage their expectations?

The most direct route is simply to communicate. Before the game, talk about your expectations. Many players will be keen to try out something new, and can be sold on a game that feels different. Stress what kind of game you would like to play, building on the heroic aspects. Make it clear that characters in Middle-earth don't need to amass wealth to be powerful or successful.

Use some examples. Where do characters "get things" in the novels? Very often from gifts, equally often by finding wonderful things in the Wild. Sting is found in a Troll cave, but an obstacle had to be overcome to win it. This is very traditional in roleplaying games, so things are not entirely unfamiliar. Remind your player group that characters rarely buy equipment in *The Lord of the Rings*, and if they do it happens off stage. *Adventures in Middle-earth* has the Fellowship phase to handle a lot of that kind of thing off stage too. A group discussion in advance of a game can be a great way to pull out some moments your players enjoyed from the novels, as well as a chance to shine a light on some of the details they need to know to build the kind of game you want.

A key point to remember is that money isn't what Middle-earth is *about*. An exploration of this very idea can be a theme for your campaign. Taking the model of Thorin's company and their burglar Bilbo, the arc of the story can be about learning that gold is not equivalent to happiness or power. You can take your players on this arc and show them that there are rewards in Middle-earth other than hoarded gold.

Go to the Source

It is worthwhile to take some time to consider individual instances at the table where the behaviour of a character in Middle-earth differs from a more generic, gold acquiring, fantasy character.

Looting of bodies for coin never happens in *The Lord of the Rings* or *The Hobbit*. As the Loremaster, you are quite within your rights to inflict Shadow points on characters who search the pockets of corpses for small change. It's kind to have an NPC show some disgust at the practice before handing out Shadow points, but it is definitely a tool to be used.

Goblins and Wargs simply do not carry around purses of coins to be harvested. They are despoilers, thugs and brutal enemies of all that is good. They simply don't have a use for coins.

Where a hoard of ancient gold is found, it can be celebrated and then buried for later, just as the Dwarves do in *The Hobbit* after encountering the Trolls. Gold can't be spent in the Wild and is very heavy indeed – just a thousand gold coins could easily weigh 75lbs. What the characters in that scene *do* take with them are *swords*.

In the Barrow-downs we witness another scene where characters could potentially fill their packs with coins, but take swords instead. And if a young Hobbit *were* to grab a handful of ancient coins, we can be sure of a couple of things. One, the coins would drive some aspect of the story, perhaps offering choices on what was more important – money or friendship, or asking what a young Hobbit is prepared to do to hang onto stolen gold. Two, those coins would surely become the stakes in a perilous scene, or be subject to a curse, or bring nothing but ill fortune.

It is worth noting that Bilbo *does* return from his quest with a relatively small amount of coin. He carries it back to the Shire on a pony in what is very clearly, in game terms, a Fellowship phase. Similarly, the horde of Troll coins buried by the Dwarves could be considered recovered in a Fellowship phase. It's there, but it's not the central theme.

Consider how Aragorn, Elrond, Galadriel, Glorfindel, Legolas or Gandalf would view the obsessive collecting of coins. Likewise, how would they react to a character trying to *pay them* gold coins. It would be an alien concept to them, and a sign of weakness, if not madness.

Long journeys transporting hoards of gold are very, very difficult, potentially dull, and – to keep true to the spirit of the novels – are best suited to the Fellowship phase, unless there's an opportunity to tell an engaging story.

So the pursuit of gold in itself isn't wholly *wrong* as a motivation for adventurers in Middle-earth, but if you are concerned with building an appropriate atmosphere, monetary wealth is best used as a plot driver, a stake to be lost, a moral question, a logistical problem, a potential source of Shadow points, a resource of lesser worth than friendship and hospitality, or just something that fades backwards into the Fellowship phase.

What Is Gold For?

We must away, ere break of day,
To claim our long-forgotten gold.

This is a worthwhile question to ask. *In character,* this varies. Gold has value in Lake-town, or Gondor, or Dale, where it can be invested in merchant caravans, or a stall in the markets there. In the Shire, vulgar displays of naked coin are surely frowned upon – witness the treatment of the avaricious Sackville-Baggins. A quiet, reserved comfort is to be admired. *Riches* are the road to ruin.

In Rohan, gold is a different matter entirely. The Rohirrim appear to live in a gift-giving culture, with wealth springing from service and fealty, rather than the ownership of gold coin. A character attempting to buy prize horses with coin in Rohan may be making a terrible mistake…

Beautiful things are admired by all in Middle-earth. Gold in the form of coin is admired by those of poor moral character.

Out of character, this is also a very important question. Traditionally in roleplaying games adventurers seek gold because gold buys better equipment, which protects them from damage, buys back HP in the form of healing potions, and buys extra capacity to inflict damage in the form of magical treasures. A character can even use it to gain levels and new powers. In Middle-earth, there are few places to buy such items, they are given as gifts or discovered in the Wild. If the story simply does not focus on these things, the acquisition of gold becomes much less significant.

In *Adventures in Middle-earth*, some of the most important assets that characters can collect are Sanctuaries and Patrons, rather than gold. Player-heroes are not independent of the world they live in, and gold alone cannot buy a safe haven in which to recover from the trials of the Road.

How to Approach Monetary Wealth in Adventures in Middle-earth

- Make gold realistically heavy so that it's not wise to carry too much – 1000 gold coins could easily weigh 75lbs. In a game with a lot of long distance travel, that's a lot of weight to carry!

- Don't provide a lot of coins as rewards – focus on other rewards, inspired by Middle-earth.

- Provide a clear purpose for larger quantities of wealth.

- Build trust in the Loremaster so that wealth can be pushed back into the Fellowship phase.

- Or you could change nothing. It's your game, your rules. Simply play as normal, assume every culture has shops of some kind that will exchange goods or services for coin.

Wondrous - Artefacts -

...an ancient horn, small but cunningly wrought all of fair silver with a baldric of green ...and there were set runes of great virtue.

Wondrous Artefacts possess characteristics that mortals wouldn't hesitate to call magical – cloaks that hide their wearers from observing eyes, war-horns capable of setting fear in the hearts of enemies and joy in the hearts of friends, staves blessed with virtues of finding and returning.

In *Adventures in Middle-earth*, Wondrous Artefacts are generally objects possessing an enchantment known as a Blessing. Most such artefacts have a single Blessing, though a second Blessing is possible. The rarest have a Greater Blessing.

> ### Too Many Wondrous Items!
> Wondrous Artefacts must be rare and unique to remain such. Just how unique wondrous items are in your campaign is a matter for you and your group to decide. They are extremely powerful, so very often less is more.

How Wondrous Artefacts Work
Wondrous Artefacts are items imbued with enchantments that exalt the natural characteristics of their owners; the more powerful in strength and will the bearer, the greater the Advantage derived from the artefact.

- A Blessing bestowed upon an artefact lets its bearer affect the result of all ability checks made using a specific skill. An object possessing two Blessings modifies the ability checks of two different skills. A Greater Blessing affects only a single skill, but with greatly enhanced effectiveness (see Artefact Bonus).

- Each Blessing may affect an ability check in two different ways: by enhancing the roll itself with an Artefact Bonus, and by letting the hero achieve a Magical Result by spending Inspiration and a variable number of their Hit Dice.

When a Wondrous Artefact is found, the Loremaster can either choose an object they have already created, or may decide to use the Blessings tables on page 131 to create one randomly.

For example, Trotter has found shelter from a storm in a ruined stone hut – to his eyes nothing more than a shepherd's refuge. The sanctuary is in fact a burial barrow, and the Hobbit finds himself sleeping fitfully among dry bones and old gold. In the morning, Trotter wakes to find a small pile of treasure, including a small ring – it is a magic ring, capable of sharpening the wits of those who wear it (conferring a Blessing to his Riddle skill).

Discovering the Blessings of an Artefact
When an artefact is first discovered, its capabilities may not be readily apparent. While it is possible that a hero discovers these while adventuring, they may learn about an item's Blessings by seeking out a knowledgeable Scholar or uncovering more through the Research Lore undertaking during a Fellowship phase. Additionally, the Loremaster might let a Player-hero guess the nature of a Blessing when the companion rolls a 20 while using a skill affected by the Blessing.

Artefact Bonus
The bearer of a Wondrous Artefact enjoys a bonus to all ability checks made using the corresponding skill.

- The Artefact Bonus is equal to the hero's Proficiency Bonus.

- If the artefact has been bestowed with a Greater Blessing, in addition to the Artefact Bonus, the hero *always* has Advantage on all ability checks made using the Blessed skill. Regardless of circumstances and difficulties, the hero retains Advantage.

For example, Trotter is trying to escape the enquiries of a nosy doorwarden in Esgaroth. He decides to put on his magic ring and befuddle the guard with his riddling.

Trotter already has proficiency in the Riddle skill, allowing him to add his Proficiency Bonus to his ability check, along with the addition of his Intelligence modifier, but the magic ring gives Trotter an additional Artefact Bonus equal to his Proficiency Bonus.

> ### Wondrous Tools
>
> There are various artisan's tools with Blessings that effectively work the same as Wondrous Artefacts. For example, a smith's hammer may have such a Blessing, causing him to add an Artefact Bonus to his ability checks made while forging.
>
> The items produced by Wondrous Tools are not magical per se, but their craftsmanship can be quite extraordinary: jewels that can catch the smallest trace of light in a room, maps that show near impossible levels of detail, cloth that feels like silk yet protects like thick leather, etc.

Magical Results

In addition to the Artefact Bonus described above, a Wondrous Artefact may also be used to directly affect the outcome of an ability check.

- A hero using a Wondrous Artefact may declare that they wish to spend Inspiration and a variable number of their Hit Dice in order to succeed at something "impossible" by turning a successful die roll made using the affected skill into a Magical Result. A Magical Result indicates that the outcome of the task did not only surpass all expectations, but achieved something beyond the hero's normal capabilities – in other words, a feat that could hardly be accomplished by the companion without magical aid.

The Loremaster decides how many Hit Dice are required for the Magical Result the player wants using the Magical Result Cost Chart as a guide. If the acting player is willing and able to spend the requisite cost, they are allowed to narrate the outcome of their ability check, disregarding what a reasonable success would normally look like. They are also encouraged to include elements reinforcing the magical nature of the event in their description – the stature of a companion may appear to grow, or their shadow to lengthen, an object may gleam or shine with an inner light, a staff may vibrate or even 'sing', the smoke from a pipe may form images, a musical instrument may conjure sounds not normally attributed to it, and so on and so forth.

Magical Results that directly seek to control another, such as by changing their perceptions, may grant the target(s) a saving throw and may be a Misdeed.

Trotter's Riddle roll has resulted in a success, but he is not satisfied, as secrecy is of the utmost importance. He declares to the Loremaster that he will invoke a Magical Result. Trotter chooses to describe how the doorwarden not only lets him go, but also soon forgets the Hobbit was ever there at all. This directly influences the will of another and is thus a large effect. The Loremaster says that Trotter

must spend Inspiration and seven Hit Dice. The guard gets a Wisdom saving throw and Trotter receives 2 Shadow points for the misdeed.

Magical Result Costs

Invoking a Magical Result always requires a character to spend Inspiration, along with a number of their Hit Dice.

This represents a hero using their spirit and will to direct the Wondrous Artefact into action.

Magical Result Cost Chart

Base Cost
Small Effect: 1 to 3 HD
Medium Effect: 3 to 5 HD
Large Effect: 7 to 10 HD
Number of Targets: +1 HD for each direct target beyond the first

Small Effect – The Magical Result directly aids the character or another, but mostly in a cosmetic way; e.g., they can do something somewhat mystical that enhances the effect of their already successful skill use.

Medium Effect – The Magical Result allows for divinatory knowledge that a character should not be able to know. The character can do something that would normally be exceedingly difficult if not impossible. In the case of some "impossible" Medium Effects, the Loremaster may declare that the ability check itself cannot be made unless the character commits to a Magical Result in advance of rolling. In such a case, if the check fails, both Inspiration and Hit Dice are still spent.

Large Effect – The Magical Result directly influences other beings, altering their perceptions or overthrowing their wills. The Magical Result is clearly, massively and unmistakably magical in nature. Large Effects that seek to control others generally grant a saving throw with a Difficulty Class equal to the companion's skill check result.

Examples of Magical Results

...Gandalf seemed suddenly to grow: he rose up, a great menacing shape like the monument of some ancient king of stone set upon a hill.

A hero might...

...run effortlessly along a slimy rope suspended over a stream (Acrobatics – Small).

...notice trembling webbing in the darkest gloom of Mirkwood indicating Spiders approaching stealthily (Perception – Small).

...give a dog detailed instructions on where to deliver a parcel (Animal Handling – Medium).

...cow a proud Elf-lord or a wild Beorning-chieftain with a look (Intimidation – Large).

...conceal an entire short sword through a methodical search by guards (Sleight of Hand – Medium – Several Targets).

...present herself eloquently and gracefully using a language she doesn't know (Traditions – Small).

...deduce the correct details of what occurred in a room hours before with little evidence (Investigation – Medium).

...locate a source of clean water in the barren waste of Mordor (Nature – Medium).

...free a patient of all pain, regardless of how grievous the hurt suffered (Medicine – Small).

...recall precise details of the great deeds of a Lord's ancestor that have been forgotten (History – Medium).

...follow Warg tracks in the woods on a night without a moon (Survival – Medium).

...discern the thoughts of someone as precisely as if the hero could read their mind (Insight – Large).

...talk a Stone-troll into believing that an imminent sunrise is still hours away (Deception – Large).

ADVENTURES IN MIDDLE-EARTH

...know about hidden facts, or occurrences happening in a far-away country (Lore – Medium).

...convince the Elvenking to borrow his most beloved white gem from his treasury (Persuasion – Large).

...derive useful information from a guarded conversation with a Dragon (Riddle – Large).

...know exactly which lair in the Misty Mountains a band of Orcs came from (Shadow-Lore – Medium).

...smoothly scale a sheer icy mountain side with bare hands (Athletics – Medium).

...make the things of which he sings so vivid they seem to appear in front of those who listen (Performance – Small – Multiple Targets).

...sneak unseen through a torch-lit hall full of cavorting Goblins (Stealth – Medium – Multiple Targets).

... get to her destination just at the right time, not too early, nor too late (Survival – Medium – Possibly climatically Large).

All Things Diminish

The lack of overt magic in Middle-earth may cause some Loremasters to question whether or not having Wondrous Artefacts about at all is a good idea. Yet, magic is not gone from the world, not yet at least. One option is to grant all Wondrous Artefacts a set number of uses, or secretly roll a d20 every time one is used. On a 1, the Wondrous Artefact is spent, its magic gone forever. Of course, the Player-hero wielding such a device is unlikely to know this has happened till the next time they try to draw on its power...

Not-so-Subtle Magic

"We're a bit suspicious round here of anything out of the way – uncanny, if you understand me; and we don't take to it all of a sudden."

A Magical Result is an outcome so remarkable and unusual that it may be unsettling to folk not used to such feats, or raise suspicion in individuals capable of recognising their otherworldy nature. Moreover, overt magical effects, even

when invoked for beneficial purposes, may sometimes be misinterpreted, as many associate supernatural occurrences to the working of sorcery. Characters that perform such feats in front of strangers may well find a cold reception, at best. Many cultures react to an individual engaging in the practice of such magics by regarding them on the Attitude Chart as Askance or worse.

Blessings Tables

If you have something in mind, you can choose which skill is affected by a Blessing (ordinary or greater), or you can determine it by rolling dice and using the charts below. The chart favours the more mental Ability Scores over the physical, both because there are more skills connected to those scores, but also because far more Wondrous Artefacts were made to enhance them. The first roll determines the Ability Score the skill is connected to, the second (if needed), chooses the skill. Repeat the procedure if the artefact has been bestowed with two different Blessings.

In brackets are listed options to help the Loremaster choose the type of object discovered, whether it is a ring, a cloak, a belt, or something else. If the same item possesses two Blessings, choose the type of object that seems more appropriate.

Other Wondrous Artefacts

'In Eregion long ago many Elven-rings were made, magic rings as you call them, and they were, of course, of various kinds: some more potent and some less.'

A Loremaster wishing to introduce magic items from other sources is certainly free to do so, but should keep a few things in mind. First, the magic of Middle-earth is generally very subtle – wands that shoot blasts of fire and lighting will likely feel a bit out of place.

When magic is overt, and frequently when it's harmful, it likely comes from Shadow. Second, any magic item that allows for swift travel by any means (such as teleporting) completely dispels the notion that travel takes a long time and invalidates the Journey system.

Player-heroes that really wish to fly to their destination should consider becoming friends with Gwaihir the Windlord, Lord of the Eagles. Last, anything that directly conjures something from nothing, or summons beings "from elsewhere" is likely to stand out as distinctly un-Middle-earth-like. With all that said, it's your *Adventures in Middle-earth* campaign. Do as you will!

Blessings Tables

1 Strength – Athletics (belt, boots, gloves, rope)

2-4 Dexterity (then roll a d6)
    1 Acrobatics (belt, gloves)
    2-3 Sleight of Hand (gloves, ring)
    4-6 Stealth (ring, cloak, shoes)

5-11 Intelligence (then roll another d20)
    1-3 History (book, scroll)
    4-6 Investigation (ring, circlet, staff)
    7-10 Lore (mirror, book, seeing stone)
    11-13 Nature (book, map, staff)
    14-16 Riddle (ring)
    17 Shadow-Lore (darkened gem, grim effigy)
    18-20 Traditions (ring, circlet)

12-16 Wisdom (then roll another d20)
    1-3 Animal Handling (ring)
    4-9 Insight (ring, circlet, collar)
    10-11 Medicine (unusual, as potions and salves quickly lose their virtue)
    12-17 Perception (ring, circlet, collar)
    18-20 Survival (boots, map, staff)

17-20 Charisma (then roll 1d4)
    1 Deception (ring, collar)
    2 Intimidation (belt, circlet, staff, weapon sheath, war-horn)
    3 Performance (ring, musical instrument)
    4 Persuasion (ring, cloak, circlet, collar)

Adventures in Middle-earth

Legendary - weapons and - armour

"These look like good blades," said the wizard... "when we can read the runes on them, we shall know more about them."

Weapons of extraordinary craftsmanship in *Adventures in Middle-earth* are generally covered using the rules for Cultural Heirlooms and armaments that have been Dwarf-forged. While those items could arguably be considered magical, their lineage can hardly be compared with that of swords forged in Gondolin for the Goblin-wars or the creations of the Dwarven smiths of old, before the coming of Smaug and the fall of Khazad-dûm. This section provides the Loremaster with rules and guidance for creating just such weapons and armour.

Most common folk never see such an extraordinary weapon in their lifetimes, much less wield one. Yet those heroes that dare stand against the Shadow of the East have a tendency to discover such arms when the time is right.

Creating Legendary Weapons and Armour

To design a magical sword or a wondrous coat of armour, the Loremaster must follow a 5-step process, making a number of choices based on their current campaign and the composition of their company of players:

1. Choose Item Type
2. Determine Craftsmanship
3. Select Banes (Elven or Númenórean weapons only)
4. Attribute Enchanted Qualities
5. Name the item

1. Choose Item Type

The first choice is the most important one: what are you designing exactly? Is it a weapon, or a piece of defensive gear, like a mail shirt or a shield? Remember to design items taking into consideration your company of heroes, or better still, with a precise character in mind; there is no place in your list of Magical Treasure for a wondrous shield that none of your players will be interested in using.

For example, the Loremaster is designing a famous weapon meant for Grimfast, a Beorning warden. The warrior uses a great spear as his primary weapon. The Loremaster selects a great spear as the item type.

Wondrous, Legendary and Healing items

2. Determine Craftsmanship

Choose Elven, Dwarven or Númenórean craftsmanship. The following paragraphs give some insight about which item types are most suited to a particular origin. Apart from defining in broad terms the history of an item, the choice of craftsmanship also determines whether a weapon should be attributed banes or not, and affects the choice of Enchanted Qualities (see Steps 3 and 4).

Elven Craftsmanship: The best enchanted weapons that may be found in forgotten hoards were made by Elvenwrights in Beleriand in the Elder Days, or in Eregion, for the wars against Sauron. Glamdring and Orcrist are good examples, not to mention Bilbo's (and later Frodo's) sword Sting.

- The Elves forged many famous long swords, short swords, daggers and enchanted spears. Other weapons or pieces of defensive war gear are not unknown, but more difficult to find.

Dwarven Craftsmanship: Many extraordinary swords, helms and suits of armour were wrought in Nogrod and Belegost by the Dwarves, either for use by their most renowned chieftains and champions, or as gifts to the greatest lords amongst Elves and Men. The works of Telchar, the smith of Nogrod, are particularly renowned: the sword Narsil and the Helm of Hador were among his chief creations.

- The smiths of Nogrod and Belegost crafted especially swords and axes, shields, helms and coats of armour.

Númenórean Craftsmanship: The weaponsmiths among the Men of Westernesse were taught by the Noldor in the making of swords, axe-blades, spearheads and knives. They acquired great skill, and put it to good use in forging many spell-bound weapons using strange metals. The barrow-blades Tom Bombadil gave the Hobbits were weapons of this sort; swords forged by the Númenóreans for their bitter wars against Carn Dûm in the Land of Angmar.

- The Men of Westernesse excelled in the making of many weapons, but rarely devoted themselves to the creation of suits of armour, recognising the greater ability of Dwarven smiths.

3. Select Banes

Bane weapons have been wrought to defeat a specific enemy. If the magical item is of Elven or Númenórean craftsmanship, then it must be attributed with one or more banes, as several of the special virtues that may be attributed to it are effective only against bane creatures (see overleaf).

Blades, spears and arrow-heads forged in Númenor may have been wound about with spells for the bane of two creature types.

- Choose two races from the following: Orcs, Trolls, Wolves, Evil Men, Undead.

Items crafted by the Elven-smiths of Beleriand or Eregion were generally created with only one type of enemy in mind.

- Choose one race from: Orcs, Wolves or Spiders.

Particularly ancient and rare Elven blades may have been wrought for the bane of the Enemy himself (or even *his* master of old), and as such be particularly dangerous to all his servants and minions.

4. Attribute Enchanted Qualities

Legendary Weapons and Armour are improved by their Enchanted Qualities, some of which are more clearly mystical than others, but all of which contribute to their might.

When you create a magical piece of war gear for your campaign, pick a selection of special characteristics, choosing from among those listed starting on page 135.

List the abilities in the order desired, keeping in mind that the Enchanted Qualities activate in the order in which they are listed according to the Proficiency Bonus of the item's bearer.

The mix and number of Enchanted Qualities attributed to an object determine how powerful the item is.

- Generally, the Loremaster should apply a total maximum of 3 Enchanted Qualities to a famous weapon or piece of defensive gear.

133

Note that a number of the Enchanted Qualities are enhanced versions of others in the listing. Enchanted Qualities sharing a common descriptor cannot be attributed to the same item (a Grievous sword cannot be given the Superior Grievous Enchanted Quality, for example). A few Enchanted Qualities also have a listed prerequisite requiring a different Enchanted Quality that must be taken first. Finally, when designing an Elven or Númenórean weapon you should be sure to bestow upon it at least one Enchanted Quality that possesses the Bane requirement.

5. Name the Item

Wondrous Artefacts rarely possess proper names. They are usually named after their maker or their most famous owner (*The Necklace of Girion, The Arkenstone of Thrain, The Phial of Galadriel*). On the contrary, Legendary Weapons and Armour often have a name, or even more than one, if the item is known by different folks.

When the Loremaster creates a piece of war gear, they should take the time to create an appropriate name, along with its historical notes. The name of an item can be revealed to its bearer who researches it or consults a Scholar or Sage (see pg 72) about it. A player is, of course, free to name an item themselves – much as Bilbo did with Sting – either because the object does not have a known name or the companion isn't interested in discovering it.

Bane Weapons

"...what they are: work of Westernesse, wound about with spells for the bane of Mordor."

In addition to being more effective against the types of creatures they were crafted to defeat, bane weapons are destructive to elements connected to the creatures that are the object of the bane and would immediately be recognised as such by them.

For example, Orcs would not dare touch a blade forged for the bane of their kind, and a sword created for the destruction of Giant Spiders would easily cut through the thickest of their webs without becoming ensnared.

How Legendary Weapons and Armour Work

Most heroes are unlikely to ever bear more than one or two such items at most in their entire adventuring careers; fortunately, the power of such items waxes with the might of the heroes that wield them.

When a companion finds a Legendary Weapon or Armour, the item displays only the characteristics of the *first* Enchanted Quality listed in its entry in the Loremaster's Magical Treasure index. The remaining features are considered 'dormant' until activated as described below.

Discovering Qualities

It is said that valour needs first strength, and then a weapon: as a companion grows in heroic stature, the more powerful their Legendary Weapons or Armour become.

- In general, a Legendary Weapon or Armour can only have a number of activated Enchanted Qualities equal to half its bearer's Proficiency Bonus, rounded up.

- As new Enchanted Qualities are revealed in a Legendary Weapon or Armour, they are unlocked in the order listed on the Magical Treasure Index.

Effectively, this means 1 Enchanted Quality for a hero levels 1-4, 2 Enchanted Qualities from levels 5-12, and 3 Enchanted Qualities from level 13 on.

When a hero bearing a Legendary Weapon or Armour reaches a character level where they are eligible to activate a new Enchanted Quality, or discovers such an item when they are already of sufficient level to have activated more than the first Enchanted Quality, the new ability may automatically activate at the Loremaster's discretion; however, neither the character (nor the player) will be aware of exactly what new ability has activated until they seek out a Scholar who can help them understand some of the history and powers of their possession.

For example, the Bride recently found the Raven Axe of Arnor in a Troll's hoard while exploring the Ettenmoors. It displayed its first Enchanted Quality – Raging – as soon as she found it. In a subsequent Fellowship phase she reached 5th level, and soon noted that her axe seemed lighter (and deadlier!) in her hands. After consulting with a Master Scholar, she discovers that the Raven Axe's next Enchanted Quality – Superior Fell – is now activated.

Some Enchanted Qualities may require a character to explicitly learn how to use them before they can be invoked, necessitating further research into old Lore about the Legendary item in question.

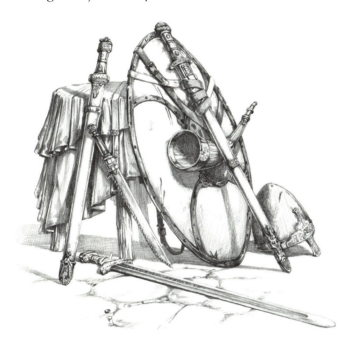

Enchanted Qualities

There was a flash like flame and the helm burst asunder. The orc fell with cloven head.

All the virtues described below set the craftsmanship of an item apart from any other. The Enchanted Quality of the object may be the result of ancient spells or graven runes, or it may be due to the innate properties of the material used for its crafting, or a combination of all such elements.

Often, the magical power of the object makes the item gleam with an unnatural light or appear as if burning with an enchanted flame, but in other cases the magical quality is more discreet, if at all noticeable. The Loremaster is encouraged to embellish the description of each Legendary Weapon or Armour with appropriately epic details.

The text of each Enchanted Quality includes any requirement that the enhanced object must satisfy for the quality to be applied to it. Enchanted Qualities indicating a specific craftsmanship (Elven, Dwarven or Númenórean) exemplify the features of war gear created by weaponsmiths and armourers belonging to that race.

All Enchanted Qualities are unique, meaning that they can only be applied once to the same item; unless directly stated otherwise, the properties of all Enchanted Qualities stack with one another.

- Loremasters should keep in mind that they should apply a maximum of 3 Enchanted Qualities to a Legendary Weapon or Armour.

Ancient Close Fitting
Craftsmanship: Elven, Dwarven
Item: Armour

This Quality enhances the AC rating of an item by +2. Aditionally once per short or long rest, if your Proficiency Bonus is +4 or more after an enemy has hit you, but before damage is rolled, you can declare that the blow missed you instead.

Ancient Cunning Make
Craftsmanship: Elven, Dwarven
Item: Armour

This Quality enhances the AC rating of this armour by +1. Reduce this armour's weight to a quarter of the normal. All Strength Requirements are waved, and its user no longer suffers Disadvantage on Stealth checks. Additionally, its wearer is immune to critical hits, taking only normal damage on such a strike.

Biting Dart
Craftsmanship: Elven
Item: Ranged weapon
Special: Bane

When you attack a bane creature using a ranged weapon possessing this Enchanted Quality, you must make two separate attack rolls. If you hit your target with both attacks, you inflict damage for both; however, your attack goes astray entirely if either roll misses. When you would have Advantage on the rolls, you instead roll 4 d20s and keep the two best.

Cleaving
Craftsmanship: Any
Item: Close combat weapon

When you successfully hit your target with a weapon blessed by this Enchanted Quality, you automatically deal an additional amount of damage equal to your Proficiency Bonus to another enemy creature engaging you in combat.

Close-fitting
Craftsmanship: Any
Item: Armour

Increase the AC of this armour by 2.

Crushing
Craftsmanship: Any
Item: Close combat weapon

This weapon deals an additional number of hit points equal to three times your Proficiency Bonus on your first successful attack. You must take a short or long rest before using this quality again.

Cunning Make
Craftsmanship: Any
Item: Armour or shield

This Quality enhances the AC rating of this armour or shield by +1. Halve this armour's weight. Strength Requirements are lowered by 3, and its user no longer suffers Disadvantage on Stealth checks.

Fell
Craftsmanship: Any
Item: Any weapon

Add +2 to all attack rolls with this weapon.

Flame of Hope
Craftsmanship: Dwarven
Item: Close combat weapon

You may take an action to hold a weapon with this Enchanted Quality aloft or similarly brandish it to rally your comrades. All of your allies within 30 feet lose the Frightened condition, get back 1d6 + your Proficiency Bonus in hit points, and gain Inspiration. You must take a long rest before you can invoke this ability again.

Foe-slaying
Craftsmanship: Elven, Númenórean
Item: Close combat weapon
Special: Bane

When you attack a bane creature, this Quality extends the critical range of your weapon by a number equal to half your Proficiency Bonus, rounded up. For example, say a 8th level Scholar bore a broadsword with this Enchanted Quality activated. With a Proficiency Bonus of +3, she extends her critical range by 2. Thus, her broadsword causes a critical on a roll of 18, 19, or 20.

Gleam of Terror
Craftsmanship: Dwarven
Item: Close combat weapon

A weapon with this Quality inspires fear in the hearts of enemies. You may take an action to force a number of creatures of your choice, up to your Wisdom modifier (minimum 1), within 30 feet of you to succeed at a Wisdom saving throw equal to a Difficulty Class of 15 + your Proficiency Bonus or become Frightened of you.

While Frightened in this way, a creature must spend its turns trying to move as far away from you as it can, and it can't willingly move to a space within 30 feet of you. It also can't take reactions. For its action, it can use only the Dash action or try to escape from an effect that prevents it from moving. If it has nowhere it can move, the creature can use the Dodge action. At the end of each of its turns, a creature can repeat the saving throw, ending the effect on itself on a success. This ability cannot be used again until you have taken a short or long rest.

Grievous
Craftsmanship: Any
Item: Any weapon

This Quality adds 2 (1d4) bonus damage to all damage rolls made with this weapon. This bonus damage is doubled as normal on a critical hit.

Keen
Craftsmanship: Any
Item: Any weapon

This weapon adds 1 to the range on which it can score a critical hit. (Without any other factors, this weapon would score criticals on both 19 and 20.)

Luminescence
Craftsmanship: Elven
Item: Close combat weapon
Special: Bane

This Quality makes the weapon's blade shine with a pale, cold light when a bane creature is within a distance equal to 30 feet times your Proficiency Bonus. You and your companions cannot be surprised by such creatures. Additionally, you have a +4 Initiative bonus if you encounter any bane creatures when so forewarned.

Mithril Armour
Craftsmanship: Dwarven
Item: Armour
Special: Requires Cunning Make or Ancient Cunning Make

This Quality adds a further +2 bonus to this armour's AC. Additionally, you have resistance to piercing and slashing damage.

Raging
Craftsmanship: Elven, Númenórean
Item: Close combat weapon
Special: Bane

A weapon graced by this Enchanted Quality deals a number of hit points in damage equal to your Proficiency Bonus to an attacked bane creature even on missed attack rolls.

Reinforced
Craftsmanship: Any
Item: Shield

+1 AC bonus to the standard Armour Class this shield normally provides. Additionally, this shield cannot be shattered or smashed by normal means.

Rune-scored Armour
Craftsmanship: Dwarven
Item: Armour

This Enchanted Quality enhances the AC rating of this armour by +3.

Rune-scored Shield
Craftsmanship: Dwarven
Item: Shield
Special: Requires Reinforced or Superior Reinforced

Gain a +1 bonus to the standard Armour Class this shield normally provides. Additionally, during the course of a battle, when an opponent misses striking you due to the Armour Class bonus provided by your shield, you may spend Inspiration and 3 Hit Dice to shatter their weapon. This does not work on Legendary Weapons but will automatically disarm them.

Runes of Victory
Craftsmanship: Dwarven, Elven
Item: Any weapon

While bearing a weapon with this Enchanted Quality you gain a +1 bonus to all saving throws. When you attack with this weapon, a roll of 1 becomes a critical hit instead of an automatic failure. Factors that increase the critical hit range expand the range from 20 as normal. For example, a weapon with Keen and Runes of Victory scores a critical hit on a 1, 19, and 20.

Superior Fell
Craftsmanship: Dwarven, Númenórean
Item: Any weapon
Special: Bane (if Númenórean)

If this weapon is of Dwarven craftsmanship, its bonus to attack and damage rolls is equal to half its bearer's Proficiency Bonus, rounded up. If the weapon is of Númenórean craftsmanship it grants a +1 bonus for attack and damage rolls. Against a bane creature, the bonus increases to be equal to half its bearer's Proficiency Bonus, rounded up.

Superior Grievous
Craftsmanship: Elven, Númenórean
Item: Any weapon
Special: Bane (if Númenórean)

If this item is of Elven craftsmanship, it adds a bonus to all damage rolls equal to 2 (1d4) plus half of its bearer's Proficiency bonus, rounded up. For Númenórean weapons, this bonus is applied for bane creatures only. When you score a critical hit, the bonus die is doubled as normal and then add your full Proficiency bonus.

Superior Keen
Craftsmanship: Dwarven, Elven
Item: Any weapon

This weapon adds 2 to the range on which it can score a critical hit. (Without any other factors, this weapon would score criticals on 18, 19, and 20.)

Superior Reinforced
Craftsmanship: Any
Item: Shield

Gain a +2 bonus to the standard Armour Class this shield normally provides. Additionally, if your Proficiency Bonus is +4 or more, once per combat after an enemy has hit you, but before damage is rolled, you can declare that the blow clanged off your shield without harming you. Finally, this shield cannot be smashed by any means.

Sure Shot
Craftsmanship: Any
Item: Ranged weapon

The bearer of a weapon with this Enchanted Quality always enjoys a clean shot, even shooting against a strong wind or when his target is protected by darkness. The wielder never suffers Disadvantage on ranged attacks and ignores all negative attack roll modifiers due to sources of hindrance.

Warding-spell
Craftsmanship: Elven, Númenórean
Item: Armour, shield, any close combat weapon
Special: Bane

When you are fighting against a bane creature, an item bestowed with such an Enchanted Quality gives you a bonus to your Armour Class equal to your Wisdom modifier or half of your Proficiency Bonus (rounded down), whichever is lower.

> ### Further Weapons and Armour of Extraordinary Craftsmanship
> The Loremaster may wish to provide their players with a chance to find additional weapons and armour that do not quite qualify for the status of Legendary, but are still worthy finds for low level characters. Creating cannily crafted weapons or armour that confer a +1 bonus is simplicity itself. Whether these have survived from long ages past when craftspeople knew better the making of things, or are imbued with a little magic of the Elves is up to the Loremaster to decide.

Magical
- Healing -

Healing in Middle-earth is a rare and wondrous thing. It is most often connected to powerful individuals, like Elrond or Aragorn, or places like the Nimrodel River. Instant healing is rare, and this makes wounds all the more significant in the game. Characters cannot charge into battle, pausing to swig from a healing potion if they happen to be hurt. Keeping healing at a low level of availability adds to the atmosphere of peril. With the structure of the Adventuring and Fellowship phases comes a clear time to be out in the world questing and testing your mettle, and a time to rest and recover.

However, a Loremaster may find they have need of helping their players with a chance to restore some hit points, or remove levels of Exhaustion in a pinch. Or perhaps your group's play style may simply be invigorated by having a greater ability to heal wounds in the Wild.

The following are a list of Middle-earth appropriate sources of healing and recovery.

Herbs, Potions and Salves

See page 154 of the *Player's Guide* for details of Athelas, Hagweed, Kingcup, Reedmace, Shadow-thorn and Water-lily.

Lembas

A rare and wonderful food, the making of which is known only to the Elves. It is only gifted to those who are not Elves in times of great need, and is a generous gift. Wrapped in leaves, one cake of Lembas removes 1 level of Exhaustion and restores 1d6 hit points per level of the creature consuming it.

Waters of Nimrodel

A flask containing the water of this river can heal the sick and restore the weary. One draught of the Waters of Nimrodel removes 1d2 levels of Exhaustion and restores 1d4 hit points per level of the creature consuming it.

Miruvor

An exceptionally rare and precious cordial from Rivendell. Small quantities of Miruvor may be gifted by Elrond, or the other powerful Elves of Imladris, in times of great need. It cannot be bought. A small mouthful removes 1d4 levels of Exhaustion and returns 1 Hit Die.

magic in middle-earth

the affairs of wizards

Dearest Thranduil,

But a few short moons have passed since our last meeting. Much thought have I spent on the matters we six discussed. I would once again call upon your better judgement - you are doubtless the coolest head of the council, and know the business of ruling your own house and the affairs of it better than any of us. Understand you have my full support in your desire to look to your own borders, and to remain strong within them. Wilder voices would have us change our ways and abandon reason in favour of risk, where there is no need. Hold fast, dear Lord of the Forest. We need not do more than we are already doing to ensure peace everlasting. Let us not endanger the peace we have by seeking out problems. Let us secure what we have.

Your friend,

Saruman

The Magic of - Middle-earth -

"For this is what your folk would call magic, I believe; though I do not understand clearly what they mean; and they seem also to use the same word of the deceits of the Enemy. But this, if you will, is the magic of Galadriel. Did you not say you wanted to see Elf-Magic?"

Magic in Middle-earth is subtle and hard to define. What is natural and unremarkable to one culture is wondrous and supernatural to another. Hobbits can hide so quickly it is as though they disappear; Elves weave ropes and cloaks that seem to change their colour; Dwarves can smith wondrous weapons. Even mortal Men have their gifts – for all the strength of the Elves of old, none of them won a Silmaril as did Beren, or slew a dragon as did Túrin.

While there is, as Sam put it, "magic like what it tells of in old tales" in Middle-earth, most magic is buried deep in the earth and bones of the people. There is also the deceits and malignant sorcery of the Enemy.

So, while magic is everywhere in Middle-earth, it is usually subtle, or manifests as part of the natural world. Gandalf kindles pinecones instead of throwing fireballs; Galadriel can see into the souls of the Fellowship, and Saruman bewitches with his speech. It's not overt spell-slinging like in other fantasy games, but Middle-earth definitely is not a low-magic setting.

Meddling in the Affairs of Wizards

"I once knew every spell in all the tongues of Elves or Men or Orcs that was ever used for such a purpose."

The Wizards – Gandalf, Saruman, Radagast, and the unseen Blue Wizards – are obviously the best-known users of magic in the tales of the Third Age. It must be remembered, though, that those wizards, the Istari, were not human – they were spirits sent from the Uttermost West and cloaked in flesh. Their power, and the power of other key figures like Galadriel or Elrond, was inherent to them. Gandalf did not study magic to learn new spells; he was given certain authority over the physical and spiritual substance of the world by his place in creation.

At the same time, it's clear that some magic can be learned, and that inherent power is not fixed. The Mouth of Sauron "learned great sorcery" in the service of the Dark Tower.

The works of the Númenóreans of old, from the *Palantíri* to the unbreakable stone of Orthanc, were clearly enchanted. Denethor's power came partly from his study of the lore of Númenor, and partly from his own strength of will.

In game terms, 'magic' is not a field of study, but a collection of strange supernatural gifts and permissions. Dwarves can create perfectly hidden doors, and no human or Elf could ever learn that art. The Elves can speak to the stones and to the trees, and this is not a talent that can be taught. The Player-heroes will never find a book describing how to brew their own Ent-draughts, any more than they could take root in the living soil and drink deep with their toes.

Creating Your Own Magic

In your campaign, you may wish to include supernatural creatures and forces of your own devising that are not directly drawn from the books. To maintain the correct Tolkien atmosphere when presenting magic, your creations should fall into one of the following categories:

- **Fairy-tale Enchantment:** Middle-earth has talking animals, enchanted clothes that fasten themselves, magical toys, and enchanted fireworks. It has streams that bring forgetfulness, and helpful sprites that are summoned by a song. If a magical idea would fit in a fairy story (or a Biblical tale), it might also be a good fit for Middle-earth.

- **Oaths and Curses:** The Dead Men of Dunharrow were held by an oath; prophecies attended the death of the Lord of the Nazgûl and the return of the king to Minas Tirith. Even Gollum's death was the work of fateful words – Gandalf reckoned that Gollum had "something to do before the end" and Frodo warned that he could use the Ring to command Sméagol to "leap from a precipice or to cast yourself into the fire". Look for words that can have greater significance placed on them.

- **Items Have Power:** Magic items are much more common in Middle-earth than spells. The Ring is an obvious example, but there are also magic swords, armour, staffs, phials, scrolls, doors, statues, stones, cloaks, ropes… In general, magic that affects the world should have a physical component or focus.

- **The Unseen World:** There is a spirit world that cannot be perceived by most people. Certain spirits exist wholly in that spiritual realm, and must cloak themselves in flesh or cloth to be visible. Those who have considerable strength of spirit are visible on both sides. At times, this spiritual world spills over into the physical – witness how Gandalf seems to grow or shrink in stature, or how the terror of the wraiths has nothing to do with the physical danger they pose.

- **Necromancy:** Sauron disguised himself as the Necromancer for centuries, and had many evil spirits and wights in his service. Undead spirits and the unquiet dead are some of the most overtly supernatural foes encountered in Tolkien's works.

- **Names & Songs:** Names have power in Middle-earth. Calling on Elbereth dismays the Nazgûl at Weathertop; speaking the Black Speech in Rivendell darkens the skies. Invoking magic often involves calling on a thing by name. Songs, too, have great power – a song is more fitting to Middle-earth magic than any chant or ritual.

OPTIONS FOR ADDING MAGIC

When considering the mechanics of magic in your game, pick one of the following options.

Default

As written, the *Adventures in Middle-earth* rules have magical effects buried within them in a way that mirrors the text of the novels. There are a few overt supernatural abilities, like Elf-Magic or Broken Spells, and there are many others that hint at miraculous intervention without being obviously supernatural. A Ranger with Royalty Revealed can heal their companions and turn away foes, but that doesn't mean the companions' wounds actually close, or that the enemies vanish into thin air. All the abilities given in the rules are drawn directly from the novels.

Limited

Loremasters who want to integrate regular OGL classes like Wizards and Clerics in Middle-earth, but still want to stay true to the tone of the books, can do so. Many OGL spells can be described in the subtle, coincidental, earthy fashion needed for Middle-earth magic. Do away with flashy spells, and focus on ones that fit with the default approach. The Bard and Druid spell lists are generally more suitable to Middle-earth than the Cleric or Wizard lists, but each list has many spells that fit perfectly with Tolkien's world (and many that don't!). See the table opposite for a list of suitable spells. Instead of material components, insist that the player describe how the spell functions differently each time it is cast. Encourage players to be creative and to integrate their magic into the world. Spellcasting is less about chanting and magical gestures, and more about adding magic to the story. For example, one can imagine Gildor the Elf casting *heroes' feast* when he meets the Hobbits in the Shire, or Galadriel casting *scrying* when looking in her mirror. In both cases, though, the magic is a natural part of their actions – Gildor doesn't stop and incant a spell. He simply invites the Hobbits for a meal, and lo! It's a magical, impossibly delicious meal that seems to spring from nowhere.

Reskinning

A middle-ground option is to allow the use of all spells, but only if the players can come up with a suitable justification or description. *Wind walk*, for example, is much too high-fantasy for Middle-earth, where people don't turn into wisps of cloud – but describe it as being carried by an Eagle, and it fits much better. Emphasise commanding and changing the natural world instead of conjuring things out of nothing – a Middle-earth *web* spell might involve existing spider-webs becoming thicker, instead of the wizard shooting a sticky ball of goo.

A *slow* spell should be described as a sickening blight that makes limbs heavy and clumsy, not a magical field that changes the flow of time. A *sleet storm* should appear to be a natural weather effect that becomes briefly more intense, like the storm on Caradhras. Be careful – spells that allow for swift travel, like *teleport*, can make journeys pointless.

Open

A final option is to make the game your own – if your vision of Middle-earth involves *fireball*, and if Sam's fear that Gandalf would *polymorph* him into a spotted toad wasn't unfounded, then use OGL magic freely. The tales of Elder Days speak of wonders that are undreamt-of in the Third Age.

Unfettered magic will remove many of the challenges in the game unless you apply it to the opposition too, of course, so give Orcs and other adversaries their own shamans and sorcerers to level the playing field.

Revealed to Them

"If there are any to see, then I at least am revealed to them," he said, "I have written Gandalf is here in signs that all can read from Rivendell to the mouths of Anduin."

Using magic in Middle-earth draws the attention of the Lidless Eye of Sauron. In campaigns set prior to the year 2951 of the Third Age, using magic simply attracts the attention of local enemies who can sense it (wraiths, servants of the Shadow, certain Spiders and worse things). After Sauron declares himself in Mordor and his gaze once more roves over the West, then any use of magic may be spotted by the Dark Tower, and the Enemy will doubtless dispatch his minions to investigate and hunt down such a threat.

List of Middle-earth Appropriate Spells

- Aid
- Alarm
- Animal Messenger
- Antipathy/Sympathy
- Arcane Eye
- Arcane Lock
- Arcanist's Magical Aura
- Augury
- Awaken
- Bane
- Barkskin
- Beacon of Hope
- Bestow Curse
- Bless
- Blight
- Blindness/Deafness
- Blur
- Call Lightning
- Calm Emotions
- Charm Person
- Clairvoyance
- Command
- Commune
- Commune with Nature
- Comprehend Languages
- Confusion
- Continual Flame
- Control Water
- Control Weather
- Cure Wounds
- Dancing Lights
- Darkness
- Darkvision
- Daylight
- Death Ward
- Detect Evil and Good
- Detect Thoughts
- Disguise Self
- Dispel Evil and Good
- Dispel Magic
- Divination
- Divine Favour
- Divine Word
- Dominate Beast
- Dominate Monster
- Dominate Person
- Dream
- Earthquake
- Enhance Ability
- Entangle
- Enthrall
- Expeditious Retreat
- Eyebite
- Fear
- Feeblemind
- Find the Path
- Find Traps
- Fog Cloud
- Foresight
- Freedom of Movement
- Geas
- Gentle Repose
- Glibness
- Greater Restoration
- Guidance
- Gust of Wind
- Hallow
- Haste
- Heal
- Healing Word
- Heroes' Feast
- Heroism
- Hold Monster
- Hold Person
- Holy Aura
- Invisibility
- Knock
- Legend Lore
- Lesser Restoration
- Light
- Locate Animals or Plants
- Locate Creature
- Locate Object
- Longstrider
- Mage Armour
- Magic Weapon
- Mass Cure Wounds
- Mass Heal
- Mass Healing Word
- Mass Suggestion
- Mending
- Message
- Minor Illusion
- Pass Without Trace
- Plant Growth
- Prayer of Healing
- Produce Flame
- Protection from Evil and Good
- Protection from Poison
- Purify Food and Drink
- Remove Curse
- Resistance
- Revivify
- Sanctuary
- Scrying
- See Invisibility
- Sending
- Shillelagh
- Sleep
- Sleet Storm
- Slow
- Speak with Animals
- Speak with Plants
- Suggestion
- Sunbeam
- Thaumaturgy
- Tongues
- True Seeing
- True Strike
- Warding Bond
- Zone of Truth

the fellowship phase

the time that is given us

Dearest Bilbo,

My apologies for such a lengthy lapse of correspondence. I am in Lake-town at last! The new town grows day by day, on great tree trunks driven into the lakebed, just as you described. What sights I have seen, such hardships we have endured, such battles fought. And won!

Scarce had we set foot in Lake-town than we received a commission from King Bard's agents, and we set off almost immediately into the wild to bring supplies to one of his survey camps in the Waste. I cannot wait to see you again and regale you with all my tales. I feel that I have become quite the adventurer! But for now I must finish this letter quickly, for tonight we feast and celebrate our victories in the Waste!

Yours in good spirits,

Celandine Took

the fellowship - phase -

"Yes, I am here. And you are lucky to be here too after all the absurd things you've done since you left home."

The Fellowship phase is something unique to *Adventures in Middle-earth* among OGL games. It is a time where the Loremaster takes a back seat, and the players take much more control of the narrative of the game. It is also a time when characters can develop their abilities, resources and connections within the world of Middle-earth.

The Fellowship phase doesn't measure time in the way the Adventuring phase does. It is a summary of events, picking out key highlights of the Player-heroes' actions, what undertakings they make and in general how they pass the time between adventures.

Despite this being the players' time to direct the story as they narrate what their heroes are doing for the duration of the phase, the Loremaster still has a job to do: steering the discussion, making sure everyone gets a turn to speak and a chance to do what they would like to do. This is especially important if the company decides to spend the Fellowship phase together in one place. In these cases, the order of proceedings might not be clear, and within a player group there is usually a range of personalities and confidence levels. To make sure everyone enjoys the Fellowship phase, the Loremaster should ensure everyone gets a bit of the spotlight. It is a terrible shame if a new Adventuring phase begins and a player hasn't had a chance to expand on their exploits during the Fellowship phase.

As Loremaster it's your job to facilitate a successful Fellowship phase, helping the players get their turn and make sensible choices together that build the atmosphere and connection to the setting. Every undertaking the players make should be woven into a broader story, so the players gain a sense of a changing developing world and their place in it. They should get a sense that their choices matter and affect the campaign unfolding around them.

The Fellowship phase shouldn't be about making hard and fast choices in the face of time pressure. Let the conversation flow, ask questions, and let the company formulate the best possible story for what they get up to.

If They Split Up

Player-heroes have the choice to disband their fellowship and head off home for the duration of the Fellowship phase. Everyone will need a bit of time with the *Player's*

Guide choosing what they want to achieve, and you should also make them aware of the additional choices presented in this Guide if you choose to use them.

While the Loremaster is used to proactively creating a coherent story, players often do less of this kind of creativity. They can be more prepared to react to situations arising, rather than prompting the narrative. Give them a chance to make their choices, and the story that accompanies it.

Each player should get an equal amount of time to tell their tale. Some players are naturally given to more florid description, and so long as everyone gets a turn this is all for the good. But that ebullience shouldn't make anyone else feel inadequate. Try to actively help less confident players with suggestions and additions that bind them into the setting. Everyone should feel able to throw suggestions into the pot to make the story, but no one voice should be allowed to dominate. Similarly, some players are simply more comfortable with a concise summary of what undertaking they made and a simple description related to that. They may not wish to elaborate, and that is a perfectly acceptable way to play.

Keeping all this on an even keel can be especially important if there is an imbalance of Middle-earth knowledge among your players. Those who know a lot about the setting may take the opportunity to show that off, which can be a great asset to any campaign. However, if it becomes too much, it is important to remind everyone that this kind of Fellowship phase is a personal affair, and a great many Player-heroes can take small, personal actions and still be telling an important tale. That a quiet Hobbit gardener may simply return to her beloved Shire and weed the herb garden for the autumn and winter, and return renewed and more capable is just as significant to their character as a mighty soldier of Minas Tirith returning to their city for a tour of duty in the ruins of Osgiliath.

If They Stay Together

A hunted man sometimes wearies of distrust and longs for friendship.

There is much to be gained by a company of Player-heroes remaining together. They can discover more experiences at a single location, giving more time for the telling of their joint endeavours. A place like Lake-town or Rivendell is full of sights and sounds that can be explored in summary in the Fellowship phase. Again, it is possible that certain players may try to dominate proceedings. Keep an eye out for it, and be sure to ask less vocal players how their Player-hero spends their time, how they feel and what contribution their Player-hero makes to the tale. Be a fair arbiter of such social imbalances and it will make your games all the more enjoyable for everyone.

Ending a Fellowship Phase

Once everyone has made their choices and told their story, the Fellowship phase ends. It is most common for the company to meet again at a Sanctuary they have opened, or which is open to them at the start of a game.

As suggested in the *Player's Guide*, it is well worth placing the Fellowship phase at the end of a play session. This gives you a chance to absorb what the players have chosen to do and make any adjustments to your next adventure in whatever way feels appropriate. You may even get sufficient plot hooks to generate the next adventure entirely based on what the company do during a Fellowship phase. Or perhaps some NPCs will be overheard talking about things that came up in the last Fellowship phase. It is recommended that, at the very least, you try to work some reflection of the Fellowship phase into the next Adventuring phase. This gives the players the feeling they are part of Middle-earth, not merely tourists who see the sights, but don't affect events.

A truly clever Loremaster can use the Fellowship phase to involve the company and their choices in key events in the story of the Third Age. The roots of many of the major events that occur happen "off stage", and it is possible to take advantage of this. For example, where does Elrond get his information in the run up to forming the Fellowship of the Ring? Where does Saruman get his knowledge of the Shire? What convinces Legolas to accept the mission to travel to Rivendell? A well managed Fellowship phase can steer the company to make satisfying discoveries or indeed become the instruments behind such events. What were the company doing while important events were occurring near them? The Tale of Years on page 21 of this volume can provide ample inspiration.

Because Fellowship phases occur outside of direct adventuring time with its direct, roleplayed dialogue, this is an opportunity to update your company on the actions of the great and the good of Middle-earth. They can meet familiar characters at an appropriate Sanctuary, and there is the opportunity to set up later events.

Alternatively you may choose to simply let your players take to the stage and drive the narrative themselves, without any sowing of seeds or intervention on your part. This too is a thoroughly enjoyable way to play. It is your game to play as you see fit.

> ### Gaining Inspiration as the Loremaster
> You can award yourself Inspiration by going back to the books and reading up on the places that would be considered Sanctuaries in *Adventures in Middle-earth*. What happens at Rivendell? Or Beorn's House? The keys to making the events of your game feel a part of Middle-earth are all to be found in the texts. They are a never-ending source of surprises and inspirational discoveries, and you should keep them close.

How Long Is a Fellowship Phase?

This is entirely up to you, the Loremaster. It doesn't have to be a set amount of time. It could credibly represent the passing of a year or two, with your Player-heroes living out their everyday lives for a sustained period, only coming together again when adventure calls. Or it could be much shorter: who knows what a person can achieve in two weeks in the hallowed halls of Rivendell, surrounded by ancient wisdom, laughter and songs of great age? Or how a deep strength is slowly gathered in the turning seasons in the Vales of Anduin?

You may well choose to have the Fellowship phase represent the end of the adventuring season and the winter months passed at the hearth. This makes good sense, and has an appropriate storybook charm, but it is all at your discretion. You are perfectly entitled to have more than one Fellowship phase in a given year.

Never underestimate the power of setting up a precedent and then breaking it. Have your company retire for the winter, let them relax into a season of recovery and good eating for their first Fellowship phase, and then when they settle into that a second time, drive them out on an unexpected wintery adventure! It will be all the more meaningful if expectations are subverted.

Experience Points

There are many ways and times in which a Loremaster may choose to award experience points. While the precise system you choose is up to you, and the topic is beyond the scope of this supplement, the beginning of a Fellowship phase is an ideal time to make major XP awards to your Player-heroes, as they complete a season of adventure and retire to rest and recuperate, and undertake such activities considered outside adventuring.

You may want to refrain from awarding XP during an Adventuring phase and award it instead at the beginning of the Fellowship phase, so that Player-heroes are seen to develop in strength of arms and ability during their time away from the Road.

- SANCTUARIES -

"Very good: I will go east, and I will make for Rivendell. I will take Sam to visit the Elves; he will be delighted."

Sanctuaries in *Adventures in Middle-earth* are very important places. Before you have some experience with the game, it can be hard to fully understand why – they sound good, certainly, but what are the mechanical underpinnings that make them significant?

> ### What Sanctuaries Do
> - They are one of two stated places (the other being 'home') that allow characters to recover all hit dice.
> - They are a place where persistent conditions can be removed.
> - They are a location in which the company may remain together throughout the Fellowship phase.
> - They allow Fellowship phase undertakings unique to that sanctuary.
> - They allow the Open Virtue undertaking.
> - At the beginning of every Adventuring phase, the company are either already at or gather at a Sanctuary.
> - Sanctuaries provide a focus for a shared story.

RECOVERY

Page 199 of the *Adventures in Middle-earth Player's Guide* details what a company can do in a Fellowship phase. At the beginning of each Fellowship phase, all Player-heroes recover all of their hit points and Hit Dice, unless they are suffering from specific conditions. While this is an automatic occurrence, it makes sense within a campaign that a Sanctuary has a part to play in this, and this shouldn't be underplayed. It offers a way to build the character and importance of Sanctuaries, which in turn builds the feeling of being part of Middle-earth. Sanctuaries are implicitly tied to the Fellowship phase and the healing that occurs.

The rules are not so rigid that this healing cannot occur elsewhere. But a Sanctuary is a convenient and logical place for this to happen, allowing the Fellowship phase to flow without spending too much time worrying about where the company are.

REMOVING CONDITIONS

While again not *strictly* limited to Sanctuaries, it makes a lot of sense for the Recovery undertaking to be centred around a Sanctuary. Rivendell, Dale or Lake-town can offer superior levels of care to a hero who has been affected by a Wight, or struck down by particularly potent Spider venom. If you wish to slow down the progress of your Player-heroes, this is something to be considered. It's also immensely thematic to Middle-earth to retire to a house of healing for a season or two.

SHARED LOCATION

During a Fellowship phase, members of the company have the choice whether to retire to a Sanctuary together, or disband to their own homes or other locations. Sharing a Sanctuary can provide a cohesive Fellowship phase narrative, with the company all remaining and growing together. Having the company go to a Sanctuary together allows them to share the story through the Fellowship phase, each partaking in the shared events. If a company disbands for the Fellowship phase, things can be a little more disparate. How much each of these options appeals will very much depend on the given player group.

UNDERTAKINGS

More detail on this can be found in the Undertakings section on page 196 of the *Player's Guide*, but being able to take new undertakings is a significant function of a Sanctuary. By opening a new Sanctuary, the company gains access to new undertakings and thus new unique abilities. Future supplements will detail new Sanctuary-specific undertakings. A Loremaster can also create their own undertakings as they see fit.

THE OPEN VIRTUE UNDERTAKING

Once every other Fellowship phase, Player-heroes may engage in an undertaking that gives them their choice of an open virtue. (See *Adventures in Middle-earth Player's Guide*, page 100, for more information on open virtues.) This virtue is gained in addition to the virtue optionally gained at 4th, 8th, 12th, 16th and 19th levels. See also the Further Undertakings section opposite for more details on gaining virtues through the Fellowship phase undertakings.

Beginning Point of an Adventuring Phase

This is probably the most easily overlooked, and yet important, role of a Sanctuary. An Adventuring phase usually begins as the company gathers in a Sanctuary. The rules are not so rigid that this must *always* be the case, but it makes sense for most Adventuring phases to begin at or near a Sanctuary that the company has open to them. It's a common point to meet up, and a place to begin a journey with ample supplies and accommodation.

At the beginning of the game, if using these default assumptions, the company has only Lake-town as a Sanctuary: Bard is recruiting adventurers, there is a lot to do in that area, and it's not too difficult a journey to many interesting adventure locations. Before too long the company will want to travel further afield, and they won't want to cross Mirkwood at the beginning of every Adventuring phase. It is a punishing journey that can leave them ill-prepared for the quest they've embarked on. Far better then to unlock a Sanctuary on the far side of Mirkwood and be able to make the assumed journey in the Fellowship phase, beginning at perhaps Beorn's House or Woodmen Town.

Reducing the need for excessive journeying is easily missed, but absolutely key. Don't be coy about letting your players know this. It is a vital part of understanding Sanctuaries. In character, it would be most unusual for a group of travellers to meet at a place they'd never gone before and where they had no certain access to the hospitality of the house.

Focus

Running through all of these points on Sanctuaries are ideas of in-world logic that save the Loremaster from having to do too much explaining. In this sense, Sanctuaries provide a shorthand: a clear place for characters to be, with some clear goals, rewards and in-world logic. While some groups may truly enjoy describing the minutiae of where they go in their Fellowship phase, others will reap the rewards of being able to say, "We all go to Rivendell together to rest and recuperate; let's decide what happens there."

As well as a focus for the Fellowship phase, opening Sanctuaries is a clear need for a party that wishes to travel far and wide. The search for Rivendell or winning Beorn's favour can be the company's aim within a campaign, whether it is the main thrust or a side quest.

What Does Opening a Sanctuary Mean?

Companies of Player-heroes have a clear drive to open Sanctuaries. Whether it's to unlock undertakings, provide local bases of healing and rest, or find a Patron, it makes sense to open a Sanctuary.

Exactly what is happening when a company unlocks a Sanctuary? This varies from Sanctuary to Sanctuary, and indeed from game to game, but here are some ideas:

Player-heroes are spending time getting to know the place and become familiar figures there. They might help the residents with their day to day problems, or assist in the expansion of a settlement. They may become familiar characters at Elrond's evenings of tales and song, or worthy protectors of the animals of Beorn's House. Your players may wish to describe exactly how they come to be welcomed without fail at a given Sanctuary. You may want to help them with some suggestions.

It is worth noting that the whole company must be present at the same place to open it as a Sanctuary.

Further Undertakings

The *Adventures in Middle-earth Player's Guide* has comprehensive section on undertakings, but there is more to do in a Fellowship phase. Future supplements for *Adventures in Middle-earth* will also present more undertakings. The three presented here have been reserved for this supplement, since they fall under the auspices of Loremaster discretion. You may well wish to have some say in whether your company of heroes can access these undertakings since they influence the accessibility of virtues and speed of character advancement, as well as allowing major plot events to be influenced

Gain an Open Virtue

Once every other Fellowship phase, Player-heroes at a Sanctuary may engage in an undertaking that gives them their choice of an additional open virtue. (See *Adventures in Middle-earth Player's Guide*, page 100, for more information on open virtues.) This virtue is gained in addition to the virtue optionally gained at 4th, 8th, 12th, 16th and 19th levels.

It should be noted that if the current Fellowship phase is particularly long and allows for two undertakings, it still counts as a single Fellowship phase.

Gain a Cultural Virtue

If the Loremaster allows it, once every other Fellowship phase in place of gaining an open Virtue, Player-heroes may make a journey back to the homeland of their culture and spend the Fellowship phase gaining an additional cultural virtue from their own culture. An open Sanctuary is not needed to make this undertaking, as the hero is at home. This allows Player-heroes the chance to gain virtues *in addition* to the chances given at 4th, 8th, 12th, 16th and 19th levels. This means that if they choose, they may concentrate on increasing ability scores at those times, while still having an opportunity to gain cultural virtues.

It should be noted that if the current Fellowship phase is particularly long and allows for two undertakings, it still counts as a single Fellowship phase.

Influence Patron

Player-heroes may spend a Fellowship phase using their charm and influence (or their perhaps gruff wilderness manners) to persuade a powerful Patron to take actions in line with what they would like to see happen in the world. For example, if they have won Thranduil as a Patron, a Player-hero may spend their Fellowship phase convincing the Elf king that he should allow King Bard to repair the Forest Road. And this change will be seen in that Patron's behaviour. In a campaign that involves itself with the fate of the Free Peoples of Wilderland, this can be an exceptionally potent undertaking and also one of the most involving.

- PATRONS -

'His heart was moved suddenly with a desire to see the house of Elrond Halfelven, and breathe the air of that deep valley where many of the Fair Folk still dwelt in peace.'

Player-heroes can make an undertaking to gain a Patron. Patrons are important figures within Middle-earth who have the power and resources necessary to take on Player-heroes as their agents in the world. A Patron can be a source of resources and information but – more importantly for the Loremaster – plot!

A Patron offers a place in the world and a sense of being part of something bigger. They can be called on for help, and to open doors to places that a company might not otherwise be able to go. In return, a debt of service is expected; how often or strictly this is extracted depends on the Patron. Perhaps Saruman the White is a jealous master, who covets the service of others in pursuit of a cause he considers noble and just. Gandalf the Grey is a wanderer who can be a mostly absent and unreliable Patron. And who knows what Radagast wants from the world? Exploring the potential relationships with these characters is very much part of the game.

A company can enjoy serving more than one Patron – they aren't limited in the number to whom they give their service, and that can generate plenty of plot in itself. The great and good of Middle-earth have many different aims and motivations: some would see the world changed and renewed. Others would have it preserved for all time, unchanging. This is a multifaceted theme of the books, and a worthy one to bring to your games.

Patrons also change over time. Where once he was a benevolent seeker of knowledge to further the power of good in the world, Saruman gradually loses hope in the light's ability to stave off darkness. His road to corruption was a long one, and he employed many helpers in his service.

Playing on the conflict between what we know as readers and what we know as characters can bring huge rewards to a game. Beorn tends towards isolation and defensiveness of his own lands and peoples, yet was convinced to take up arms in the greater struggle before the gates of Erebor. That character arc can be reflected in your games, and your Player-heroes can play a key part in it. We know that there was a great battle at Dale in the War of the Ring, but that is all we know. Who were Bard's lieutenants? Who helped his new kingdom reach the place where it could fight armies of Mordor?

Patrons in *Adventures in Middle-earth* are there to provide structure for adventures and hooks on which to hang the happenings you come up with. Making some decisions on the motivations of the great and the good, and allowing their plans to proceed across the years in the background, really makes the world come to life. Equally, giving the company a chance to influence those plans with their undertakings, as well as with what they do in Adventuring phases, adds hugely to the feeling of being part of a living, breathing world.

Note that a powerful NPC can send the company on adventures without being their Patron. Patrons can also come in less grand forms than Gandalf or Elrond. The elders of the Woodmen, or a merchant-noble of Lake-town could just as easily be a Patron to a company of adventurers.

Potential Sanctuaries and Patrons of Wilderland (and slightly beyond)

Rivendell	Elrond
Beorn's House	Beorn
Lake-town	The Master of Esgaroth
Dale	King Bard
Erebor	King Dáin Ironfoot, Thorin's company of Dwarves
Rhosgobel	Radagast
Isengard	Saruman the White
Wilderland	Gandalf the Grey
Mountain Hall	Hartfast (see *Wilderland Adventures*)
Woodmen-town	The elders of Woodmen-town
Woodland Hall	Ingomer Axebreaker (see *Rhovanion Region Guide*)
Lothlórien	Galadriel, Celeborn

Adventures in Middle-earth Player's Guide Errata and Rules Clarifications

The Dúnedain cultural virtue Royalty Revealed (page 104, *Player's Guide*) states that this virtue applies to "Northern Dúnedain only".
The virtue counts for all Dúnedain.

Do Cultural Reward weapons, Dwarf-forged Weapons, or Warrior's Birthright Weapons count as magical?
Yes, though this is of limited utility in *Adventures in Middle-earth* compared to other settings. The range of monstrous adversaries is different, and have different weaknesses.

Are all weapons made by Dwarves considered "Dwarf-forged" (page 152, *Player's Guide*)?
No. "Dwarf-forged" is a shorthand for artefacts made by Dwarven craftspeople of sufficient skill, and in sufficiently ideal circumstances, such as the forges within Erebor. A wandering Dwarf may be of sufficient skill to craft Dwarf-forged weapons anywhere, though this is unlikely. He or she is likely to be able to make very well made weapons and armour anywhere, but not those considered Dwarf-forged in the rules. Similarly, apprenticed or inexperienced Dwarven craftspeople may not yet have the skill to make what the rules considers Dwarf-forged weapons, even in the most ideal of circumstances with the very best materials. Dwarves themselves, however, may argue this point...

What constitutes an official "region" for the Wanderer class's Known Lands (page 82, *Player's Guide*)?
The different colour regions on the Loremaster's map count as a single region. Lone Lands have many regions – each self-contained area on the Loremaster's map of Eriador counts as an individual region for the purpose of Known Lands.

In the Wanderer virtue, Hunter of Shadows (page 85, *Player's Guide*), undead aren't listed under "Foe of the Enemy".
Not all enemy creatures count as servants of the Enemy. Undead, in as much as they exist in Middle-earth, are not uniformly servants of the Enemy – those that are being covered by "any other creature that willingly serves the Lord of Mordor".

In the Warrior Class, under the Knight Archetype, for the ability Sworn Defender, (page 93, *Player's Guide*), how or when does the temporary hit point pool recharge?
While you are either protecting your charge, or performing the quest that counts as your charge, the extra hit points are regained as a bonus whenever you regain your regular hit points.

The example for the Wanderer class feature, Unflagging, (page 84, *Player's Guide*) refers to suffering only a "-1 to ability checks and attack rolls".
This doesn't match the standard Exhaustion chart. Those with Unflagging do indeed suffer Exhaustion at two levels less, as written. The example erroneously mentions attack rolls, and this should be ignored.

The Wanderer archetype, Hunter of Beasts (page 84, *Player's Guide*) has the ability "Swift Shot". Does it use up a reaction?
No, it is a bonus action.

When on a journey, can a Player-hero refuse a role to allow it to be filled by a Wanderer to the mechanical benefit of the company?
The final decision rests with the Loremaster, though it contravenes the spirit of the rules – what is the Player-hero doing during this journey where he or she refuses to help choose a route, catch food, find a campsite or watch for enemies? There should certainly be an XP cost to such a cynical action, and perhaps a Shadow point penalty for leaving all the work to others.

Rations seem awfully expensive at 120c per day.
This is an error. They should be 60c per day.

- Index -

A
Acidic Drool — 121
Adding Wandering Monsters and Scripted Encounters — 57
(Beginning Point of an) Adventuring Phase — 152
(The) Adventuring Phase — 44
Adventuring Rules — 50
Adversaries — 88
Adversaries and Battle — 87
Aggressive — 118
All Enemies of the One Enemy — 42
All Things Diminish — 130
Artefact Bonus — 127
Artisans' District — 30
Artisan's District Adventure Seed — 31
Assembling a Company — 11
Attercop — 105
(Final) Audience Check with Gella — 85
Audience with Gella — 84
Audiences — 80
(Planning) Audiences — 80
   Expectations — 81
   Motivation — 80
   Outcomes — 81
(Running) Audiences — 82
   (The) Final Audience Check — 84
   (The) Introduction — 83
   Outcomes — 84
   Roleplaying the Audience — 83
Audiences Summary — 85

B
Bandolier of Knives — 118
Bane Weapons — 134
Barding Nobles — 33
Barding Swordsman Cultural Virtue — 53
Battle in Middle-earth — 88, 89
Before the Game — 38, 40
(The Land of the) Beornings — 15
(The Land of the) Beornings Adventure Seeds — 16
Beorning's Great Strength — 53
Beorn's House — 15
Berserk — 118
(A Wilderland) Bestiary — 97
Big — 116
Bite Attack — 116
Biter — 118
Black Uruk — 100
Blessings Tables — 131
Blood Driven — 121
Bloodthirsty — 119
Boatmen of Esgaroth — 35
Bowmen of the Guild — 35

C
Call for Aid — 116
(The) Carrock — 16
Cave-Troll — 107
Characters of Middle-earth — 68
Chieftain — 68
Clobbering Sweep — 120
Clumsy — 116
Commanding Voice — 119
(The) Council of the North — 26
Coward — 116
Craftspeople — 31
Creating Your Own Magic — 143
Creature Actions and Abilities — 116
(List of) Creature Actions and Abilities — 116
Creature Bonus Actions — 118
Creature Specific Actions and Abilities: Orcs & Goblins — 120
Creature Specific Actions and Abilities: Spiders — 121
Creature Specific Actions and Abilities: Trolls and Ogres — 120
Creature Reactions — 118
Creature Specific Actions and Abilities: Wargs and Wolves — 121
Cruel Lash — 120

D
Dale — 12
Dale Adventure Seeds — 13
Deeply Sinister — 117
Deliverance Arrives As All Seems Lost — 42
Denizen of the Dark — 119
(The) Departure of Aragorn — 26
Describing Middle-earth — 58
Desperate — 117
Dirty Brawler — 117
Disarming Strike — 117
Discovering the Blessings of an Artefact — 127
Discovering Qualities — 134
Distraction Attack — 117
Don't tell me how I feel! — 58
Drums — 120
Dwarf — 77
Dwarf-Lord — 78
Dwarf Notables — 33
Dwarf Smiths — 30
Dying Frenzy — 121

E
Eightfold Gaze — 121
Elf — 76
Elf-Lord — 77
Elven Quarter — 32
Elven Quarter Adventure Seed — 32
Enchanted Qualities — 135
Erebor — 13
Erebor Adventure Seeds — 14
Evil Maw — 121
Excessive Strength of Arms — 119
Exhaustion — 52
Experience on the Road — 61
Experience Points — 150

F
Farmer — 71
Fell Speed — 118
(New) Fellowship Phase Undertakings for Lake-town — 36
   Go to the Market-pool — 36
   Secure a Supply of Marsh Herbs — 37
(Ending a) Fellowship Phase — 149
(How Long is a) Fellowship Phase? — 150
(The) Fellowship Phase — 148
   If They Split Up — 148
   If They Stay Together — 149
Fierce Bees — 120
Focus — 152
Folk Along the way — 66
Foreword — 6
Foul Alliance — 119
Foul Liquor — 120
Foul Reek — 118
Further Undertakings — 153

G
Gain a Cultural Virtue — 153
Gain an Open Virtue — 153
Gaining Inspiration as the Loremaster — 150
Gandalf and Balin visit Bilbo — 26
Gatehouse and Bridge Defenses — 28
Gatehouse and Bridge Defences Adventure Seeds — 29
(The) Gathering of Five Armies — 25
Gathering Shadows — 25
Gella, the Village Elder — 82
Gimlet Eyed — 117
Goblin Archer — 104
Gollum seeks the One Ring — 26
Great Bats — 114
(The) Great Hall of Rhosgobel — 17
(The) Great Hall of Woodland Hall — 17
Great Leap — 117
Great Orcs — 97
Great Spider — 106
Great Spider Actions — 121

(The) Grey Pilgrim	26	2. Determine Craftsmanship	133	(The) Nazgûl enter Dol Guldur	26
Grim Banner	120	3. Select Banes	133	No Quarter	120
		4. Attribute Enchanted Qualities	133	Non-Player Characters	
H		5. Name the Item	134	and Audiences Expanded	64
(The) Hall of Balthi	18	(How) Legendary Weapons and		Not-so-Subtle Magic	130
(The) Halls of the Elvenking	20	Armour Work	134	Northern Mirkwood	19
Hard Eyed	119	Lembas	139		
Hatred	117	Long Arms	118	**O**	
Heart of Mirkwood	19	(The) Long Defeat in a Fallen World	42	Old Ford	16
Herbs, Potions and Salves	139	(The) Long Marshes	15	Old Lore	21
Hideous Toughness	119	(The) Long Marshes Adventure Seed	37	(The) Open Virtue Undertaking	151
High Pass	16	(The) Loremaster	46	(What Does) Opening a Sanctuary Mean?	152
Hill-Troll	108	(The) Loremaster as Director	47	Options for Adding Magic	144
Hill-Troll Chief	107	Consistency	47	Orc Adventure Seed	102
Hobgoblin	98	(The) Loremaster as Narrator	48	Orc Guard	104
Hobgoblin Adventure Seeds	98	Creativity	48	Orc of Goblin-town	102
Hospital Healers	34	(The) Loremaster as Referee	47	Orc of Mount Gram	102
Hound of Sauron	114	Fairness	48	Orc Soldier	103
				Orc-Chieftain	102
I		**M**		Orcs	97
Ideas for Things Seen on the Road	58	Magic in Middle-earth	140	Orcs of the Misty Mountains	101
Ill-prepared for Battle	119	(The) Magic of Middle-earth	142	Other Lands	20
In the Sack with You!	120	Magical Healing	139	Out of Character Treasure Hunters	124
Influence Patron	153	Magical Result Costs	129	Go to the Source	125
Inspiration	52	Magical Result Cost Chart	129	What Is Gold For?	126
About Inspiration in Middle-earth	53	Magical Results	128	Outlaw	74
Gaining Inspiration	52	(Examples of) Magical Results	129		
Inspiration as a Tool for Guiding		Marsh-Hag	99	**P**	
your Game	52	Marsh-Hag Adventure Seeds	99	Paralysing Attack	121
Starting Inspiration	53	Marsh-Ogre	108	Patrons	154
Using Inspiration	52	Marsh-Ogre Adventure Seed	109	Playing Characters from the Book	67
Introduction to Gella	83	Meddling in the Affairs of Wizards	142	Playing Members of the Free Folk	67
(The) Iron Hills	14	(The) Men of Bree Cultural		Dwarves	67
		Virtue: Desperate Courage	53	Elves	67
J		Merchant	69	Men	67
(Suggested Places to End a) Journey	60	Merchant's District	29	Other Folk	67
Journeys	56	Merchant's District Adventure Seed	30	Poorly Armed	117
(Interrupting) Journeys	59	Merchants	30	Poorly Protected	117
Journeys Expanded	54	Messenger	70	Precepts of Middle-earth Play	40
(Making Your own) Journey Events Tables	61	Messenger of Lugbúrz	100		
Arrival Table: Raw	63	Mewling	117	**R**	
Embarkation Table: Raw	61	(The) Middle-earth Loremaster	47	Raft-elves	32
Journey Events Table: Raw	62	Miles Are Miles	40	Ranger	75
		Mirkwood	18	Really Big	117
K		Mirkwood Adventure Seeds	19	Recent Past	24
Keen Mounts	121	Miruvor	139	Reckless Hatred	118
King Bard's Proclamation	11	Misty Mountain Goblin	102	Recovery	151
		(How to Approach) Monetary Wealth in		Removing Conditions	151
L		*Adventures in Middle-earth*	126	Residential District	34
Lake-town	14	Mordor-Orcs	100	Residential District Adventure Seed	34
(A Guide to) Lake-town	28	Mountain Hall	16	Rests	50
(The) Lands about the Mountain	12	Mountain-Troll	109	Rests on the Road	57
Last One Standing	119	Mountains of Mirkwood	19	(The) Return of Arwen	26
Last Stand	120	Multiattack	117	Revealed to Them	144
Legendary Weapons and Armour	132	Multiclassing	53	Rhosgobel	17
(Creating) Legendary Weapons and				Rotting	120
Armour	132	**N**		Royal Archers of Dale	36
1. Choose Item Type	132	(The) Narrows of the Forest	20	Rubbery Skin	117

S

Sage	72	Last, but Not Least...		49	Wondrous Artefacts	127

Sage 72
Sanctuaries 151
(Potential) Sanctuaries and Patrons of Wilderland 154
(What) Sanctuaries Do 151
Sauron Declares in Mordor 26
Savage Assault 118
Savage Attack 117
Scenery in Combat 90
    Atmosphere 96
    Caves 95
    Mirkwood 93
    Ruins 94
    Weather 96
    (The) Wild 90
    Woodland 91
Screamer 117
Secret Shadows 115
Setting and the Tale of Years 8
Shared Location 151
Shield Smasher 121
Shipyards District 34
Shipyards District Adventure Seeds 35
Seize Victim 120
Silvan Elf Emissaries 32
Singer 73
Snaga Tracker 101
Snake-like Speed 118
Sneaking 117
(Using the) Sources 10
Southern Mirkwood 19
(The) South 21
(List of Middle-earth Appropriate) Spells 145
Spiders of Mirkwood 105
Spiders of Mirkwood Adventure Seed 105
Starving Cannibal 117
Stone-Troll 110
Stony Hide 117
(Especially) Strong Abilities and Actions 119
(The) Strong Die First 119
Stupid 117
Survivor 120

T

(The) Tale of Years 10, 21
Terrifying in Aspect 119
Terrifying Howl 121
Thick Hide 121
Thug 73
Tittering Laugh 117
Tolkien's Canon 48
    Filling the Blanks 49
    It is all about Characters 49

Last, but Not Least... Subjective Sources 48
Town Councillors 34
Town Guard 68
Town Guards 29
(The) Town-hall Quarter 32
Town-Hall Quarter Adventure Seed 33
Town Watch 31
Treasure and Rewards 124
Troll Adventure Seed 108
Trolls 107
Troupe Abilities, Actions and Bonus Actions 118
Two Guiding Lights 50

U

Unclean Stench 121
Undertakings 151
Unsuccessful Journeys 51

V

Vampires 114
Vampire Adventure Seed 115
Vengeful Band 119
Venomous 117
Vicious Hiss 118
Vicious Wounds 120
Vile 118
Vile Gang 119

W

War Cry 119
War Paint 118
Wargs 111
Warrior 71
Waters of Nimrodel 139
Weak in Limb 118
Weak Willed 118
Weak Willed Alliance 119
Weakling 118
(Further) Weapons and Armour of Extraordinary Craftsmanship 138
Welcome to Middle-earth 10
(The) Werewolf of Mirkwood 113
Werewolves 113
(The) West 20
Western Mirkwood 20
Wild Wolf 111
Wilderland 10
Wilderland & Beyond 12
Wilderland Player's Map 27
Wolf Leader 112
Wolves of the Wild 111
Wolves of the Wild Adventure Seed 111

Wondrous Artefacts 127
(Other) Wondrous Artefacts 131
(How) Wondrous Artefacts Work 127
(Too Many) Wondrous Items! 127
Wondrous, Legendary and Healing items 122
Wondrous Tools 128
Woodland Hall 17
Woodland Realm 20
(The Land of the) Woodmen 16
(The Land of the) Woodmen Adventure Seeds 17
Woodmen-town 18
Woven from Darkness 121

Y

Year 1050 21
Year 1980 21
Year 1999 22
Year 2063 22
Year 2210 22
Year 2460 22
Year 2463 22
Year 2480 23
Year 2510 23
Year 2570 23
Year 2589 23
Year 2590 23
Year 2740 23
Year 2747 23
Year 2758 23
Year 2770 23
Year 2790 24
Year 2793 24
Year 2799 24
Year 2841 24
Year 2850 24
Year 2851 24
Year 2890 24
Year 2900 24
Year 2911 24
Year 2931 24
Year 2941 25
Year 2942 25
Year 2943 25
Year 2944 25
Years 2944-2945 25
Year 2946 25
Year 2947 26
Year 2948 26
Year 2949 26
Year 2951 26
Years Are Long 41
You're in Charge 57

Adventures in Middle-earth™

Adventures in Middle-earth
Player's Guide
CB72300

Adventures in Middle-earth
Wilderland Adventures
CB72302

Adventures in Middle-earth
Rhovanion Region Guide
CB72303

Adventures in Middle-earth
Mirkwood Campaign
CB72304

Adventures in Middle-earth
The Road Goes Ever On
CB72305

Adventures in Middle-earth
The Eaves of Mirkwood &
Loremaster's Screen
CB72306

Find out more about the entire *Adventures in Middle-earth* line at cubicle7.co.uk

OPEN GAME LICENSE Version 1.0a

The following text is the property of Wizards of the Coast, Inc. and is Copyright 2000 Wizards of the Coast, Inc ("Wizards"). All Rights Reserved. 1. Definitions: (a)"Contributors" means the copyright and/or trademark owners who have contributed Open Game Content; (b)"Derivative Material" means copyrighted material including derivative works and translations (including into other computer languages), potation, modification, correction, addition, extension, upgrade, improvement, compilation, abridgment or other form in which an existing work may be recast, transformed or adapted; (c) "Distribute" means to reproduce, license, rent, lease, sell, broadcast, publicly display, transmit or otherwise distribute; (d)"Open Game Content" means the game mechanic and includes the methods, procedures, processes and routines to the extent such content does not embody the Product Identity and is an enhancement over the prior art and any additional content clearly identified as Open Game Content by the Contributor, and means any work covered by this License, including translations and derivative works under copyright law, but specifically excludes Product Identity. (e) "Product Identity" means product and product line names, logos and identifying marks including trade dress; artifacts; creatures characters; stories, storylines, plots, thematic elements, dialogue, incidents, language, artwork, symbols, designs, depictions, likenesses, formats, poses, concepts, themes and graphic, photographic and other visual or audio representations; names and descriptions of characters, spells, enchantments, personalities, teams, personas, likenesses and special abilities; places, locations, environments, creatures, equipment, magical or supernatural abilities or effects, logos, symbols, or graphic designs; and any other trademark or registered trademark clearly identified as Product identity by the owner of the Product Identity, and which specifically excludes the Open Game Content; (f) "Trademark" means the logos, names, mark, sign, motto, designs that are used by a Contributor to identify itself or its products or the associated products contributed to the Open Game License by the Contributor (g) "Use", "Used" or "Using" means to use, Distribute, copy, edit, format, modify, translate and otherwise create Derivative Material of Open Game Content. (h) "You" or "Your" means the licensee in terms of this agreement.

2. The License: This License applies to any Open Game Content that contains a notice indicating that the Open Game Content may only be Used under and in terms of this License. You must affix such a notice to any Open Game Content that you Use. No terms may be added to or subtracted from this License except as described by the License itself. No other terms or conditions may be applied to any Open Game Content distributed using this License.

3. Offer and Acceptance: By Using the Open Game Content You indicate Your acceptance of the terms of this License.

4. Grant and Consideration: In consideration for agreeing to use this License, the Contributors grant You a perpetual, worldwide, royalty free, non exclusive license with the exact terms of this License to Use, the Open Game Content.

5. Representation of Authority to Contribute: If You are contributing original material as Open Game Content, You represent that Your Contributions are Your original creation and/or You have sufficient rights to grant the rights conveyed by this License.

6. Notice of License Copyright: You must update the COPYRIGHT NOTICE portion of this License to include the exact text of the COPYRIGHT NOTICE of any Open Game Content You are copying, modifying or distributing, and You must add the title, the copyright date, and the copyright holder's name to the COPYRIGHT NOTICE of any original Open Game Content you Distribute.

7. Use of Product Identity: You agree not to Use any Product Identity, including as an indication as to compatibility, except as expressly licensed in another, independent Agreement with the owner of each element of that Product Identity. You agree not to indicate compatibility or co adaptability with any Trademark or Registered Trademark in conjunction with a work containing Open Game Content except as expressly licensed in another, independent Agreement with the owner of such Trademark or Registered Trademark. The use of any Product Identity in Open Game Content does not constitute a challenge to the ownership of that Product Identity. The owner of any Product Identity used in Open Game Content shall retain all rights, title and interest in and to that Product Identity.

8. Identification: If you distribute Open Game Content You must clearly indicate which portions of the work that you are distributing are Open Game Content.

9. Updating the License: Wizards or its designated Agents may publish updated versions of this License. You may use any authorized version of this License to copy, modify and distribute any Open Game Content originally distributed under any version of this License.

10. Copy of this License: You MUST include a copy of this License with every copy of the Open Game Content You Distribute.

11. Use of Contributor Credits: You may not market or advertise the Open Game Content using the name of any Contributor unless You have written permission from the Contributor to do so.

12. Inability to Comply: If it is impossible for You to comply with any of the terms of this License with respect to some or all of the Open Game Content due to statute, judicial order, or governmental regulation then You may not Use any Open Game Material so affected.

13. Termination: This License will terminate automatically if You fail to comply with all terms herein and fail to cure such breach within 30 days of becoming aware of the breach. All sublicenses shall survive the termination of this License.

14. Reformation: If any provision of this License is held to be unenforceable, such provision shall be reformed only to the extent necessary to make it enforceable.

15. COPYRIGHT NOTICE
Open Game License v 1.0a Copyright 2000, Wizards of the Coast, LLC.

System Reference Document 5.1 Copyright 2016, Wizards of the Coast, Inc.; Authors Mike Mearls, Jeremy Crawford, Chris Perkins, Rodney Thompson, Peter Lee, James Wyatt, Robert J. Schwalb, Bruce R. Cordell, Chris Sims, and Steve Townshend, based on original material by E. Gary Gygax and Dave Arneson.

END OF LICENSE